Whole Language
for Second Language Learners

Whole Language
for Second Language Learners

Yvonne S. Freeman
David E. Freeman
Fresno Pacific College

Heinemann
Portsmouth, NH

HEINEMANN
A Division of Reed Publishing (USA) Inc.
361 Hanover Street, Portsmouth, NH 03801-3912
Offices and agents throughout the world

Library of Congress Cataloging-in-Publication Data

Freeman, Yvonne S.
    Whole language for second language learners / Yvonne S. Freeman, David E. Freeman.
        p.   cm.
    Includes bibliographical references and index.
    ISBN 0-435-08723-1
    1. Language and languages—Study and teaching.   2. Second language acquisition.   3. Language arts.   4. Education, Bilingual.   5. English language—Study and teaching—Foreign speakers.
    I. Freeman, David E.   II. Title.
    P53.F73 1992
    418'.007—dc20   92-765
                                                                                          CIP

Cover design by Jenny Jensen Greenleaf.
Cover photos by Kay Armijo, Joan Buchbinder, Ellen Kunz,
and Bunny Rogers.
Printed in the United States of America.
93 94 95 96 9 8 7 6 5 4 3

To all the teachers of bilingual students in our schools and especially to our two daughters, Mary and Ann, who are proof that being bilingual can be natural and enriching.

Contents

Acknowledgments

This book was written because we have had the privilege of learning about second language students from creative, concerned, and dedicated teachers. In this book you will read about stories of teachers and second language students at many different grade levels. Although each story is unique, all of these teachers have the common goal of making a difference in the lives of their students. Many thanks to the following talented educators:

Kay Armijo
Steve Bell
Blanca Camargo
Carolina delaluz Cervantes
Lorna Cube
Steve Demeter
Nancy Fino
Alan Hollman
Jane Jones
Charlene Klassen
Cyn Koukos
Ellen Kunz
Debbie Manning
Linda Medel
Sam Nofziger
Mary Perich
Susan Rodriguez
Kelly Rosales
Barbara Senneway
Julie Suderman
Rhoda Toews
Vince Workmon
Katie Bausch-Ude

Charlotte Brown
JoAnne Campbell
Julie Craig
Lonna Deeter
Rose Marie Dixon
Linda Gage
Larry Jason
Marilyn Hutchins
Arnie Kriegbaum
René Lebsock
Miriam Marquardt
George Mason
Irene Munoz
Bunny Rogers
Teresa Calderón Parker
Michael Roberts
Jill Rojas
Sonia Ruan
Cathy Stokes
Diane Tew
Nancy Triguerio
Denette Zaninovitch

This book would not have been possible without the support provided by our mentors, Kenneth and Yetta Goodman.

Introduction

Assumptions about Whole Language

Whole language brings together modern, scientific knowledge of teaching, learning, language, and curriculum and puts it into a positive, humanistic philosophy, which teachers can identify with and which offers them strong criteria for their professional decisions and teaching practice (Goodman, Bird, and Goodman 1991, p. 10).

Whole language. We hear about it everywhere. With all the publicity, it's hard not to have heard something about it. Professional journals and newsletters are filled with articles about whole language and with ads for whole language materials. Experts offer whole language seminars, workshops, conferences, and videotapes. School districts are transitioning to whole language and providing inservice for their teachers to show them how to use new "whole language" approaches and materials. However, each time we hear about and read about whole language, we may be given different messages about what it is, who it is good for, and how best to implement it.

Some Misconceptions about Whole Language

What is whole language anyway? Is whole language big books? Is it process writing? Is it thematic teaching? Is it a revolt against basal readers and phonics? Is it just good teaching? Is it the latest fad? Although each of these may be part of whole language, whole language is more than any one of them or even all of them together.

For example, the idea that whole language is big books or process writing suggests that whole language consists of particular approaches to teaching language arts. It is true that in the early grades whole language teachers often use big books to introduce reading rather than using basal reading programs, and many whole language teachers use process writing rather than worksheets and copying exercises, but whole language is not only language arts. Whole language teachers do whole language in all areas of the curriculum. Math and science are integrated. As students use the scientific method to explore natural phenomena, they develop necessary math skills when they estimate, weigh, and measure. They also keep math journals and write about what they discover. In social studies, students carry out community surveys and report results both in writing and orally (Freeman and Freeman 1991). Teachers incorporate art and music across the curriculum, realizing that the fine arts offer different ways of knowing for students from kindergarten through college (Gardner 1984).

Often, whole language teachers organize their lessons around themes or units, drawing on resources such as *The Web*, a publication from The Ohio State University that suggests literature and activities appropriate for certain themes. Freeman and Mason (1991) have suggested organizing themes around big ideas and powerful contrasts. Not all teachers who use themes would consider themselves whole language teachers. There is a difference, too, between doing a unit on apples or spiders, and using broad themes as a basic organizing principle (Edelsky, Altwerger and Flores 1991). In short, although many whole language teachers find that they can provide more continuity for their curriculum by using themes, not all whole language teachers use thematic teaching, and not all thematic teaching is done by whole language teachers.

Another popular idea about whole language is that it is a revolt against certain practices and materials. It is true that whole language teachers are more apt to use real literature than to use basal programs, and they prefer to engage students in authentic activities rather than drilling them on worksheets. They generally avoid the direct teaching of skills as the prerequisite for reading and writing. They prefer to teach skills in the context of real reading and writing activities. In fact, this has led to the misconception that whole language teachers don't teach skills at all (Newman and Church 1990). Whole language teachers may avoid using certain materials or techniques, but this is not the defining characteristic of whole language teaching. In some schools where teachers are required to use basals and to teach skills directly, teachers are still able to apply whole language.

Finally, whole language has often been dismissed as either "just good teaching" or as the latest fad. We do believe that whole language is good teaching. Often, during workshops, veteran teachers have commented to us that what we are calling whole language is what they have been doing all along. It is what they always considered good teaching. The difference, though, between whole language and successful practice is that whole language has a solid research base. Miller (1990) has traced the history of whole language. He shows how whole language practice is grounded in the ideas of educators such as Rousseau, Montessori, Dewey, and others. Whole language teachers examine the assumptions about teaching and learning upon which they operate, they become researchers in their own classrooms, and they refine their practices in light of the research they conduct as well as the research that they read.

Certainly, whole language could be seen as a fad. Publishers and others with commercial interests are jumping on the bandwagon. Nevertheless, because whole language is a grass roots movement led by teachers and grounded in research, it is not likely to fade. Whole language practices are becoming the standards against which other practices are judged. Major organizations such as the California Association for Bilingual Education and the National Council of Teachers of English are sponsoring whole language conferences. The Whole Language Umbrella, a confederation of more than four hundred whole language groups across the United States, Canada, and other countries, not only provides a network but also holds a large conference yearly. In a few short years, whole language has moved from the fringe to the center of the educational arena.

The Research Base for
Whole Language

What all these statements about whole language have in common is that, like the blind men and the elephant, they capture only part of the reality. There seem to be as many versions of whole language as there are practitioners. However, there is also a growing consensus about the basis for the whole language movement and the principles that drive it.

First, whole language is a grass roots movement centered in classrooms. Teachers in these classrooms are finding ways to empower both their students and themselves. These teachers are showing their professionalism by reading research, conducting research in their own classrooms, sharing successful practices with other educators, and working with their colleagues and with their students to implement a meaningful curriculum.

Whole language is grounded in the recent research on language, learning, and teaching that shows that learning is natural. In first language, Goodman (1986b) and Smith (1985) have pointed out that learning seems easy outside of school but difficult in school. They suggest ways to reform education and make learning in schools as easy as learning outside schools.

In second language, Krashen (1982) makes a similar point when he distinguishes between learning and acquisition. People acquire language in natural settings outside school, and they learn language in schools when instruction is sequenced and there is practice and correction. Krashen suggests ways to make classrooms places where students can acquire a second language. He points out that students acquire language most easily when they use language for authentic purposes rather than focusing on language and teaching grammar directly.

In addition, Cummins's research has shown that it takes longer for students to develop the kind of language called for by academic tasks than the kind of language needed for interpersonal communication. Both Cummins (1989a) and Freire (1970) have written extensively about the need for student empowerment. Cummins offers a framework for intervention that calls for interactive and experiential learning. Freire explains that students are not "banks" into which teachers "deposit" knowledge, but that learning must have a relationship to students' needs and interests.

All these researchers argue that students learn as they construct their own knowledge. Knowledge can't simply be transmitted from a teacher to students. What has emerged from this research and from the reflective practice of whole language teachers is a philosophy, a set of beliefs about what makes teaching and learning easy and natural.

The Students in
Whole Language Classes

There are as many ideas about what whole language is as there are about who whole language is for. For example, kindergarten teachers often find whole language easy to implement because many of their practices are consistent with whole language philosophy, whereas many high school teachers have difficulty visualizing how they would do whole language. In some schools, whole language is only for the most advanced students, those who have already mastered basic skills; in other schools, teachers only use whole language with students performing below grade level expectations.

When whole language is seen as a philosophy about teaching and learning, a philosophy grounded in current research, it becomes apparent that whole language should not be restricted based on student age or ability. We believe that whole language is good for all ages: young children, teenagers, college students, and adults. We also believe that whole language is good for all kinds of learners, those who are exceptional learners as well as those considered by the system to be average or below average.

The Need for Whole Language
for Bilingual Learners

For those students whose first language is not English, whole language is not only good teaching, it is essential. Whole language may be the only road to success for bilingual learners. The instruction that many bilingual learners have received in schools has been for the most part fragmented and disempowering (Crawford 1989; Cummins 1989b; Flores 1982). Teachers and administrators want to do what is best for all children, but frequently they are unprepared for students who come from different cultural and linguistic backgrounds and do not speak English. As a result, the drop-out, or push-out, rate among second language students is high. Studies have shown that among Hispanics, for example, nearly 45 percent fail to complete high school (Kollars 1988).

The high drop-out rate for language minority students is of particular concern because the number of these students has increased significantly in recent years. Dramatic shifts in demographics have filled schools with a rich mix of students from diverse ethnic backgrounds. Olsen (1991) reports that during the 1989–90 school year 5 percent of all students K–12 in the United States were classified as Limited or Non-English Proficient (LEP or NEP). In some states the percentage of language minority students is much higher. In California public schools, one child in six is a second language learner. In 1990, nearly 862,000 California students were identified as LEP.

Traditional methods are not working well for bilingual students. Even among those who complete high school, only a small number go on to four-year colleges. To reverse this trend of school failure, a new approach is required, and for many teachers, whole language seems to be the answer.

Commonsense Assumptions about Bilingual Learners and Whole Language Principles

Whole language is a philosophy. All teachers make educational decisions based on the beliefs they have about teaching and learning. Because many educators have little information about how to work with second language students, instruction in their classes has been based on a set of commonsense assumptions. These assumptions, we believe, serve to limit the potential of bilingual learners (Freeman and Freeman 1989a; Freeman and Freeman 1989b; Freeman and Freeman 1989c). To help define whole language, particularly for bilingual students, we contrast each of seven commonsense assumptions with a whole language principle that expands the potential for educational success (Goodman 1986b; Hudelson 1984; Hudelson 1987; Rigg 1986; Urzúa 1989).

Commonsense Assumptions

1. Learning proceeds from part to whole.
2. Lessons should be teacher centered because learning is the transfer of knowledge from the teacher to the student.
3. Lessons should prepare students to function in society after schooling.
4. Learning takes place as individuals practice skills and form habits.
5. In a second language, oral language acquisition precedes the development of literacy.
6. Learning should take place in English to facilitate the acquisition of English.
7. The learning potential of bilingual students is limited.

Whole Language Principles

1. Learning proceeds from whole to part.
2. Lessons should be learner centered because learning is the active construction of knowledge by the student.
3. Lessons should have meaning purpose for students now.
4. Learning takes place as groups engage in meaningful social interaction.
5. In a second language, oral and written language are acquired simultaneously.
6. Learning should take place in the first language to build concepts and facilitate the acquisition of English.
7. Learning potential is expanded through faith in the learner.

As we have worked with teachers who have bilingual students in their classrooms, we have found that when they base their instruction on the whole language principles rather than on commonsense assumptions about bilingual learners, teachers can help all students, and especially second language learners, succeed in schools. A brief look at each principle provides an overview of whole language.

1. Lessons should proceed from whole to part.

Students need the big picture first. They develop concepts by beginning with general ideas and then filling in the specific details. Organizing curriculum around themes helps teachers move from whole to part. Second language learners need to know where they are going as they learn their new language. For this reason, preview and review in the primary language is especially helpful.

2. Lessons should be learner centered because learning is the active construction of knowledge by students.

Whole language focuses on the whole student. Lessons begin with what the student knows, and activities build on student interests. Teachers create contexts in which students can construct knowledge because they know that learning is not simply the transmission of information.

3. Lessons should have meaning and purpose for students now.

Students learn things that they see as meeting a present need. Students are given choices in what they study. They reflect upon what they are learning and apply what they learn to their life outside, as well as inside, school.

4. Lessons should engage groups of students in social interaction.

When students share their ideas in social settings, individual concepts are developed. Working in groups, students also learn the important life skill of collaboration.

5. Lessons should develop both oral and written language.

Especially for students learning English as a second language, the traditional view has been that the development of oral language must precede the development of literacy. However, involvement in reading and writing from the start is essential for developing academic competence. Both written and oral language can be developed simultaneously.

6. Learning should take place in the first language to build concepts and facilitate the acquisition of English.

When students come to school speaking a language other than English, teachers can build on strengths by helping the student develop concepts in the first language. Full development of the primary language facilitates the acquisition of English, and recognition of the first language and culture builds self-esteem.

7. Lessons that show faith in the learner expand students' potential.

Teachers who believe in their students, including their bilingual students, plan activities that show their faith in the learner. All students can learn if they are engaged in meaningful activities that move from whole to part, build on students' interests and backgrounds, serve their needs, provide opportunities for social interaction, and develop their skills in both oral and written language.

Conclusion

In the following chapters we examine the seven principles in detail. We look particularly at how each one applies to bilingual learners. For each principle we give examples from whole language classrooms and suggest specific activities that could be used with all students and especially second language learners.

Whole language is not a panacea. It won't cure all the problems that bilingual students and their teachers face. It won't be easy to implement, and there will be resistance to many practices consistent with whole language. Nevertheless, we are convinced that teachers who discard the seven commonsense assumptions listed and replace them with practices that follow the whole language principles we have outlined will offer all of their students a better chance for school success.

1

Learning Goes from Whole to Part

Introduction

Picture a fictitious classroom filled with thirty inquisitive second graders, many of them second language learners. The teacher is conducting a lesson centered around a food theme. First she passes out some pieces of oregano. She asks the children what they can tell her about it. They look at the oregano, they smell it, they feel it. "It's green and it smells funny," says Manuel. "I think I know what it is, it's *perejil* (parsley)!" pipes up María. The teacher records the children's answers on a large piece of butcher paper.

She collects the oregano and passes around some mozzarella cheese. The children know that this is cheese, that it's white, and, after tasting it, that it doesn't have much taste. Francisca declares that it is definitely not *queso Oaxaca* that her mother uses to make enchiladas. Again the teacher records the children's responses. Garlic and tube-shaped Italian sausage follow the mozzarella and then comes tomato sauce. The children are interested, but they aren't sure where all this is going. The teacher passes out uncooked, wide noodles with scalloped edges. The noodles are brittle and dry. They look nothing like the noodles the Laotian students in the class eat daily.

"Now," the teacher announces, "we are going to cook a special meal. Using all these things you have looked at, we will make lasagna. How do you think it will taste?"

"Yucky!" shout several students. "I'm not going to eat it," claims Mo. "Nothing you passed out smelled good or tasted good either."

"It might be good," countered Alicia. "Noodles and tomato usually means Italian food, and I like spaghetti."

"You always cook things we like," added Mai. "I'll try it."

The students in this class are intrigued by the food the teacher has passed around. They try to use their own past experiences with food to predict what lasagna will be like. However, despite the fact they may have smelled and even tasted each of the ingredients, they can't mentally put the odors and tastes together into a final product. The individual tastes of oregano, garlic, sausage, mozzarella and tomato sauce simply don't add up to the taste of lasagna.

The lesson we've described here might be part of a unit developed around cultural differences in which children study foods from different cultures. In many ways the lesson is consistent with a whole language approach. The children are engaged. There is lots of talk. The children read what the teacher writes up on the butcher paper. Later they will cook and eat the lasagna. They will write about the experience.

Although this is a good lesson in a literal sense, on a metaphorical level it suggests why some educational practices make learning hard for students. The teacher presented all the ingredients that make up lasagna. Even though the students experienced all the parts of the recipe in isolation, they couldn't predict what the whole, the lasagna, would be like. The taste of lasagna is different from the tastes of its constituent parts. Knowing about the parts doesn't ensure knowledge of the whole.

In this chapter, we look more closely at the commonsense view that, when we break a subject down into parts, we make learning easier. We argue that the whole is more than the sum of the parts and that students, especially second language learners, need first a sense of the whole to understand the parts. The whole provides an important context in which the parts are naturally embedded. We contrast the commonsense part-to-whole approach to teaching with a whole language alternative: Learning is easier when it goes from whole to part.

To explain this whole language alternative we do three things. We consider what first and second language researchers have said about how language learning takes place. We look specifically at the importance of context, which provides the whole, in second language learning. And we give examples of classrooms where whole language teachers teach bilingual students from whole to part.

Language Learning Takes Place Whole to Part

The process of acquiring a first or a second language involves moving from whole to part, although it sometimes doesn't look that way on the surface. In learning oral language, for example, babies first utter single words like *Mama* or *milk*, then they produce two word sentences *want milk*, and only later develop complete sentences. This suggests that language develops from the parts, the single words, to the whole, complete utterances.

However, though it is true that children first utter single words, those words often represent complete ideas. *Milk*, for example, could mean *I want some milk, I spilled the milk,* or *That's milk over there.* Russian psychologist Vygotsky (1962) believed that word meanings develop in a functional way from whole to part:

> In regard to meaning . . . the first word of the child is a whole sentence. Semantically, the child starts from the whole, from a meaningful complex, and only later begins to master the separate semantic units, the meanings of words, and to divide his formerly undifferentiated thoughts into those units. (p. 126)

Children start with ideas that they express in a single word, and later they learn to use more words to express that idea. They are able to add more detail with time and move toward the conventional adult way of speaking. In the same way, when children first start to use written language, they often write a single letter to represent a whole word. This is true also for children learning to write English as their second language. In early stages of writing English, Sonia, a native Greek speaker, wrote *Iwtmh* to represent *I went to my house* (Cambourne and Turbill 1987, p. 46). As students write more, they begin to represent words by first and last sounds. Manuel, a fifth grader recently from Mexico, wrote the following from the teacher's dictated weekly spelling list, which included the words *birds, bison, feathers, furs, laws, ocean, plants, protect, safe,* and *gone.*

1. BS	6. On
2. bn	7. PS
3. fs	8. Pt
4. fs	9. sf
5. LS	10. gn

Unfortunately, Manuel's teacher did not know about writing development and did not recognize that Manuel was actually representing the whole with first and last letters. Manuel got no credit for any of the words he wrote.

Students who are encouraged to write using their own hypotheses about spelling often move next toward representing each syllable with a letter as Reina, a first grader from Mexico, did with *LDBG* for *Ladybug*. Finally, students come to realize the alphabetic principle, that letters represent individual sounds, not syllables or words. Though students do not move neatly through these stages, these examples are typical of learners who experiment with representing their ideas through writing. Throughout the process of their written language development, students always first represent the whole, not the parts. In the development of both speech and writing, then, children begin with a whole and only later develop an understanding of the constituent parts.

Goodman (1986b) explains this phenomenon. He says that when we learn language we are "first able to use whole utterances" and that "Only later can we see the parts in the whole and begin to experiment with their relationship to each other and to the meaning of the whole" (p. 19). Parts are harder to learn than wholes because they are more abstract. We need to have the whole to provide a context for the parts. Of course, what is difficult here is deciding what is a whole and what is a part. Teachers who use a *look–say* method of teaching reading, for example, may think they are providing wholes by giving students whole words. However, in reading, words are not the whole. Similarly, second language teachers may feel they are providing the whole by having students memorize dialogues rather than focusing on individual words. Again, a dialogue is not what we mean by a whole.

Unfortunately, instruction in schools has too often been organized from part to whole. This has been especially true in the area of reading. A clear understanding of the reading process helps to clarify why reading instruction for first and second language learners should move from whole to part.

Why Part-to-Whole Reading Instruction Doesn't Work

Most schools in America have adopted an industrial model of education. Following this model, information is packaged in small units that are transmitted, one at a time, to students as they pass along education's assembly line. Writers such as Shannon (1989, 1990), Goodman (1986b, 1988), Smith (1986), and Weaver (1988) have documented the historical development of this model, and they have argued that what seems to have worked for industry does not work for education. As Goodman (1986b) puts it, the part-to-whole approach is logical, but it is not psychological.

Phonics

Much of the evidence against part-to-whole learning comes from research in reading. Phonics instruction is a clear example of instruction that starts with small parts, individual sounds, and attempts to build up to the whole, the ability to read effectively.

Words are made up of sounds, and texts are made up of words. If students can recode visual symbols into sounds that represent the words in a story, it follows logically that they should be able to comprehend or "read" the story. However, as in the lasagna lesson described at the beginning of the chapter, the problem with studying the parts in isolation is that students cannot visualize how the parts go together. As a result, students often come to the end of the educational assembly line with only bits and pieces of information. They may have the parts of reading, but they cannot put them together to make sense of what they read.

Though proponents of phonics believe that phonics instruction is essential to teach reading, this part-to-whole approach has several problems. Smith (1985), for example, has shown that a very large number of phonics rules and exceptions is needed to account for even the one- and two-syllable words taken from basal readers for young children.

Still another problem with using phonics to identify words is that it is inefficient. For example, reading proceeds from left to right, but phonics requires a right-to-left progression. We often need to know the end of the word to be able to pronounce the first part of the word. Consider the following two words:

City
Cite

To know how to pronounce the *c*, the reader needs to know the next letter. If the next letter is *i*, for example, the *c* has an *s* sound, but the reader still doesn't know how to pronounce the *i*. It is not possible to determine the pronunciation of *i* until the end of the word is reached. It has the short sound in *city* and the long sound in *cite*. Until the whole word is perceived, the reader cannot assign phonetic values to the individual parts. This example is not an exception. To sound out words part to whole with phonics, it is necessary to go to the end of the word and work backward.

The Look–Say Alternative

A phonics approach to reading is not effective. It is too slow and often is painful. Students who depend on phonics to sound out words letter by letter often decide that reading is simply not worth the effort. An alternative to phonics that some educators have suggested is a "look–say" method. In this approach, students are shown flash cards of whole words to memorize. However, whole words are still not the "whole" necessary for reading to have meaning. Consider the following series of words (taken from Smith 1985).

minute

the

read

permit

print

on

the

When we have asked different people to read the words on this list aloud, we have gotten different results. Sometimes the first word is \min-et\ but other readers say \mə-n'(y)üt\. The second word can be \thə\ or \thē\. Readers can't decide whether the third word rhymes with *reed* or with *red*. It isn't until readers know the whole sentence, "Read the minute print on the permit," that they know how to pronounce the words or even what the individual words mean. To pronounce individual words, we often have to know what syntactic role they play in a sentence.

Still another example shows that even when we know all the words and can understand individual sentences, we may not be able to make much sense out of text. We have often given teachers the following paragraph to try to make this point.

With hocked gems financing him our hero defied all scornful laughter that tried to prevent his scheme. "Your eyes deceive you," he had said. "An egg, not a table correctly typifies this unexplored planet." Now three sturdy sisters sought proof, forging along, sometimes through calm vastness, yet more often over turbulent peaks and valleys. Days became weeks as many doubters spread fearful rumors about the edge. At last, from nowhere, welcome winged creatures appeared, signifying momentous success.

Readers who first encounter this text usually complain that it is poorly written, that it doesn't make any sense, and that the parts don't go together. They understand all the words, but they can't tell us what "hocked gems" refers to or what the phrase "an egg, not a table" means. When we ask them to tell us what would help them understand this text, they often ask for a title. These readers have all the parts, but they need the whole, the main idea. They know intuitively that titles often supply that information. If we supply a title such as "Columbus' Voyage to America," all the parts seem to come together for most readers. Instead of perceiving the story as a series of unconnected sentences, the teachers see that the text is cohesive and coherent.

One last consideration should be mentioned here. When we work with second language learners, the above passage about Columbus could present an additional problem. For immigrant students who have no knowledge of Columbus, the title is not a useful clue. The reference to Columbus provides the whole only if we have the requisite background knowledge and experience. For our second language students, "Columbus" may simply be one more unconnected part. They need more than a title as background for understanding this passage.

To summarize, part-to-whole instruction makes learning hard for several reasons. First, as the phonics examples show, it is hard to understand the individual parts outside the context of the whole. Second, the whole is more than the sum of the parts, so even if we know all the parts, as we did with the passage about Columbus, we may still not understand the whole. Third, and most important, if we give students only the parts, they may decide they are not much interested in them because they really don't know what the whole might be like. That's what would probably happen to us if we first experienced lasagna one part at a time the way the children did in the first lesson described. As a result, whole language teachers attempt to teach reading and other subjects from whole to part.

Teaching Reading Whole to Part

In René's first grade classroom, language is kept whole. There are thirty-five children in the classroom representing five different ethnic groups, including African-Americans, Hispanics, Hmongs, Anglos, and Laotians. Although many of the children enter René's classroom at the beginning of the first grade unable to read, they all leave as readers.

Print is visible everywhere. There are books of different sizes in the book racks, charts with poetry and songs, lists of the students' favorite children's authors with the books they have written, stories written by the children, and a message board for leaving messages to other classmates. The teacher and children read, write, and talk together daily. René reads favorite stories that the children soon memorize and read with her, with peers, or by themselves in the book corner. (This early memorization is a stage of reading and is not the same as the conscious memorization that goes on when, for example, one memorizes a poem.) The students read books by one children's author and discuss how that author's books are the same or different. They read songs and poetry from charts.

The children write their own stories representing whole words by single letters, by letters representing the first and last sounds, and by letters representing syllables as they move toward conventional spelling. Although various children may be at different stages of the writing process at any given time, they read their stories to their teacher and to each other. They read and write messages for the message center. The children are constantly writing, reading, and discussing whole texts of interest to them.

When asked how she teaches reading, René explains that she doesn't teach reading directly. Her students learn to read by reading, not by being taught sounds or words in isolation. Not all children in her classroom become independent readers at the same time, but the constant exposure to the reading of whole, meaningful texts eventually leads all her students, including her second language students, into reading. Her students become skilled language users (Lebsock 1988).

Whole Language: Skills in Context?

In René's classroom, students develop literacy using a whole-to-part approach. However, the question she most commonly is asked is, How do you teach reading skills in a whole language approach?

Teachers who ask this question may see whole language as just another way to teach skills such as phonics or vocabulary. The assumption is that whole language teachers simply teach these skills in context. However, as Edelsky, Altwerger, and Flores (1991) point out, getting to the parts and teaching the skills is not the goal of whole language teachers:

> What one child learns is not necessarily what other children are learning, and most importantly, what is taught or learned is triggered by what the children need for the language they are actually using at the time. That is, to become skilled language users, the focus of both teachers' and children's activity is whatever purposes the children themselves are trying to accomplish. By contrast, to learn language skills, children work on exercises according to a curricular sequence, and above all, the focus of teacher's and children's activity is the skill. (p. 38)

The goal of whole language teachers like René is to enable students to become skilled language users. Her goal is not to teach separate language skills. The focus on skills has been largely the result of confusing causes and effects. Good readers can do phonics. But children don't need to practice phonics to read and write. Children in René's classroom can pick out sounds from their reading and write by sounding out words. Good readers develop large vocabularies. But children do not need to develop large vocabularies to learn how to read, write, and speak. René's students carry on class discussions using sophisticated vocabulary and write using a wide range of words. The focus is always on the whole, on communicating through reading and writing as well as speaking and listening, and in that process the students develop the parts, the sounds and words.

As students actually read and write whole texts, they become more aware of the parts. Teachers may help learners focus on these parts. When René worked with her students as they were writing, she often asked them the beginning sound of a word they were trying to write. When the children were reading, she would ask what sounds letters made. However, she only asked these questions about words that occurred in the stories children were reading or writing and only when those questions helped students understand or express an idea. The focus on parts was not designed to refine or practice specific skills.

As they worked with their teacher, René's students learned more about literacy. Goodman and others (1987) describe learning as "coming to know through the symbolic transformation and representation of experience" (p. 98). The knowing cycle involves three stages: *perceiving, ideating,* and *presenting.* René's students perceived written language as they read. Beginning readers don't really "see" all the words or letters, but when they write as well as read, they begin to "read like a writer" (Smith 1982). That is, they begin to perceive the smaller parts of words. In this process, they also ideate, or build concepts about words. In their writing, the children present their ideations to others. By examining students' written presentations, teachers can assess children's conceptualizations of print.

Involving students in reading and writing complete texts allows them to come to know as they move through the three stages of the learning cycle. Whole language teachers understand that language is learned best when it is kept whole. When we break that whole down, we make learning more difficult. We are attempting to do for students what they must do for themselves if they are to construct their own understanding of literacy processes. The goal of literacy instruction is to produce skilled readers and writers, not to teach reading and writing skills.

Two Scenarios of Second Language Classrooms

Whole language teachers realize that attempts to transmit knowledge directly by teaching skills or attempts to divide knowledge up for the learner only subvert natural learning processes. These approaches do not make learning easier. What, then, should the teacher's role be if learning develops whole to part? To help illustrate the differences between whole-to-part and part-to-whole approaches, we will contrast two classrooms of second language learners.

Scenario #1

Betty teaches English as a Second Language (ESL) in a large, inner-city high school in California. Her students are mostly Hispanics and Southeast Asians who have varied educational backgrounds. Betty's class is a fairly traditional ESL class in which students work to improve their linguistic competence, their ability to manipulate linguistic units, rather than their communicative competence (Hymes 1970). To do this, Betty uses several part-to-whole activities to build vocabulary and improve grammatical accuracy. For example, students memorize and repeat dialogues, complete worksheets, study word lists, and take spelling and grammar tests.

In a typical period, Betty turns on the tape recorder as soon as the bell rings, and the students listen to the ten-line dialogue from the week's lesson. After listening to the dialogue, the students repeat each line after the speaker on the tape while looking at the dialogue in their books. Betty then turns off the tape and asks the students to practice the dialogue in pairs for five minutes. Next, Betty leads oral substitution drills from the dialogue. She reads a sentence, and the students give the contracted form:

Teacher	Students
I am hungry.	I'm hungry.
She is laughing.	She's laughing.
They are in class.	They're in class.

After the students have practiced the drills orally, they do a written exercise on contractions in their workbooks. During the last fifteen minutes of the class, Betty dictates a list of vocabulary words and asks the students to write sentences using the words.

Scenario #2

Lonna's classroom is also a high school classroom for second language learners. Her students come from many different countries, although the majority are Southeast Asian students whose first languages are Hmong, Laotian, Khmer, and Thai. Lonna's class is called a content reading class, and her goal is to prepare her students to be mainstreamed into regular content classes. Lonna believes that her students must be involved in authentic, meaningful reading and writing to become competent readers and writers of English. In Lonna's classroom, students read whole texts on topics that are important to them and write about their reading. There are no isolated vocabulary lists, no oral repetition drills, or grammar lessons. A description of a unit on newspapers gives an idea of how Lonna approaches teaching (Freeman and Freeman 1989c).

A general discussion of the purpose and value of the newspaper began the unit. A speaker from the local paper came and explained to the class the various parts of a paper, such as headlines, the masthead, the index, and the different sections. During this talk, students were able to examine the various sections of the newspaper, since the school had purchased enough newspapers so that each student could have one. In addition, the students toured the newspaper offices.

Later Lonna posted on a bulletin board an article, which had just appeared in the local newspaper, about the Ban Vinay refugee camp. Her students, many of whom had lived at the camp, read the article with interest. When Lonna invited students to write about the article, the response was enthusiastic. Mai began her response by reflecting on her experiences at the camp:

> My memories of Ban Vinay in Thailand is very sad. When we live in Ban Vinay my brother is very sick. He almost died there. We were very poor. We have to get in a line to get our food. I was very small at that time. When we get in line, all the older people always step over me, because I was so small they couldn't see me.

Mai's writing and that of her classmates was put up on the board, around the news article. This activity generated a great deal of interest. Students from ESL classes across the campus came to the room to read the news article and the student responses and then added their own writing.

Mai's teacher created an activity in which learning could move from whole to part. In the Ban Vinay lesson, students responded to a whole article, not part of an article or an adapted, simplified version of an article. Full, unadapted texts provide more comprehensible input than do adapted or simplified texts (Freeman and Goodman in press). The students' written responses were full pieces of writing, not constrained or limited by the teacher. Both Graves (1983) and Calkins (1986) have argued that only when writers produce whole texts from the start do they develop an adequate understanding of the writing process. Lonna used a whole-to-part approach to reading and writing instruction.

The two scenarios provide examples of part-to-whole and whole-to-part teaching of second language students. In the first scenario, Betty used a modified audio–lingual method as she had students repeat dialogues and practice drills. She also worked on isolated grammar points and lists of words. Lonna, by contrast, kept language in authentic context. To understand whole language for ESL students more fully, it is important to consider the role of context in learning. All learning occurs in a context, and the richer that context, the easier the learning.

Cummins's View of Language Acquisition

Research on second language acquisition by Cummins (1981, 1989) has helped highlight the important role context plays in developing language proficiency. Cummins explains that learners may develop two different types of proficiency. Conversational proficiency is the ability to use language in face-to-face communication, whereas academic proficiency is the ability to carry out school-related literacy tasks. To explain the difference between academic and conversational proficiency, Cummins developed a framework that places any instance of language use into one of the four quadrants on the chart presented here as figure 1–1.

Cummins found that it took immigrant students about two years to develop conversational proficiency (quadrant A) but five to seven years to reach grade level norms in academic tasks (quadrant D). A closer examination of the two scales Cummins uses to define language proficiency provides additional evidence for the need to teach whole to part.

In figure 1–1 the horizontal scale places instances of language use along a continuum from *context-embedded* to *context-reduced*. An example of context-embedded language is a discussion between a salesperson and a customer deciding which of several sweaters to buy. The two can negotiate meaning by referring to the sweaters as well as by using gestures, changes in intonation, and so on. Telephone conversations are much more context-reduced. Although callers can infer meaning from intonation, they can not rely on facial expressions, gestures, or reference to things both people can see. Cummins (1981) describes context-embedded communication as deriving from "interpersonal involvement in a shared reality that reduces the need for explicit linguistic elaboration of the message" (p. 11). In context-reduced communication, on the other hand, "that shared reality can not be assumed and thus linguistic messages must be elaborated precisely and explicitly" (p. 11). In particular, academic language requires "the ability to make complex meanings

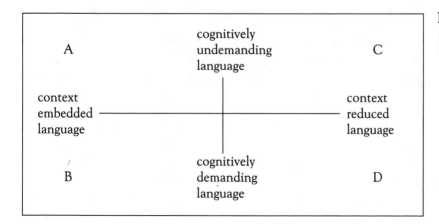

Figure 1.1
(Cummins, 1981, p. 12)

explicit in either oral or written modalities by means of language itself rather than by means of paralinguistic cues" (Cummins 1989, p. 30).

Cummins emphasizes that to facilitate the development of academic proficiency, teachers must begin by providing context-embedded instruction: "academic growth will be fostered by context-embedded instruction that validates students' background experiences by encouraging them to express, share and amplify these experiences" (p. 29). Language develops as we have increased opportunities to use it in authentic contexts for real purposes. For that reason, whole language teachers of second language students teach language and content by beginning with the experiences of their students and building on those experiences. They "teach to and from the experiences of the students" (Olsen and Mullen 1990, p. 56). Rather than teaching isolated language parts, then, Cummins suggests that the role of the teacher is to keep language in meaningful contexts, that is, to provide authentic language events and to ensure that students are working with whole language, not simplified parts.

Providing Context to Support Language Development

One way to embed language in context is to provide the kind of extralinguistic support found in authentic language use. For example, if two children on the playground are talking about who is going to use the swing first, their conversation is embedded in the situational context. The extralinguistic cues include objects, such as the swing, and actions, such as pointing, as well as gestures and intonation cues.

Second language teachers know that the greater the contextual support provided by objects and actions, the lower the necessity for students to rely solely on their new language itself. In traditional language classes teachers frequently provide extralinguistic cues by developing lessons around things and people found in the classroom including the teacher and the students themselves. Further, teachers may bring objects from home into the classroom or ask students to bring things in to talk about. "Show and tell" is popular in both mainstream and ESL classrooms with good reason.

When conversations are about things or people that are not present, teachers can still provide context by bringing in pictures that show people and places outside the classroom. If they are reading to students, teachers may use big books that contain illustrations all the students can see. Acting out situations that do not occur naturally in the classroom is another way teachers can provide context. Such role-play allows students to communicate without having to rely solely on the words that are spoken. Further, teachers may use gestures such as holding a hand to their ear to mimic talking on the telephone, and, in this way, enrich the context.

In some cases the only context available is linguistic. Cummins uses the term "context-reduced" rather than "decontextualized" to describe cases in which the primary context is the language itself. He recognizes that language offers a range of possible contextual support. An expository text or a lecture is easier to understand if there is an introduction that outlines the main points. Stories are easier to understand if they follow a familiar pattern. Children who have heard many stories learn these patterns. Often stories begin with "Once upon a time . . .," then a problem arises, and usually there is a resolution with a happy ending. As students come to understand this pattern, subsequent stories become more predictable.

Teachers of second language students may also use the students' first language to provide contextual support for the second language. Bilingual teachers often use a method called *preview, view, and review.* In the first phase, they preview the lesson in the students' first language. This helps ensure that the students understand the big picture. It helps them follow the "view," the actual lesson conducted in their second language. Finally, the teacher may provide additional context for the lesson by reviewing the main concepts again in the first language.

A summary of the kinds of possible contextual support for communication are represented in figure 1–2.

This figure suggests that teachers facilitate language learning when they keep authentic language in context by providing either extralinguistic or linguistic cues. This approach contrasts with many methods of language teaching that rely on simplified materials. Attempts at simplifying language forms or functions often result in inauthentic language. Practice with simplified language forms may cause students to form false ideas about natural language. Above all, simplification limits the range of cues available and reduces the context. The importance of the role of context in developing language proficiency becomes more apparent when we examine the way in which context is related to cognitive demand.

Figure 1.2

	Language	
Context-embedded		*Context-reduced*
Extralinguistic cues provided by situation objects or actions.	Linguistic cues provided by use of cohesive, coherent language.	Language lacks linguistic or extralinguistic cues.
Teacher uses role play realia, or pictures, and gestures.	Teacher uses stories with predictable patterns, outlines, and story maps.	

Cognitively Demanding Language

The second dimension Cummins uses in figure 1–1 to define language proficiency is a scale from *cognitively undemanding* to *cognitively demanding* language. Cummins explains that this continuum "is intended to address the developmental aspects of communicative competence in terms of the degree of active cognitive involvement in the task or activity" (p. 12). At an early stage, an activity may require a high level of cognitive involvement. Over time, as the task is mastered, the activity becomes more automatic, and the cognitive demand lessens. The scale is intended to be developmental in that a task that is demanding at one stage becomes less demanding at a later stage. For example, certain aspects of phonology or syntax are very demanding for a three-year-old but relatively undemanding for a six-year-old. A three-year-old may have trouble pronouncing a word with *r* and say *wabbit* rather than *rabbit*, but *r*'s generally present six-year-olds with no problems. When a person acquires a second language, tasks that are at first cognitively demanding are later less demanding. For example, second language learners might form negatives at first by using constructions such as "I no like it." Later, these learners produce the conventional form easily.

Cummins equates cognitive demand with the amount of conscious attention required by a task. This aspect of proficiency is developmental in that familiarity with a task makes it less demanding. For example, when learning to drive a car, a person must focus a great deal of conscious attention on details such as steering, engaging the clutch, and shifting. Fairly soon, these tasks become automatic, and the driver's mind is freed to concentrate on other matters. After a long trip, we might arrive at our destination having solved a complex academic problem and realize that we can scarcely remember any of the actual details of driving the car. Because we drive frequently, driving occupies little conscious attention.

Although performing a task frequently may reduce cognitive demand, this should not suggest that we can simplify learning by breaking a task into parts and practicing those parts in isolation. We learn to drive a car by actually driving a car, and if we drive frequently, we do so because driving serves a real function for us. We develop separate driving skills in the context of actual driving.

When we are familiar with a task, it is less cognitively demanding for us. We don't need to pay as much conscious attention to it. In the same way, language in context seems easier than context-reduced language. Is there a connection between these two concepts Cummins uses to explain language proficiency? That is, how can we explain the relationship between cognitive demand and context?

The Relationship between Context and Cognitive Demand

Context is often viewed as something external to the learner. However, if the concept of context can include both *external* context (the swings on the playground) and *internal* context (previous experience or background knowledge), then the relationship between Cummins' ideas of context-embedded language and cognitively demanding language becomes clearer. Our previous experience or background knowledge serves as a context for each subsequent instance of language use. When we can use background to make sense of new ideas, we find those ideas less cognitively demanding. Even when there is no external contextual support, if we can make use of an internal support system developed through previous experience, tasks demand less conscious attention.

This helps explain why certain subjects are not, in themselves, necessarily more cognitively demanding than other subjects. It is true that some subjects are more complex than others. Calculus is harder than algebra. Further, to study some topics it is helpful to study other topics first. However, while different topics have different potentials for the demands they might put on a person, the demand a particular topic makes depends on a person's previous experiences with that topic. To a mathematician, both algebra and calculus may seem quite easy.

Consider the following example of how previous experience interacts with cognitive demand. If we have lived all our lives in a country such as the United States where temperatures are given in Fahrenheit, it is not cognitively demanding for us to decide what to wear when someone reports that the temperature outside is 22 degrees. However, if we travel to Canada and someone reports that the temperature is 22, we have more mental work to do. We have to make some connection between the Fahrenheit scale and the Celsius scale so that we can relate our past experiences. We can figure out what to wear, but the task is more cognitively demanding because we lack the necessary background.

The effect of previous experience also shows up in reading. If a person reads narrowly as Krashen (1985) suggests, reading is easier. Narrow reading focuses in on one topic or one author. By the time a teenager reaches the second or third *Sweet Valley High* book, he or she can easily predict many elements of character and plot. The teen has built up a context from reading the earlier books in the series. The language of the new book is context-embedded, so it is less cognitively demanding.

Cummins's framework has two scales, and this suggests that context and cognitive demand are separate concepts. Wald (1984), who has suggested that Cummins's framework does not adequately address sociolinguistic factors associated with the development of language proficiency, notes that the framework "weds the seemingly social concept of context-embedding with the psychological concept of cognitive demand" (p. 62). Whole language approaches to literacy are frequently labeled *socio-psycholinguistic* because there is the recognition that individual psychological processes always occur in a social context. If Cummins's horizontal scale may be thought to reflect social factors and the vertical scale embodies psychological factors, as Wald suggests, it should be possible to combine the two into a single scale. Our background knowledge helps determine how cognitively demanding a subject is, and background knowledge can be considered as part of the context, so language that is context-embedded is less cognitively demanding than language that is context-reduced. The two concepts may be represented as shown in figure 1–3.

Figure 1–3 suggests that as we learn something, whether it is a new language or a new subject, we rely most heavily at first on external cues. Over time, we learn which features to attend to; that is, we discover the conventional patterns. Foreign language students

Figure 1.3

Cog. undemanding language ————→ Cog. demanding language

Context-embedded		*Context-reduced*
the learner uses external cues provided by things, people, or language.	the learner has internalized external cues and can use this background knowledge even when external cues are not present.	the learner is not yet able to use external cues and has not yet constructed internal cues to provide background knowledge.
social aspects	psychological aspects	

often report that speakers of the language they are studying talk very rapidly. They get this impression because they don't know which parts of the language count. For example, in English it does not matter whether a sound like *p* is aspirated or not. Although there is a physical difference between the *p* in *pot* and the *p* in *spot*, native English speakers can ignore that difference. When English speakers learn Korean, however, they find they have to attend to aspiration because differences in aspiration produce different meanings in words. Since students learning a new language do not know which features to attend to, they try to listen to all the details at once, and this results in cognitive overload.

Krashen (1982) has hypothesized that we acquire a language when we receive *comprehensible input*, which he defines as messages that we understand. We only understand messages in a new language when the cognitive demand is not too high, when it is below a certain threshold. Second language teachers make input comprehensible by embedding it at first in a rich extralinguistic context. Over time, students begin to build an internal representation of the language they are studying, a specialized background knowledge, that allows them to understand messages even when they are not context-embedded.

Context cues are important in all learning. Goodman (1984) argues that much of learning involves making predictions. We use all available cues to reduce our uncertainty and confirm our predictions. Here again, there is a connection between context and cognitive demand. The more cues that are available, internal or external, the less uncertainty there is to reduce and the less cognitively demanding is the task. It is easier to make successful predictions when we have adequate background knowledge.

For example, my knowledge of English spelling patterns makes it fairly easy for me to predict which word can be formed by unscrambling the letters *h, c, l, a, k*. I know that the normal pattern for English words is consonant-vowel-consonant, so I place the *a* in the middle. I also know that only certain consonant clusters can begin and end words. Words often end in *ck* and few English words begin with *kl*. Even though this knowledge helps me unscramble "chalk," the task is still context-reduced because I am dealing with a word in isolation. It would be easier to predict the word if it appeared in a story as part of the line, "The teacher picked up the _____ and wrote on the blackboard." In fact, I don't really need the letter cues to make an accurate prediction in this context because the sentence reduces my uncertainty and allows easy prediction. This example demonstrates the importance of keeping language in authentic context.

Learning involves constructing meaning using all available cues. Teachers who teach whole to part provide as many cues as possible, knowing that the greater the number of cues, the less demanding the task of comprehending. Unscrambling an individual word like *chalk* is more difficult than reading the same word in a story, because in the story the word is embedded in context. In the process of comprehending a story, when learners can use background knowledge to make predictions based on the whole, they can understand the parts more easily. Language is less cognitively demanding when it is more context-embedded, so whole language teachers teach whole to part to provide as much context as possible.

Part-to-Whole
Vocabulary Instruction

One area of the curriculum where part-to-whole instruction predominates is the teaching of vocabulary. It is a common practice in both first and second language classrooms to teach isolated vocabulary words apart from any real context, either by presenting lists of words or by teaching word parts. Sometimes teachers make up word lists by selecting from a story or from a textbook chapter words that they think would be difficult for their students. However, experience shows that it is hard to define words when they appear on a list. The first thing most parents do when their child asks them to help with vocabulary homework by defining a word like *condolences* is to ask the child to put the word in a sentence. Parents know intuitively that it is easier to define words in context. Taking words out of a text takes them out of context and limits the available clues that would help students understand them.

Other problems emerge when using word lists to teach vocabulary. For one thing, it is hard to predict which words all the students will have trouble with. In addition, students may find a meaning for a word that is not the meaning that applies in the text it came from. Besides, if we were limited in our vocabulary to words we learned each week on a list, we simply wouldn't have enough words to communicate effectively.

Some teachers attempt to make learning vocabulary more efficient by breaking the words down into their parts and teaching word roots, prefixes, and suffixes (Freeman 1991). The critical question, then, is, Does a knowledge of word roots and affixes allow students to predict the meaning of words? Is the meaning of the whole word equal to the sum of its parts?

Let's look more closely at this common approach to teaching vocabulary through its parts. Examples here come from a workbook series designed to teach phonics by Herr (1959), who states:

> A root word is a small word from which a larger word is made. About 65 percent of the words in our dictionary come from Latin and Greek roots. A few of the most-used Latin and Greek roots are given below. It will help you increase your word power if you know these. When you come to a word you do not know, try to pronounce it with your knowledge of phonics, then if you still do not recognize the word or its meaning, look at a base word and then look for the prefix and suffix. (p. 75)

According to Herr, the first step in determining the meaning of a word is to pronounce it. If that doesn't work, apply your knowledge of affixes and roots. This approach appears to work well in some cases. Consider the following prefixes, roots, and suffixes.

Prefix	**Root**	**Suffix**
re- back, again	cogn- know	-ize to make
con- with	bene- good	-tion state or condition
un- not	dic(t)- say	-al relation to
de- from, down	greg- flock	-ate to make
	capit- head	

Using the information from these parts, we can arrive at definitions of complex words:

con+greg+ate+ion+al = relation to the state or condition of being with the flock
un+re+cogn+ized = not made known again
bene+dic+tion = the condition of saying something good
de+capit+ate = to make the head (go) from

We can connect the meanings of the parts and the meaning of the whole. But which came first, our knowledge of the meaning of the whole word or our knowledge of the meaning of the parts? In answering this question, it is helpful to consider what must be done to use word parts to determine meaning. A person must overcome certain potential problems:

1. Deciding which parts are prefixes, roots, and suffixes
2. Deciding what the root really is
3. Deciding which meaning of a root or affix applies

For example, is *cognate* made up of *co* + *gnatus* or *cogn* + *ate*? Which meaning of *re* should we use to determine the meaning of *retire*, *back* or *again*?

Often these problems are not apparent to someone who knows both the meaning of the word and the meanings of the parts. For the teachers who use prefixes, roots, and suffixes to teach vocabulary, it makes perfect sense to look at the parts to understand the whole. However, this process breaks down when someone does not already know the meaning of the words.

We would like to try to put you, the reader, in the situation that many students find themselves. That is, we would like to have you apply your knowledge of roots and affixes to some words that may be less familiar.

Try using your knowledge of roots and affixes to define the following words (you may use the meanings previously listed if you wish): (1) capitation, (2) capitular, (3) cognomen, (4) beneficiate, and (5) benefice.

Now try defining these words: (1) regregation, (2) unconcapitize, and (3) decognal.

Here are some possible answers for the first five words.
capitation—a direct, uniform tax imposed upon each person
    (head)
capitular—of or relating to an ecclesiastical chapter (chapter =
    head)
cognomen—surname or nickname

beneficiate—to prepare iron for smelting

benefice—an ecclesiastical office to which revenue for an endowment is attached

How did you do on the first set of words? Most teachers we have worked with find that unless they already knew the meaning of a word on the list, their definitions were not too close to the dictionary definitions we have provided here. Even when they were given the meanings of the parts, they were not able to guess the meaning of the whole.

As you may have suspected, the second list consists of words we made up. It is interesting to see how many different definitions a group of teachers comes up with in trying to define the words on the second list. This exercise shows that knowledge of the meaning of word parts does not necessarily lead to knowledge of the meaning of words. It is only when we know the meaning of the word *and* we know the meaning of the affixes and root that we can make a logical connection. When we know the whole, the parts make sense.

Vocabulary instruction, whether it consists of memorizing weekly word lists or of learning word parts, is a prime example of a part-to-whole approach. We make learning easier when we go whole to part. Otherwise, our students may not ever see the forest because they are too busy trying to identify the individual trees. This is particularly true for our second language students.

Part-to-Whole Instruction with Second Language Students

Students who speak English as a second language face all the part-to-whole instruction that other students face. Beyond that, though, they often have to contend with part-to-whole methods particular to second language teaching. Most adults who studied a foreign language in high school or college can remember this kind of teaching. In the *grammar-translation method*, students studied the verb *to be* one week and the next week they began to study the regular verbs (in the present tense only, of course). They memorized lists of words and translated sentences from English to the target language and from the target language to English. And after three or four years of studying French or Spanish or German, they could ask a few questions in the new language, but they certainly couldn't understand the answers. In fact, no one really expected them to be able to actually speak the foreign language at the end of the course. The goal of the course was to expand the intellect by doing the exercises and to be able to translate works of literature in the foreign language (Larsen-Freeman 1986).

Another second language teaching method that goes from part to whole is the *audio–lingual method*. The lesson (in Scenario #1) taught by Betty followed principles of this method. Textbooks for this method were written by structural linguists. This group of linguists divided language into subsystems (phonology, morphology, syntax, and semantics) and described the structures within each system. Some language educators believe that it is logical to teach language using the organization of subsystems as proposed by the structural linguists. In the audio–lingual method, structures are presented one at a time and students drill those structures until they have mastered them. Unfortunately, this is another case of something that is logical but not psychological. This part-to-whole teaching makes it hard for students to actually communicate in the new language. This is one reason that many adults who studied a foreign language in high school or college cannot speak the language now.

A Shift Toward Whole-to-Part Language Teaching

The recognition that all learning, including language learning, involves a gradual process of differentiating the parts out of the whole has led to a change in second language teaching. Instead of beginning with discrete bits of language, teachers attempt to surround students with a wide range of the target language. These teachers use specific techniques to make the new language understandable. They do this by embedding the linguistic elements of communication in a rich nonlinguistic context. They recognize that language is easier to learn when it is kept whole. They know that plunging a student into a new language, the old sink-or-swim method, is not the best way to teach. Instead, they create situations in which students dealing with the full range of the target language get clues from the context that help them make sense of what they are experiencing. In Krashen's (1982) terms, they make the input comprehensible.

In addition, these teachers, even when they are teaching a class called English as a Second Language (or French or German), keep language in its larger communicative context. Rather than focusing on the language itself, they create situations where students can use language for authentic purposes. They recognize that language is best learned in the functional context of use, so they teach language through the content areas.

Whole Language Teachers Teaching Whole to Part

In a summer program for secondary high school students that we observed, the teachers were encouraged to apply whole-to-part teaching in their content classrooms for second language students (Freeman and Freeman 1989a). Rather than having their students focus on language or memorize bits and pieces of information about biology or history, these teachers taught language through content by concentrating on key concepts.

In a U.S. history class, Rob, the teacher, began the unit on the American Revolution by asking students to talk about what revolution meant, why countries had revolutions, where there were revolutions right now, and finally what they knew about the American Revolution. Both Rob and the students brought in current periodicals with articles about present-day revolutions. Rob read the students a short story about the American Revolution to help make the characters and setting of the period come alive. He also showed a film about the American Revolution. Students then read the social studies text, compared what they read with the information about revolutions they had already gathered, and worked in groups to decide what the major causes of the American Revolution were, what events and people were important to the outcome, and how the American Revolution could be compared to other revolutions discussed in class.

Rob was working with students who had not been successful in previous classes. They were language minority students and had scored low on standardized tests. However, they did well in Rob's class. Part of their success can be attributed to the rich context Rob provided. Rather than teaching isolated vocabulary, he built a strong background for concepts such as "revolution" long before the students encountered that term in their text. By itself, the textbook offered context-reduced language, but the class activities provided the context that made the textbook understandable.

In a second class, the biology teacher organized a number of activities in which his students worked in cooperative groups and examined real plants and animals. For example, one day he brought in a variety of fruits and vegetables. The students, working in small groups, studied the samples. They began with very general observations. Bananas had only one outer layer of skin while onions had many layers. Oranges could be divided into equal sections, but turnips were not so conveniently organized.

As the students examined various fruits and vegetables, they categorized them according to different criteria. They became more adept at making accurate observations, either directly or under a microscope. They began to see the world as a biologist sees it and to ask the kinds of questions a biologist might ask. As their investigations continued, they worked in teams to explore particular aspects of the topic that interested them.

These kinds of activities provided the whole, the context the students needed to develop the concepts and the language necessary for their study of biology. The language was embedded in experiences with real fruits and vegetables, and students received added support from one another as they interacted in small groups. The teacher did not rely exclusively on the textbook but, instead, opened the whole world of biology to his students and yet did it in a way that helped them understand it.

Conclusion

In this chapter we have examined the commonsense assumption that learning goes from part to whole. Part-to-whole teaching dominates in our schools. Teachers and textbooks attempt to make learning easier by dividing it up into bite-sized chunks for student consumption.

Part-to-whole approaches to teaching and learning, we have argued, are logical but they are not psychological. The parts are more difficult to learn outside the context of the whole. In many cases, students lose interest in the whole after they struggle with the parts. Tasting oregano, tomato sauce, and mozzarella doesn't whet their appetite for lasagna.

Whole language teachers keep language whole. They know that whole language is richer in context than adapted or simplified language. Language embedded in context is less cognitively demanding than context-reduced language. Whole language teachers also recognize that an important part of learning is the process of constructing meaning by determining which parts count. They believe that students will only develop a love of reading or writing or social studies if they have the opportunity to read and write complete texts and talk about ideas that make sense in their world. The students are not expected to memorize and reproduce information; instead, they construct their own understandings.

Whole language teachers realize that whole-to-part teaching is good for all students, but that it is especially important for second language students. These students need context-rich language so that they can understand instruction. They need to see the whole so that they know what to do with the parts. They need to be immersed in meaningful activities, not submerged in the grammatical details of a new language.

Whole-to-part teaching is not easy for the teacher because school days are fragmented. Standardized tests encourage teachers to have students learn bits and pieces of subjects. Teachers may never have personally experienced learning in a whole-to-part classroom and, in many schools, few other teachers may be trying to teach from whole to part. Yet, despite the obstacles to this approach, whole language teachers reject the commonsense view that learning progresses from part to whole and attempt to teach whole to part, because they know this makes learning easier for their students.

2

Lessons Should Be Learner Centered

Gangs Fight
BY ROGELIO SANCHEZ AND GEORGE GADISON

There have been many reports of fighting all around Fresno, L.A. and some alleys by Red Rags, Blue Rags, F-14ers, Midnight Cruisers, L.A. Cruisers and some other gangs.

They steal, kill, fight, get revenge and go cruising out of town. They usually fight with their fists, sticks, knives, guns and possibly some other weapons.

Many people think that they fight because they hate each other and they are prejudiced to each other.

Many meetings have been done by our government to stop gang fighting. Will they stop? No one knows.

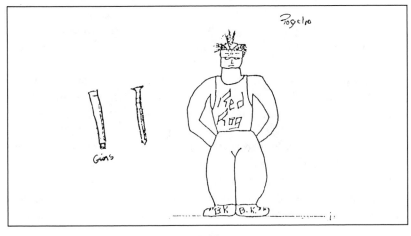

This item in *Top Action News* (June 15, 1988), a newsletter published in Charlene's fourth grade classroom, is an example of students writing about what is important to them and what is part of their world. The publication of this newsletter was just one of the many ways that Charlene helped make the instruction for these students learner centered.

Because most of Charlene's students were second language learners coming from a variety of first language backgrounds, it was critical that the curriculum for them draw on their background, their interests, and their strengths. To build on what her students knew about and were interested in learning, Charlene had them read and discuss books about young people from various cultures in literature studies, worked with them on a unit on the theme of "prejudice," arranged for them to be "reading buddies" for first graders, and involved them in group work for presentation to peers on content topics of their choice. All of these activities were learner centered because they follow Dewey's (1929) advice that "the child is the starting point, the center, and the end" (p. 14) of all curriculum decisions.

Charlene's classroom exemplifies a second important principle of whole language—*classes* should be learner centered rather than teacher centered. Y. Goodman, a leader in the field of whole language reseach, has said that the cartoonist, Bil Keane, can summarize years of Goodman's whole language research in one cartoon. This learner-centered principle is illustrated in one of Keane's "Family Circus" cartoons in which Billy leads his younger sister, Dolly, into the house after school explaining to their mother, "Dolly's school would be better if they didn't have that lady up front talkin' all the time."

The idea of the teacher as the source of all knowledge standing up front and directing instruction follows from commonsense assumptions of how schooling should be. This traditional image is even more strongly supported when bilingual learners are involved. With second language learners, the temptation to have a teacher-centered classroom arises because the perception is that the teacher has the English proficiency the students need. Therefore, all knowledge must come from the teacher. However, it is important to remember that second language learners are not deficient just because they do not speak English. They bring a rich and varied background of experiences and talent to the classroom. Whole language teachers find ways to use their students' knowledge, including their first language and culture, even when the students do not speak English.

To explore this idea of a learner-centered curriculum for second language learners, in this chapter we first review two approaches to teaching a second language, the *empiricist* approach and the *rationalist* approach. Methods for organizing curriculum consistent with the rationalist approach appear to be more student centered than those based on the empiricist approach. However, a closer analysis of two popular rationalist methods of teaching ESL reveals important differences between the rationalist approach and the approach used by whole language teachers. Following this discussion of traditional ESL teaching, we suggest one method for organizing learner-centered lessons by using a questioning lesson plan format. Next, we look at student publishing, one specific activity used in many learner-centered classes. Many whole language teachers like Charlene have published student work. Finally, we describe a sample unit that is strongly learner centered. This unit is organized around the questioning lesson plan and involves students in writing and publishing materials based on their lives and interests and in reading and writing about others whom they admire.

Two Approaches to Language Teaching

The Empiricist Approach

A brief history of the philosophical approaches to language teaching can provide a base for understanding the kind of instruction for second language students we frequently see in schools. From the end of the 1800s to the middle of the 1900s, foreign languages were taught by the grammar-translation method, which we discussed in chapter 1 and will further discuss in chapter 4. The grammar-translation method of teaching a second language had many limitations, and with the advent of World War II, two of these in particular stood out. Students who had studied a foreign language under a grammar-translation method could read and translate the written language, but they could not comprehend or produce the oral language. Since the U.S. Department of Defense had an interest in finding espionage agents who could function behind enemy lines, the U.S. Government became interested in effective ways of teaching people to speak and understand foreign languages, not just read and write them.

It seemed logical for members of the Defense Department to go to linguists, people who studied language, for advice about language teaching. The approach to linguistics at this time was *structural*. Structural linguists sought to describe observable features of human languages. They believed that language study should be based on descriptions of what people using the language really say rather than prescriptive rules mandating what they should say. These linguists studied languages, especially those that had never been written down, identified the salient sounds, the vocabulary, and the structural patterns. With this information, they wrote dictionaries and grammars to describe the languages they were studying.

At this time, beliefs about learning were strongly influenced by *behavioristic psychology*. Like structural linguists, behaviorists were also interested in what was observable, what could be recorded and measured. Experiments such as those with Pavlov's dogs and Skinner's boxes led to the belief that learning takes place by operant conditioning, by repetition and practice (Brown 1980).

From the influence of the structural linguistics and the behavioral psychologists, an empiricist approach to teaching language emerged. Empiricists felt that the scientific way to teach a language involved using behavioral techniques to practice and form habits with the structural patterns of the language that had been identified by linguists. This approach relied on research based on controlled experiments with animals. Empiricists held certain premises about language learning:

1. Language is speech, not writing.
2. A language is a set of habits.
3. Teach the language, not about the language.
4. A language is what its native speakers say, not what someone thinks they ought to say.
5. Languages are different. (Diller 1978, p. 19)

It is apparent that these premises constitute a reaction against methods like grammar-translation, which emphasized grammatically correct written language. In addition, the empiricists added the idea that learning was habit formation and that, since all languages are different, it is important to contrast the student's first language with the language they are learning. This comparison, called *contrastive analysis*, was designed to determine which areas of the language to be learned would cause difficulties. Then drills could be devised to avoid errors and create good language habits. For example, students of many language backgrounds would be predicted to have trouble learning that in English an *s* is added to the third person singular verb forms in present tense, so drills were written to help students practice this form.

An Empiricist Method of Teaching a Second Language

The influence of these beliefs about language gave rise to the *audio-lingual method* (ALM), which stresses oral language, memorization of dialogues, and pattern drills and de-emphasizes grammar. In an audio–lingual classroom, teachers treat second language learners as passive and believe that learning depends on a teacher-centered classroom where students are led through repetitious drills and exercises to form correct habits of pronunciation and sentence word order. Students respond to direction from teacher and text. They have no input in what they learn or how they learn it. Since they don't speak the target language, it is assumed that learners have nothing to contribute to decisions about curriculum. Despite the emergence of new understandings about linguistics and psychology, the influence of the empiricist approach is still evident today in materials and practices in many second language classrooms. ALM is still the most widely used method for teaching a second language.

The Rationalist Approach

Just as structural linguistics and behavioral psychology provided the base for an empiricist approach to language teaching, *generative* linguistics and *cognitive psychology* gave rise to the rationalist approach. Influenced by the work of Chomsky, the generative-transformational school of linguists brought about a revolution in linguistics as they sought a "distinction between the observable surface level of language and the deep structure of language, that hidden level of meaning and thought which gives birth to and generates observable surface linguistic performance" (Brown 1980, p. 11). In the same way that generative linguists posited abstract levels of meaning, cognitive psychologists considered the effect on behavior of factors, such as motivation, that could not be directly observed. Cognitive psychologists saw learners as creative, and they saw learning as being influenced by meaning and motivation. In a cognitive view, the learner is not passive but active. For second language teaching, these new understandings led to a set of premises about language that differ radically from those of empiricists:

1. A living language is characterized by rule-governed creativity.
2. The rules of grammar are psychologically real.
3. People are specially equipped to learn languages.
4. A living language is a language in which we can think.
   (Diller 1978)

These beliefs about language changed second language instruction dramatically because learners were now seen as being capable of generating their own rules for language if they received sufficient comprehensible input (Krashen 1982) or messages they could understand in that language. For example, students could create their own past tense forms for verbs. In other words, they could construct their own internal grammars when exposed to their second language without direct, explicit teaching of grammar or repetitious drills on forms. Instead of relying on teachers or texts to teach students language, rationalists believed that learners were responsible for their own learning and would learn if actively engaged in using language for real communicative purposes. For these reasons, methods consistent with the rationalist approach are more learner centered.

Rationalist Methods of Teaching a Second Language

The rationalist approach to language learning has given rise to various methods for language teaching. Two well-known and commonly used methods of teaching a second language that come from the rationalist approach are *The Silent Way* and *Community Language Learning*. We will review each of these methods to determine whether or not they are learner centered.

The Silent Way

The Silent Way, developed by Gattegno, makes students responsible for their own learning and encourages learners to become independent of the teacher. The method gets its name from the fact that the teacher is silent much of the time. During Silent Way lessons teachers model an expression only once, and then students are responsible for working together to try to reproduce what the teacher has modeled. Gattegno believes that teachers should give students only what is absolutely necessary to promote learning and that students will develop their own internal understanding of the language they are studying as they work together with classmates.

Although these ideas seem to support a learner-centered method and the rationalist view about language, several aspects of the Silent Way actually make it teacher centered and inconsistent with whole language beliefs. First, the curriculum is entirely in the hands of the teacher. Beginners are initially taught the sounds of their new language from color-coded sound charts. Next, teachers focus on language structures, sometimes using Cuisenaire rods to visually represent parts of words and sentences. For example, for a noun plural, such as *boys*, a long white rod could represent the base, *boy*, and a short blue rod could represent the inflectional affix *s*. As students begin to understand more of the language, they are taught stories using the Cuisenaire rods as props. For example, in a story about a little girl walking her dog near a park bench, the teacher might use a red rod to represent the little girl, a green rod for her dog, and a yellow rod for the park bench. At all stages of the method, the teacher models as little as possible and students try to repeat after careful listening with help from each other. The teacher leads them toward correct responses by nods or negative headshakes.

It may be true that in Silent Way classes students are in charge of their own learning, but the curriculum could hardly be called learner centered. It is the teacher who decides what should be taught, when it should be taught, and how it should be taught. In learner-centered classes, the students help determine curriculum. In Silent Way classes, students receive a curriculum that has been formulated by someone else.

In other ways, as well, Silent Way classes are not consistent with whole language principles. Language lessons that focus on sounds on a color-coded chart or language structures or stories taught with colored rods do not move from whole to part nor do they center on the students' needs and interests in the real world. The method may attempt to make the student responsible for learning, but for a curriculum to be learner centered, students must be involved in deciding what is to be learned and have a clear understanding of how the learning has relevance to them.

Community Language Learning

Community Language Learning is a method for teaching a second language that was developed by psychologist Curran. Curran based his method on Rogers's principles of humanistic psychology. Rogers saw learners as a group in need of counseling and a kind of positive therapy. In Community Language Learning (CLL) teachers serve as counselors charged with facilitating learning. They join together with students to form a learning community characterized by an accepting atmosphere. The goal is to lower students' defenses and encourage open communication.

In a typical CLL lesson students, who have previously come to know each other, sit in a small circle. The teacher/facilitator stands behind one of the students. This student makes a statement or asks a question in his or her native language. In a gentle, supportive voice the teacher translates what the student said from the student's native language to the language being learned. The student repeats what the teacher says until comfortable enough to record the new phrases or sentences on a tape recorder. This procedure is repeated with others in the circle until a short conversation is recorded. Then students listen to their conversation and the teacher writes it on the board. The textbook actually becomes what the students said in their recorded conversation. Students often copy the written conversation from the board to take home and study. As time goes on, students use more complex language and eventually come to need the teacher/facilitator less and less.

Many aspects of CLL make it a learner-centered method consistent with whole language. Not only do students take charge of their own learning, but they also set the curriculum. The language that is studied is based on what students want to say. However, though the curriculum is learner centered in the sense that it is generated by the students, there are differences between a CLL class and a whole language class.

The curriculum in a CLL class does come from the students themselves, but the curriculum is restricted by the fact it *only* comes from the students. In whole language learner-centered classrooms, the students' own language and interests are valued, but they are also expanded on by the availability of a wide variety of resources, including the teacher, books, magazines, realia, and media. Although much can be said in favor of the supportive CLL method of teaching a second language, it could also be said that it is limiting because it does not introduce new academic content to students. Students in CLL classes learn how to say in a new language what they already know. In whole language classrooms, on the other hand, the goal is to teach language through content so students get both a new language and new content area knowledge. Whole language classes are balanced. Curriculum begins with students' interests and experiences, but it uses those interests and experiences to lead students into a greater awareness of how others have attempted to answer the questions the students themselves are raising.

There is a difference, then, between the way CLL and whole language classes are learner centered. Other differences exist as well. What is done with the language once it is written down is important. Often, this language is analyzed for vocabulary or grammar study. For example, if students use the verb *to be* in an early lesson, the teacher might isolate this verb for the students to conjugate and then compare with a regular verb such as *walk*. In other words, once the conversation is completed, it may become the basis for direct instruction in grammar. This sort of instruction goes from part to whole and is not meaningful for learners.

Second Language Methods and Whole Language

Most methods for teaching second languages are based on either empiricist or rationalist approaches. Whole language teachers generally find methods based on the rationalist approach more compatible with their own teaching. Rationalists, unlike the empiricists, believe that learning depends crucially on the activity of the learner, so methods such as Community Language Learning and Silent Way begin with the learner and actively involve the learner in each lesson. However, although the learner is active, students still depend on the teacher to provide the direction and/or the knowledge for learning to take place. For example, a teacher using the rationalist approach might ask students to find vocabulary definitions in the dictionary. The students may be actively engaged, but the teacher directs the activity and determines the correctness of the results. For these reasons, whole language teachers have not adopted specific ESL methods such as Silent Way for use with their second language students.

Instead, whole language teachers follow a *transactional* approach. This approach stresses the activity of both the teacher and the learners. The teacher does not simply facilitate learning for the students. Instead, the teacher learns with the students as they explore knowledge together. Topics for exploration may come from either the students or the teacher, and together all members of the class, including the teacher, determine how to find answers to the questions they have posed. Second language students learn language in the process of exploring content area questions.

In classes where teachers and students work together to negotiate curriculum, structure is still needed. Many teachers would be uncomfortable simply playing each day "by ear" and exploring whatever comes up. This is one reason that teachers of second language students teach language through content. They know that a long-range plan is needed for learning to take place. Both the teacher and the students can help create the plan. In the next section, we discuss a way to organize curriculum that is consistent with a transactional approach and that is learner centered, yet still carefully structured.

Questioning Strategies Begin with the Student

One way to engage student interest as they learn language through content is through the use of students' questions. Clark (1988) has pointed out that curriculum should involve students "in some of the significant issues in life" and therefore encourages teachers to design their curriculum around "questions worth arguing about" (p. 29). Clark suggests questions for different grade levels such as, How am I a member of many families? (K–1); What are the patterns that make communities work? (2–3); How do humans and culture evolve and change? (4–5); and How does one live responsibly as a member of the global village? (6,7,8).

Sizer (1990) draws on the the same idea by suggesting that organizing around "Essential Questions" leads to "engaging and effective curricula." In social studies teachers responsible for teaching U.S. history might begin with broad questions such as "Who is American? Who should stay? Who should stay out? Whose country is it anyway?" (p. 49). Sizer suggests larger questions for long-term planning and smaller, engaging questions to fit within the broader ones. For example, an essential question in botany might be "What is life, growth, 'natural' development and what factors most influence healthy development?" A smaller, engaging question might be "Do stems of germinating seedlings always grow upwards and the roots downwards?" (p. 50).

In all of the preceding examples, the goal is to make the curriculum learner centered rather than teacher centered by involving students in answering relevant, real world questions that they help to raise. In the following chapter, we present steps for organizing long-term themes using Don Howard's "A Wonderfilled Way of Learning." In this chapter we suggest a way of using questions for day-to-day lesson planning and then give a sample unit based on this kind of questioning approach to planning. We should add that in a learner-centered class, the questions come primarily from the students; however, as a member of the learning community, the teacher also can raise questions.

Questioning Lesson Plan

Teachers at all levels are required to do long-term and day-to-day planning. Too often the day-to-day planning becomes routine, a kind of rote exercise completed because it is required by administrators. In our work with teacher education candidates, for example, we have found that student teachers are tempted to fulfill the requirement of preparing lesson plans by making lists—lists of page numbers students will read; lists of exercises students will complete; lists of activities students will be doing; or lists of materials that will be needed.

Although we try to get away from this mechanical type of lesson planning, we also realize that it is critical that all teachers have some plan for the general direction in which the curriculum is headed. For whole language teachers, it is important that they be able to show administrators, parents, and other teachers that their whole language curriculum does fulfill district and state curriculum guidelines. At the same time, whole language teachers must keep in mind that they should always keep the learner at the center of all curriculum decisions. A method for planning that we have suggested for student teachers and that we recommend for experienced teachers is the "Questioning Lesson Plan" (fig. 2–1). This lesson plan format is designed to help teachers reconceptualize curriculum as a series of questions generated by the students and the teacher as they explore topics together. This format also encourages teachers to remain focused on the broad concepts they are studying. It asks them to consider how each lesson might connect to broader themes. Planning lessons with this format is one way teachers can put whole language theory into practice. In addition, we suggest that they use the Whole Language Checklist (Freeman and Freeman 1988) (fig. 2–2) to review their lessons. The checklist is also a series of questions drawn from whole language principles.

Critical to any lesson plan is the idea of learner centeredness. When lessons begin with students' interests and experiences, students are naturally more motivated to engage in learning. If they are not interested in learning something, their learning is apt to be short-term rote memorization at best. In whole language classes we hope that students' interest is not based simply on the desire to do well on a test or get some other kind of extrinsic reward, but instead we hope that students will "buy into" the curriculum because they honestly are interested in answering the questions that they have helped raise. We have found that teachers who plan lessons with the Questioning Lesson Plan and review them with the Whole Language Checklist create learner-centered classrooms.

An example of a questioning plan that draws on student interest and involvement comes from Kelly, a fourth grade teacher, who teaches in a small farming community. Kelly's classroom has several Hispanic students whose first language is Spanish. The students'

Questioning Lesson Plan

1. **What is the question worth talking about?** (Can the topic for this lesson be formulated in a question? What is the engaging smaller question that fits into your broader question for your overall theme?)

2. **How does the question fit into your overall plan?** (What is the broad question/theme that you and your students are exploring over time? How does the smaller, engaging question support the concepts you are working on with this broad question?)

3. **How will you find out what the students already know about the question?** (What are different ways your students might show what they already know about answering the question? You might brainstorm, do an experiment, interview someone, etc.)

4. **What strategies will you use together to explore the question?** (What are ways the question might be answered? You and your students might read, do an experiment, brainstorm, ask an expert, work out a problem together, etc. Ask the students if they have ideas about how to answer the question.)

5. **What materials will you use together to explore the question?** (List the resources, including people, that students might use to answer the question. Again, ask the students if they have ideas about this.)

6. **What steps will you and the students take to explore the question?** (In order to be sure that you are keeping in mind principles about learning, consult the WL Checklist (see below). Do the activities you suggest incorporate whole language principles?)

7. **How will you observe the students' learning?** (What are some different ways to evaluate the process of your students' learning? Be sure to consider alternatives to traditional tests including group presentations, a group produced book or newspaper, the results of an experiment, a drawing or schemata, etc.)

facility with English varies greatly; yet, Kelly wants to be sure to involve all her students in her lessons regardless of their English proficiency.

Kelly and her students had been working on the theme of drugs. Their broad question was, How do drugs affect my life? As they explored this topic, the class looked at the surgeon general's warning

Whole Language Checklist 1. Does the lesson move from the general to the specific? Are details presented within a general conceptual framework? 2. Is there an attempt to draw on student background knowledge and interests? Are students given choices? 3. Is the content meaningful? Does it serve a purpose for the learners? 4. Do students work together cooperatively? Do students interact with one another or do they only react to the teacher? 5. Do students have an opportunity to read and write as well as speak and listen during the lesson? 6. Is there support for the students' first language and culture? 7. Does the teacher demonstrate a belief that students will succeed?

Figure 2.2
Whole
Language
Checklist

against smoking and the effects of tobacco on health. The question of why people would still buy cigarettes and smoke despite the medical evidence arose naturally from the students during discussion. Kelly thought that if she and her students looked at different advertisements, they could see how the media used propaganda. Following the Questioning Lesson Plan, Kelly's unit on drugs might look like this:

Questioning Lesson Plan

1. What is the question worth talking about?
How does the media (newspapers, magazines, T.V. in Spanish as well as English) use propaganda to encourage smoking?

2. How does the question fit into your overall plan?
The students realize that tobacco is a drug that is harmful, and they need to be aware of the ways the media can encourage this unhealthy addiction in their lives.

3. How will you find out what the students already know about the question?
We will see if we can remember seeing any cigarette ads. What language were they in? Where did we see them? What were the ads about? We will look for ads and write down what they are about or, if possible, bring the ads to class.

4. What strategies will you use together to explore the question?

We will brainstorm what we have seen in the media. Students will interview people and collect ads. We will use cooperative groups as we discuss and look at ads. We will compare and contrast different ads. Students might make up their own ads about smoking.

5. What materials will you use together to explore the question?

Magazines/newspaper ads in both English and Spanish; Video.

6. What steps will you and the students take to explore the question?

(Consult the WL checklist to be sure each step is consistent with WL principles).

a. Do a quickwrite (write for one minute anything that comes to your mind on the topic or question) on ads they can remember for cigarettes. (Be sure to allow for ads in Spanish and English.)
b. Brainstorm familiar ads.
c. Interview others and collect ads.
d. Cut out cigarette ads from English and Spanish newspapers and magazines and categorize them according to how they appeal to the public (i.e., smokers are beautiful, smokers are athletic, smokers are rich, etc.).
e. Make a bulletin board of the ads in their categories.
f. Write and act out ads against smoking.
g. Videotape ads to show to other classes.

7. How will you observe the students' learning?

a. Students' contributions to the small and large group discussion and the bulletin board display will be observed.
b. Group presentations (including videotapes) and written advertisements will show that the students have answered the question for this lesson.

Kelly did more than facilitate this unit of study. She was an active colearner. She was as excited and interested as the students in finding ads in magazines and noting down billboard ads as she drove around town. During class discussions and activities, Kelly added her examples. Reviewing Kelly's unit with the Whole Language Checklist clarifies how a series of lessons drawing on students' questions is consistent with whole language.

Whole Language Checklist

1. Does the lesson move from the general to the specific? Are details presented within a general conceptual framework?

Kelly started with what the students knew about ads in general and then moved on to an analysis of specific ads.

2. Is there an attempt to draw on student background knowledge and interests? Are students given choices?

The students wrote and brainstormed about what they already knew. Then they chose specific ads to bring in and discuss. They also chose the ad to make up for the video.

3. Is the content meaningful? Does it serve a purpose for the learners?

This topic was one students were very interested in because there is a great deal of pressure on them to use various kinds of drugs, including tobacco.

4. Do students work together cooperatively? Do students interact with one another or do they only react to the teacher?

The students interacted in several of the activities, particularly in creating the ad.

5. Do students have an opportunity to read and write as well as speak and listen during the lesson?

Yes, all four modes were included. In addition, the students used drama and the visual arts as they made the video.

6. Is there support for the students' first language and culture?

The discussion of ads in Spanish focused on their culture. Spanish speakers translated the Spanish ads. Group could choose to do their anti-tobacco ad in English, Spanish, or in both languages.

7. Does the teacher demonstrate a belief that students will succeed?

Yes, especially with the video for the other classes. The students realized that Kelly had confidence in what they could do.

With units such as this one, which are learner centered and encourage participation, students often contribute in ways teachers cannot plan for. One of Kelly's students interviewed his grandparents about smoking. When they realized what their grandchild was doing, they offered to loan the class a video they had that included cigarette ads from a television show produced in the 1950s. With this resource, students were able to compare ads for cigarettes before the surgeon general's warnings were required with current ads and to look at the difference in the claims that advertisements made in the past and make today. Several students were surprised that there had been a time when cigarettes were advertised on TV. They began to raise questions about who regulates media—questions that could form the basis for future units.

Another interesting and unexpected outcome of looking at ads came from the Spanish-speaking media. The students noticed that there were more ads for smoking in Spanish language magazines than in English magazines. This led to a discussion about whether more Hispanics smoked than Anglos and what the reasons for this might be.

Lessons such as those that Kelly involved her students in are learner centered because they draw on student interests, include experiences from the students' own lives, encourage the active involvement of all the students, and encourage students to creatively share what they are learning with peers. These kinds of activities could lead to others; for example, teachers and other adults who still smoked could be interviewed to get their opinions on the effect ads had on them. Guest speakers from the American Cancer Society and other health organizations could be invited to come to the class to help answer questions, such as how many Hispanics smoke in relation to other ethnic groups.

The Questioning Lesson Plan and the Whole Language Checklist encourage teachers to take a critical look at the rationale for the activities they plan with their students as they explore different content areas. As students and teachers answer real questions that interest them, they learn together.

Publishing: A Learner-Centered Classroom Routine

Kelly's class wrote and performed ads against tobacco to conclude their study. The ads were videotaped so that members of the class and others at the school could view them. Another way that teachers have been able to make public the products of their students' learning is through classroom book publishing. Teachers with immigrant students, especially, have discovered that students want to tell about their own experiences, and that they can do this through writing.

The article from the newsletter published in Charlene's classroom is just one example of the type of publishing possible and the kinds of topics that students find important to write about. We have seen newsletters, individual books published for the classroom library, whole class books, books for school distribution, books published with hardback covers, and even professionally published books. All of these help bilingual learners share their experiences with others.

Publishing can be as simple as a very small, hand-printed, and hand-illustrated book and as complex as a professionally published collection of student writings. Topics can vary from concerns and interests students have about their daily lives to the philosophical retellings of life-changing experiences. Sometimes publishing is done in a language other than English. In learner-centered classes, students choose to write in their first language or in English about their own experiences and about the things they have learned. When teachers publish their students' own stories, other students can read them, and in this way, the reading and writing curriculum becomes learner centered.

Simple Classroom Publishing: From Handmade Books to Newletters

In many whole language classrooms students publish books almost daily. Often a "publishing corner" occupies a place in the classroom where students can find pieces of paper of various sizes, shapes, and colors and many types of writing implements, including multicolored pens, pencils, and markers. During a daily writer's workshop time, students write, share, and edit various kinds of writing including books. These pieces of writing are often read to the rest of the class by the author during an "author's chair" time. For young emergent writers a book may be a series of a few pictures or it may be the result of a language experience activity in which the student dictates the story, the teacher acts as scribe, and the student then illustrates the finished book. For older learners who have a great deal of experience writing and publishing their own work, a book might consist of many pages and be divided into chapters. What is important is that the students choose their own topics and celebrate their writing as respected authors.

This type of writing has been found to be especially successful with second language students. Since students may choose what is important to them and the students' message is accepted and valued even when the form is not always conventional, writing becomes a way for all students to contribute. To include even non-English-speaking students, some teachers encourage their students to write stories in their first language. Another way to support student writing is to encourage students to coauthor books. Carolina, a student teacher in a fourth grade classroom, suggested that three of her reluctant Spanish-speaking writers collaborate on a book. The result is the hand-written and illustrated book *Viva Tijuana* (*Long Live Tijuana*) shown in figure 2–3. This book shows the reader the value the writers still place on things about their own country and how they are learning to compare life in Mexico with life in the United States.

What impressed Carolina about the writers of this book was the ownership and pride they took in the project. Not only did they dedicate the book proudly to "all the famaliys that know spanish," but they also ended their book with self-portraits and a personal greeting from each of the authors, "¡Ola! Nuestros nombres son Jorge, Jose y Hector. Jose tene 9 ayos Hector y Jorge tenen 10 anos. (Hello! Our names are Jorge, Jose and Hector. Jose is 9 years old Hector and Jorge are 10 years old.) Though the book is filled with nonconventional forms in both Spanish and English, their story is readable and the finished product gave each of the boys confidence in himself as a learner.

In Julie's high school ESL class, students are also publishing books on topics of interest and concern to them. After a discussion on pollution, Carmela wrote and published a creative story that included her solution to the problem (fig. 2–4).

Carmela "invents" several syntactic and semantic forms in English relying on her knowledge of Spanish. For example, she uses *contamination* for *pollution* because *contaminación* is the Spanish word for pollution. She says, "In one country about the here exist a very big Ghost the name Smog," which draws on the Spanish structure "En un país por aquí existía una fantasma que se llamaba 'Contaminación'" (In a country around here there was a ghost who was called Smog). Although Carmela frequently relies on her knowledge of her first language as she writes in English, her story and illustrations show that she is becoming confident in English. By allowing Carmela to publish and share her book, Julie is giving her second language student the opportunity to begin to express thoughts and concerns in her new language.

Both *Viva Tijuana* and *The Ghost of Contamination* were very simply constructed books. On plain white paper, students drew their own illustrations with marking pens and hand wrote their texts. Covers for their books were designed on construction paper and simply stapled around the pages. In some classrooms the student books that are published look more like professional books. Students

Figure 2.3
Pages of story
"Viva Tijuana"

4-30/90

Dedecated
to
all the
famaliys that
know spanish

①

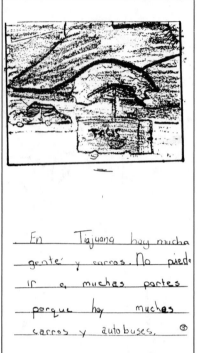

En Tiajuana hay mucha
gente y carros. No piedo
ir a muchas partes
porque hay muchas
carros y autobuses.   ③

hechos de tortilla,
carne, cebolla y le
echan chile. Hay agua
de jamaica. Hay Coca-Cola
Los platilbs que   ⑤

Hay carros como
como los que tenemos
aqui. En muchas partes
de Tiajuana hay donde
puedes comer. ¡Hay tacos! ④

nos : gustan   a
nosotros son el pozole
taquitos , tacos , birria ,
tamales, tostadas grandes,
aguas Frescas, Coca-Cola (6

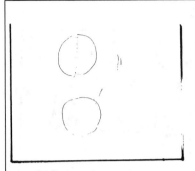

carne, asada sedos de
chicharrones, carnitas , pua
nico, cocos, Si   ya te
acabaste el   agua puedes
partir el coco y comerte la (7

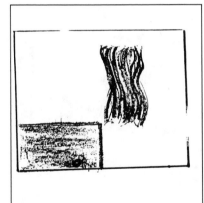

Hay tiendas donde
puedes   comprar cosas
y   comida. Si hay algo
que   questa diez peso
Puedes decirle   al hombre (8

lo   quiere a   por cinco pesos
y te   lo   dan . La agua
no   esta´   buena. La tienes
que   comprar en botellas.
                              (9

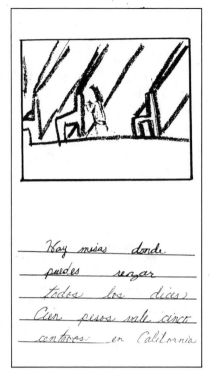

Hay misas donde puedes rezar todos los días. Cien pesos vale cinco centavos en California

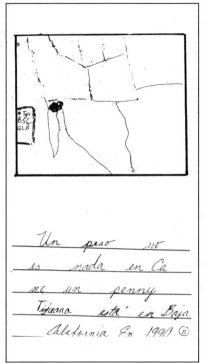

Un peso no es nada en Ca ne un penny Tijuana está en Baja California. En 1990 (ii)

Tijuana era un pueblo chiquito de 242 habitantes

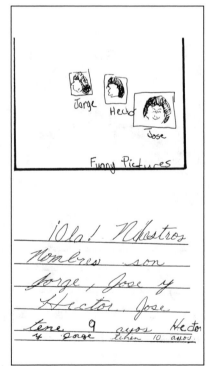

Jorge   Hecto

Jose

Funny Pictures

¡Ola! Nuestros Nombres son Jorge, Jose y Hector. Jose tene 9 años Hector y Jorge tienen 10 años.

Figure 2.4
Carmela's
story "The
Ghost of the
Contamination"

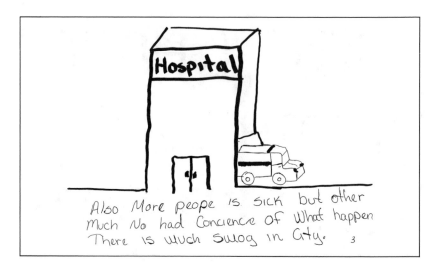

Also More people is sick but other Much No had Concience of What happen There is Much Smog in City.   3

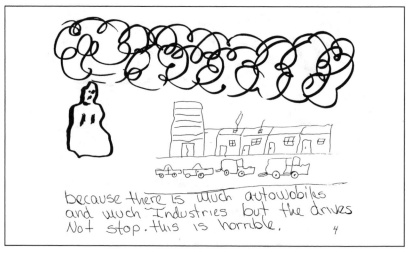

because there is Much autowobiles and Much Industries but the drives Not stop. this is horrible.   4

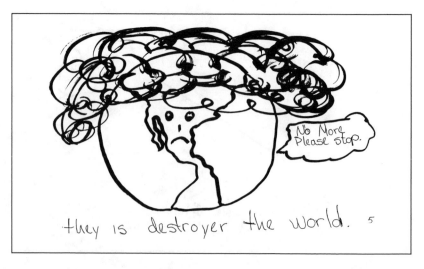

they is destroyer the world.   5

But some young people have conciencie of that
Are destrayed the world. they have took a decition
they want help the world.
6

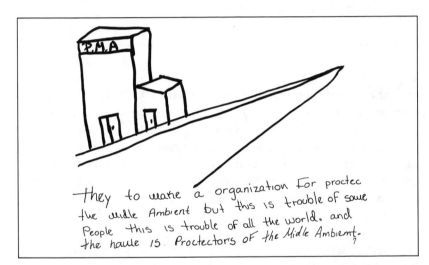

they to make a organization For proctec
the midle Ambient but this is trouble of some
People this is trouble of all the world. and
the name is. Proctectors of the Midle Ambient.
7

they to make a big manifestation, and
Much people Listen and took conciencie and
help for Safety the World of Ghost.
8

write the text of their stories, plan where they want illustrations and then type the text. After the text is typed on separate pages, students illustrate their books. The covers for these books are cardboard, covered with decorative pieces of wallpaper or contact paper. The pages are either stapled or sewn so that the final product looks more like a commercially produced book. As computers become standard equipment for schools and classrooms, teachers are finding it easier to do more sophisticated desktop publishing of books and even class newsletters.

Newsletters are a simple way of allowing students to share their experiences in writing. Class-published books may have a somewhat limited audience, whereas newsletters are usually duplicated and distributed more widely. They are often sent home for parents, to neighborhood organizations that the students are involved in, or to other classes in the school. Sometimes newsletters are even distributed more widely and mailed across the country to other classes.

Topics that appear in newsletters might vary widely. In the issue of Charlene's class newsletter where "Gangs Fight" appeared, students also wrote about a field trip to the zoo, activities around their school and within their classroom, local news, national sports figures, news from a nearby high school, and things they had learned in their current unit on prehistoric animals. Tou Vue and Mo Vue chose to write about something that had happened to a classmate. Their article is titled "Dog Bites Kid":

Dog Bites Kid
by Tou Vue and Mo Vue

A boy named Chanthalansy Keovilayvanh was coming to school when he was bitten by a dog. The dog was one foot, five inches long, one foot tall, and the fur was yellow brown. The dog thinks that Chanthalansy was stealing something in their yard. There were five dogs and two went away. Three attacked him. He got bitten on his left leg. It happened on Friday, May 27th at 7:45. He lives at 3329 E. Belmont Avenue in an apartment. The dog has been taken to the dog pound.

"Dog Bites Kid" showed Charlene things her students knew and also what they were interested in talking and writing about. The style and detail of this article revealed that the authors were familiar with journalistic writing. Tou and Mo included details that appear in police reports and wrote in an impersonal, descriptive style. It is clear that there was much discussion with Chanthalansy about the incident. The details they chose to include in the article show what they felt was most interesting and most important. Teachers who are "kid watchers" (Goodman 1985) learn a great deal from observing both the style and the content of what their students write.

Formally Published Books

Teachers who publish student work use formal as well as informal formats. Sometimes the books that are published are individual books that have clothbound covers and pages that have typed text. These books often are made part of the class library and are checked out like books written by professional authors (Calkins 1986; Graves 1983). What is important about classroom publications by second language students is that they draw on the students' experiences and give us a picture of their lives. Themes for the books are chosen by the students and often center around their experiences coming to this country or adjusting to this country after arrival. A description of three different formal publications will give an idea of the potential this kind of activity has.

We Came to America (1983) is a collection of the writings of fourth and fifth grade refugee students put together by the Migrant Education Program in Fresno County, California. Frances McConnel, the teacher who coordinated the project, explains the purpose and effectiveness of the project in her preface:

> As a small child, one of my favorite stories was the true story of how my grandparents came to America. . . . My students are all Laotian or Hmong. They began telling me some of their stories of how they came to America, and I could hardly believe my

ears. When I suggested they write these stories for me, it was like striking oil. Some of the children couldn't write fast enough. It was as if they had bottled it up inside, and now it could finally all come out.

Thirty children published their illustrated stories in the book that was typed and spiralbound with a construction paper child-illustrated cover. Phouvieng's story (fig. 2–5) will give an idea of what the stories were like. This book has been very popular among teachers who want to encourage their students to write. As a result, it has been reprinted. Although the idea is a simple one, the book has become a powerful teaching tool.

Drawing on the experience of teachers like Frances, who had published books with younger children, Bunny Rogers decided that her high school ESL class could also publish a book. The students chose the title *The Big Experience (1990)* and assisted in all aspects of the publication, including the cover design (see fig. 2–6).

In *The Big Experience* students wrote about a time they were afraid, needed help, or were happy. In the introduction, Bunny expresses what she hopes the publication will accomplish:

Figure 2.5
Phouvieng's Story How I Came to America

How I Came to America

When I was born, my family lived in Laos. The Vietnamese told us to leave our house. We left the house because they were going to shoot us. We moved to Thailand.

My father had a boat, so we crossed the Mekong River in his boat. In Thailand we lived on a farm. My father built a house in two days. Some people from Laos helped my father to build it, and he helped them. We planted rice to eat.

When I came to America, I rode a big airplane. In the airplane they gave us something to eat, and they gave us something to drink. When I came to America, we went to San Diego, where we lived for two years.

I couldn't speak English. I was ten years old. I was scared and didn't want to go out of the house. When I went to school, I learned how to speak English. I had an American friend, but I could not talk to him. He was in my class. Now I speak English and am learning how to write. I live in Fresno now.

Figure 2.6
Cover of *The Big Experience*

It is hoped that all who read these pages will be touched, as we have been, by the eloquence and indomitability of the human spirit as expressed by these young people.

Through pieces in this publication, students shared topics of interest and concern to them, such as Yia's story (see fig. 2–7).

New Americans (1990) is a publication by Wayland Jackson's middle school ESL class. This is the third year that his seventh and eighth grade students have produced a hardcover book that contains

Figure 2.7
Yia's Ghost
Story and
Illustration

When I was 7 years old I went to the farm, and when I come back home I saw something like a ghost. When I screamed I looked back and I didn't see the ghost.
I don't know what was wrong, but when I saw it, it was not big like a man. The one I saw was small like little boy, but I never saw that ghost again.
When I lived in Thailand mostly the little boys and girls when they were a little kid might see something like ghosts. But sometimes the men or women saw them too. When you see it you must look carefully because if you move you will not see it again.
In Thailand there are many dead people and so most people will see something like ghosts or something very different. I saw something like a cat but not a cat.
I don't know how to call that animal. Some are very small, but I saw something small, too.
But now in this country I never see something like that again.
—*Yia Xiong, Laos*

photographs of students and the school as well as drawings done by the students to illustrate the typed stories and articles. All the students worked on putting the book together, including typing the text and organizing the artwork and pictures. Several gave up after-school hours and vacations to help meet deadlines. When the text was done, it was sent to a local library bindery to be bound with a hardback cover. Once the books were bound, the students actually used them in their class as one of their textbooks. The low cost of publication was covered by sales to students, parents, and community members.

A short piece written by José Valencia and illustrated by Vang Lor (fig. 2–8) shows how second language learners write and draw about what is important to them. Students who enroll in Wayland's class each year realize they will probably be involved in a book project. They enter the class ready with ideas. The books have always had a particular theme until recently. The themes had centered around the lives of the new immigrants and their past experiences. In 1991 Wayland and his students decided to write a book on folk medicine. The students began their research enthusiastically, but the project was abandoned after a freeze killed the plants their family

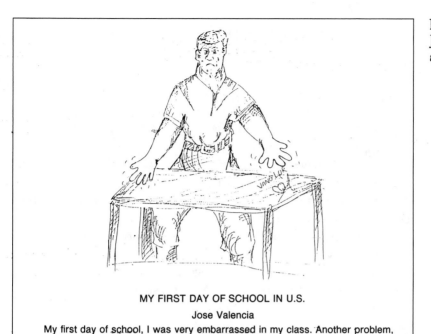

Figure 2.8
Jose Valencia
and Vang Lor

MY FIRST DAY OF SCHOOL IN U.S.

Jose Valencia

My first day of school, I was very embarrassed in my class. Another problem, I don't even know any words in English. When the teacher talk to me, I don't understand. But I have luck, because in the class was a person who speak Spanish, and he translate me. I was embarrassed, because they change me to another class. But this never happen again, because I learn a little bit English.

members grew for the home remedies. In 1992 Wayland and his students began another book. This time the students and the teachers together decided that the book would have no theme. They agreed that writing has to come from the experiences and interests of each writer. Although some students may choose to pursue last year's theme of folk medicine, others will choose topics that interest them right now including jobs, family activities, concerns about gangs, and the problems of poverty.

Classes that are learner centered often include book projects that feature student writing. The writing may be a collection of individual stories around a common theme or a collection of writing centered on the students' own interests and experiences. In other cases, the writing may focus on what students are studying. One class we observed published a book on various sea creatures as the culmination of their unit on oceanography. Whether the books are fiction, stories of students' lives, or summaries of students' research, all of these publications are learner centered because they have drawn on student interests and strengths. For many second language students, these publications are a first step toward future school success.

Me and Other Great People: A Study of Heroes

Whole language teachers use a transactional approach to explore questions together with their students. They recognize that their second language students can learn language through content, especially when they see a connection between the content and their own lives. We have suggested that one way to make classes learner centered is by having students publish stories that reflect their experiences, interests, and research. We have also described a learner-centered lesson plan format organized around questions worth talking about. To conclude this chapter, we combine these two ideas by using the Questioning Lesson Plan format to outline a unit that involves students in reading and writing autobiography and biography. As we describe the unit, we suggest possible activities that can be adapted for different grade levels.

1. What is the question worth talking about?

How am I similar to and different from others?

2. How does the question fit into your overall plan?

This self-analysis is one step toward answering the larger question, What are my values and who are my heroes?

3. How will you find out what the students already know about the question?

Students can learn about themselves through reflection on their own characteristics. They can interview or read about others to establish a basis for comparison.

4. What strategies will you use together to explore the question?

Strategies will include responding to a book, brainstorming, interviewing classmates, reading about sports and sports heroes, and writing autobiography and biography.

5. What materials will you use together to explore the question?

Materials include the book *People*, questionnaires made by the students, newspapers, books, and magazines about sports, a camera for taking class or school pictures, and butcher paper to put up charts or other displays.

6. What steps will you and the students take to explore the question?

(1) Begin the lesson by reading the book *People* by Peter Spier. Since the book discusses physical characteristics, interests, customs, and languages of people around the world, have the students brainstorm in groups about all the ways people in the book are the same and all the ways they are different.

(2) Move from the discussion of people around the world to those in the classroom. How are the people in the book the same as or different from each of the students in our class? Have students brainstorm questions they could ask their peers for an interview to find out the interests, customs, language backgrounds, and so on of their classmates. The students can then interview each other and write about each other.

7. How will you observe the students' learning?

There will be frequent opportunities to observe students as they interview, read, and write.

A number of possible extensions for this lesson could help to answer the bigger question, What are my values, and who are my heroes? These would be part of the extended unit on this topic.

(1) Several activities are possible using the data collected from the interviews: (a) Find Someone Who, (b) Who Is It?, and (c) Introductions. In Find Someone Who, students make up "Find someone who. . . ." forms from the interview information. These forms contain sentences with characteristics of people in the class. For example, "Find someone whose first language is Laotian" or "Find someone who likes to roller skate." All students then question each other to find people who fit the descriptions and fill in their names on the forms. The descriptions might also be used as a "Who is it?" guessing game. Students read descriptions from the interviews they did and the other students guess who they wrote about. In addition, the write-ups from the interviews could be used as introductions. Students could tell important things and interesting stories as a way of introducing each other.

(2) A next step might be to have students look at themselves and their own lives. Students could ask themselves, What things, symbols, or objects represent me? They could make posters with their names in large script and a symbol that represents them. In some classes, as a variation, students have designed a personal coat of arms. A next step after the visual representation could be to

create a book of basic information called *All About Me*. Students can brainstorm as a group all the information they would like to include in their individual books.

(3) Following the making of individual *All About Me* books, students might choose to compile the information into a class book. This could include a picture of each student with basic information printed underneath. The class pictures could also be one section of a longer book about the school that would include other people such as the principal, the vice-principal, the attendance secretary, the nurse, the cafeteria staff, and the couselors. Students could take pictures and interview these people and include them in the book.

(4) To get students reading about the lives of personalities who interest them, teachers or students could bring in newspapers with sections from the sports pages, entertainment, or teen pages. The students could read articles and share what they learn with their classmates. Each student or pair of students could report on one newspaper personality.

(5) Teachers might ask students to brainstorm, What do you know about sports? Then they could allow students to look through and discuss together different issues of *Sports Illustrated for Kids* and, working individually or in pairs, pick a sports hero to become an expert on and to share with the rest of the class. They might prepare a "vital statistics" chart on their hero and different groups could compare heroes.

(6) Several other activities that would encourage language development also are possible using resources such as newspapers, magazines like *Sports Illustrated for Kids*, and biographies or fictional accounts of sports heroes. Students could make charts listing vocabulary specific to different sports. They could read the sports pages daily, following certain teams, and they could chart results of their games. Students who become experts in one sport could teach others how to read box or line scores. In *Sports Illustrated for Kids*, there are many letters written by kids to sports heroes. Students might wish to write to their sports hero and ask questions they could not find answers to in their reading. To learn more about particular sports heroes, students could also read factual accounts of athletes' lives or read novels such as *In the Year of the Boar* and *Jackie Robinson*, which include information about sports heroes.

(7) As students become experts on different sports heroes, they could produce books following the same format they used in *All About Me*. Since many sports heroes are from foreign countries or are recently naturalized citizens, students could explore the different backgrounds of sports heroes. The question, What does it take to

make a sports hero? might lead to some interesting discussion. Students could also explore reasons that certain countries produce great athletes in specific sports.

(8) As a culminating activity students could choose to write about a sports hero, and these accounts could be published in a class book or newspaper. Or students could create a collage of pictures about a particular athlete or sport. Students could also present in dramatic form scenes from important points in the life of the sports hero they have studied.

This unit begins by asking students to reflect on who they are and then involves them in reading, writing, and talking about other people they admire. A unit such as this might be a way to help second language students, and all students, begin to consider what they might become. In our example, we have used sports heroes. It would be easy to expand or refocus this unit to include heroes from a number of other fields. The choice would depend on the age and interest of the students.

Conclusion

When teachers build on the strengths of second language learners, all students benefit. Recently, a teacher education candidate at our college was observing a learner-centered classroom when a new student arrived. Steve wrote about his observation experience:

> The teacher had a new student who came from Ethiopia and spoke no English. She could not speak the student's first language . . . but rather than allowing him to languish, she chose to allow him to teach the class enough of his native language so that they could all communicate a little bit. . . . The children got excited about discovering a new language. This led to the teacher doing a unit on Africa complete with a wall-size relief mural of the entire continent. The end result was that the Ethiopian student was treated as a valued part of the class. He was able to contribute the richness of his culture while learning about his new home.

When teachers center their curriculum around their learners' experiences and interests, they build students' self-esteem. They show that they value their students by including students' lives and questions in the shaping of curriculum. In a learner-centered classroom, the potential of bilingual learners is expanded.

3

Lessons Should Have Meaning and Purpose for Learners Now

Why Do I Deserve My Ball

I deserve to have my ball becous it cost alot of money. And my dad will get mad at me for loesing it. And my mom will get mad at me becous she will say that she waisted all of her money to some man for a teacher could take it away. All I want is my ball. I was playing with it when the bell rang because when I got to school evrybody had the courts and I was board so when the bell rang I started to have some fun. Becous I didn't have fun befor the bell rang. Please may I have my ball back? Thank you. Miguel

Miguel hasn't mastered all the conventions of English writing yet; however, he does know how to present an effective argument. Jane, a resource teacher, has found that the bilingual students she works with produce very convincing arguments when they write to get themselves out of trouble. In this piece of writing Miguel includes clear reasons why he deserves his ball back as well as an explanation of why he was playing with his ball after the bell had rung. This piece of writing is much better in many respects than the writing Miguel generally produces in class. Why is this?

We have found that when students write or complete other assignments that they perceive as meeting a real and immediate need, the quality of their work is superior to what they typically produce. These are the kinds of assignments that Edelsky (1989) has called *authentic*. During these assignments, students are using language naturally to fulfill real purposes, and for that reason, the assignments are meaningful to the students. Of course, not every assignment will have the immediacy that Miguel's letter had. But teachers can attempt to find ways to make assignments authentic.

A goal of whole language teachers is to involve students in activities that are meaningful and have a purpose for the students right now. For an assignment or activity to be meaningful, it must be understood by the student. In the case of second language students, some assignments are not meaningful simply because the students don't understand the language of the assignment. To use Krashen's (1985) term, the input must be comprehensible. Miguel certainly understood his assignment. If he wanted his ball back, he would need to write a convincing letter.

The letter Miguel wrote to Jane also met a second condition for a meaningful assignment. Getting his ball back meant something to Miguel personally. Completing the assignment successfully would serve a purpose for Miguel right now. When students understand an assignment and see that it serves a function for them personally, they may be more willing to take the risks involved in completing it. Older students learning a new language, for example, may not be willing to risk the embarrassment of answering the teacher's question in front of their classmates. They may worry about getting the pronunciation or the grammatical form wrong. But when the question is a real one and they see the purpose of answering it, students are willing to take a risk. Risk-taking occurs more often with authentic assignments. In whole language classrooms where teachers involve students in meaningful, authentic activities, students take risks, and in this process, they learn.

In his classroom writing, Miguel often produces short essays with simple words. Miguel doesn't risk using complicated grammatical structures or words he might spell unconventionally. Yet when he is asked to write a letter that has real meaning for him, he takes some chances. He focuses on the content, not the form. And in the process, he learns. He pushes himself beyond what he knows he can do and tries to do new things. Smith (1983) says that out of school we learn all the time as we solve problems. What Jane has done by asking Miguel to write a letter is to create a condition where Miguel can use language in school to solve a real problem, and as he uses language in this way, Miguel learns language.

Halliday (1984) has pointed out that we learn language, we learn through language, and we learn about language. In this chapter we briefly discuss how second language students learn language and use language to learn when they are engaged in meaningful assignments. We then look at some of the ways that students have traditionally been taught a second language. We suggest a whole language model for organizing curriculum that contrasts with traditional models of second language curriculum but is consistent with the way people learn and use language naturally. This model—"A Wonderfilled Way of Learning," developed by Don Howard—builds curriculum around thematic units using a series of steps. As we examine language learning, traditional language teaching, and a whole language alternative, we develop a theoretical rationale as well as practical ideas for teachers wishing to apply whole language with bilingual learners.

Functional Use of Language

Children learn their first language by using language to solve problems. They learn language that serves a useful purpose for them (Halliday 1975; Smith 1983). Babies' first words are ones that identify primary caregivers—mamá (Spanish), *dada, bapa*—or immediate need that they have—*wawa, agua* (Spanish for water), *mov* (Hmong for food or rice) and *mis* (Hmong for milk). As children grow older, they continue to learn the language that is necessary for them to get what they need. They also learn when to use the language they know. They gain a knowledge of the system of language and the uses and purposes for language (Barrs, Ellis, Hester, and Thomas 1988).

By the time they reach school, children have considerable control over the forms of language. They use language for a range of purposes. They have begun to develop different registers, different forms of language that accomplish their purposes in different contexts. Heath (1983), in her study of children in two different communities, has shown that although children coming to school have developed sophisticated uses of language, they may not have developed the functions of language expected in school. What they know about language doesn't help them in the new, school context, and, thus, they fall behind.

Heath worked in communities where English was the first language of the children. To succeed in school, the children she studied had to learn a new variety of English, the language they already spoke. The task for a child who speaks English as a second language is even more formidable. What complicates the task is that the teacher may not recognize that the child who doesn't speak English still has language. The problem is that although the child does have language, it is not a form of language that is useful in school.

By age five most children have learned to use the main structural features of their native language, its sound system, and a great deal of its vocabulary. In addition to this knowledge of their language, children also have knowledge of the uses of language. They know, for example, how to initiate conversations, ask and respond to questions, and how to take turns in conversations (Barrs et al. 1988). Halliday (1975) has identified specific functions of language that young children use as they develop language, such as the regulatory function as they give orders or the personal function as they describe things they can and like to do. Not only do young children give orders orally, but they also learn that print serves different functions. In her pre-first classroom Katie was amazed when Andy came to her with his daily journal entry for her response. The class had read a story about a cowboy and a wolf. After doing his drawing, he made a box on his journal page, and he directed her exactly where to write with RTINHIR (Write in here) (fig. 3–1).

As long as they are actively engaged in school activities, children learn the language of school. They learn when it is appropriate to talk and when to be quiet. They learn to talk differently with their teachers, the peer tutor, and their friends on the playground without ever being explicitly taught how to do this. This learning about the use of language continues throughout all our lives. Our teenage daughters, for example, speak one register with their friends that includes specialized vocabulary for describing music, cars, and their peers. However, when they are with our adult friends, they use a different vocabulary and even grammar.

Second language learners, whether small children or adults, also learn the language they need to function in the different social settings they find themselves, including school. For many immigrant students, their first English words are learned from their peers as these new students try to gain social acceptance. Sometimes, the words they learn are not acceptable in the wider society. The story of Mara's first words in her third grade bilingual classroom as reported by her teacher are a classic example of this:

> Since our classroom maintains a positive, encouraging atmosphere, it was natural for Blanca and Jessica to come running up to tattle that Mara had told them, "Shut up." . . . I exclaimed "That's great!" These were Mara's first words in English. I explained my reaction to the two girls as we went over to tell Mara

some nicer ways to say "Shut up" in English. She was receptive to our offers of new ways to express herself, and she also walked away armed with new English words to meet her need for quiet or to be left alone. (Morrissey 1989)

So much more is involved in learning language than studying the vocabulary and grammar. Newcomers to school are often overwhelmed by their surroundings. An eighth grade Vietnamese girl described the confusion she felt on her first days of school:

> You don't know anything. You don't even know what to eat when you go to the lunchroom. The day I started school all the kids stared at me like I was from a different planet. (Olsen 1988, p. 71)

However, it doesn't take long for students to learn the importance of the social context in their new school situation. A Filipino boy in the tenth grade described how difficult it is for teenagers to feel free to risk speaking their new language:

> There is lots of teasing me when I don't pronounce right. Whenever I open my mouth I wonder, I shake and worry, will they laugh? They think if we speak Tagalog that we are saying something bad about them, and sometimes they fight us for speaking our language. (Olsen 1988, p. 38)

Schools try to provide safe places to use English by offering ESL classes, but these classes are not always the answer either. Second language learners soon realize that this special classroom setting further labels them. A Vietnamese teen explains:

> Here ESL is a bad word to be called. At first I like ESL because the other kids and the teacher were nice to me not knowing English. But I want to get out now. (Olsen 1988, p. 63)

This teenager realized she needed to learn the academic language of school as well as the language necessary to fit in socially.

For older second language learners, the social, functional, everyday uses of their new language may be all they ever learn. These older learners need to shop and find their way around. Most of their English is learned in carrying out these everyday activities. We recall Francisca, a sixty-year-old refugee from Yugoslavia, who attended Yvonne's adult ESL classes with her eighty-year-old husband. She was uncooperative with other students and usually refused to participate in English until discussions about shopping, cooking, or gardening came up. Even though she claimed she was unable to read or understand English, she found all the food bargains in the local paper and shared them each week with the entire class, including the teacher!

Students who speak English as a second language acquire English as they engage in meaningful activities. They use the language they know to learn the language they need. However, when we review the way second languages have been taught traditionally, we don't often find an emphasis on meaningful learning. As a result, many of us who studied a foreign language in high school or college are not proficient in the language today. To understand why most of us never learned a second language in school, it is helpful to review traditional language teaching methods.

Second Language Teaching Methods

Grammar-Based Approaches

In natural learning situations, people seem to learn those things that are meaningful to them. They attend to whatever helps them solve their own problems. It is the learner who decides what to learn. In traditional second language classes, this process is reversed. The things second language learners are *taught* in school are selected by the teacher, and those things may not be meaningful to students. The situation is further complicated if the teacher relies heavily on a textbook. Although the teacher knows the students and can respond to their needs, the textbook was written by someone who has had no contact with the students.

In traditional second language classes the content is the language being learned. Students are asked to focus on the language itself rather than on using language to solve their problems. Can you imagine telling a baby that she can't have her bottle until she identifies milk as a concrete, noncount noun? Yet, in a sense, that is what we do with second language students when we teach them the grammar of English. We are really telling them that they need to learn the grammar and the vocabulary first, and then they will get to use the language later. This reverses the natural process and makes learning a new language much harder.

When the content of a class is grammar, the additional problem is that most students do not understand what it is they are being taught. Smith (1983) says that people do not learn when (1) they already know it, (2) they don't understand it, or (3) they don't want to risk. When the content of a second language class is grammar, all three of these conditions for *not* learning are present. Some students already know the grammar because it has been taught before. We have taught Japanese university-level students who knew English grammar better than we did. Unfortunately, they didn't know how to order a hamburger at McDonald's, so our class on grammar was not helping them learn. Other students do not have any concept of grammar. They don't see how the parts—the nouns, the verbs, and the adjectives—make up the whole of grammar, so they do not understand it at all. Francisca could find the best price in town for corn, but she certainly couldn't (and wouldn't) spend time trying to find an antecedent for a pronoun. Still others are threatened by the fact that most grammar exercises have one correct answer for each question. Grammar exercises are not sufficiently meaningful for them to risk the embarrassment of giving a wrong answer in front of their classmates. In short, in second language classes where the content is grammar, students are not involved in authentic tasks that encourage them to take the risks necessary for real learning.

In second language teaching, traditional grammatical approaches call for a carefully sequenced introduction of language structures and vocabulary. Grammar-based textbooks control the use of tenses and complex structures until the students have "mastered" the forms necessary to move on to more sophisticated language. This sequential system almost guarantees failure because mastery of advanced structures depends on control of simpler structures, and the class moves on whether all the students have learned a particular form or not. Attempts to control language learning create contexts in which language use is inauthentic. Students may learn forms of language that fulfill classroom functions. For example, they may learn to put a series of different nouns in the blank slot during a substitution drill. However, students in controlled classrooms do not learn forms of language that will serve their purposes in the world outside the classroom.

The language used outside of school is not controlled in the same way workbook exercises and oral drills are. Outside of school, students learn to understand and use, though not with perfect accuracy, language that they find they need. K. Goodman (1988) explains that there is a tension between *invention* and *convention* as people learn language. As learners try to make meaning, they are, in a sense, inventing language. The forms of this "invented" language are monitored or controlled by the social conventions of language use:

> In their inventions children make use of the linguistic resources around them. They use sequences from the ones they hear. But they invent the rules by continually modifying their expressions toward those which are best understood by adults around them. This can be seen again as an interplay between two forces, personal invention and adult convention, which eventually are in equilibrium at the point where their personal language is broadly within the social language. (Goodman 1988, p. 4)

For example, a young child will try different ways of telling her parents what she wants until she is close enough to the conventional form to be understood. The next time that child expresses herself she will use the more conventional form that got her what she wanted.

The same kind of tension in learning happens with second language learners. Gustavo, an El Salvadoran teenager and family friend told us, "I am boring in my U.S. History class." When we laughed at what this outgoing young man had said and explained that he was "bored" not "boring," we were taking his invention and helping him move toward a more conventional form. Gustavo took what he already knew about the word *boring* from having heard it and "invented" a use that was not quite conventional. Through our social interaction with him, he began to move from invention to convention.

Our recent interaction at our college with Tong, a young Hmong man, also demonstrates the importance of social interaction, purpose, and function in learning conventional English. Tong mentioned the name of a Hmong woman who studied at our school and then began to tell us about his desire to continue his education. He explained, "I first generation here to go to college. I study B.A. degree." He wanted to continue study at our smaller college and was trying to get the necessary forms and investigate possible programs of study. We immediately began to explain that in our office, we had programs for teacher education *after* the B.A. degree was completed or for a Master's degree only and that he should go to the undergraduate office. He quickly explained he had *finished* a B.A. degree already at the large, local university. He was interested in pursuing studies at a smaller college. In the course of the conversation the past *-ed* ending on the verb *study* became important for communication, and Tong made a point to use the past tense for the rest of the conversation when describing what he had already completed.

Unfortunately, in many traditional, grammar-based second language classes, students are not given opportunities to invent or construct meaning. The language in these classes is controlled by the teacher or the text. The exercises are taken from someone else's experience. The drills are intended to teach correct forms of English, but students only learn the correct forms when they find themsleves in situations where they need them, as Tong did when he realized that we thought he hadn't finished his B.A.

This is not to say that teachers and classrooms are not important for second language learners, however. Learners do need classrooms and involvement with others. Students can learn more effectively in schools than outside schools, if they are involved in authentic activities in their classes rather than being involved in grammar drills.

Whole Language Alternatives to Grammar-Based Approaches

Learners need to be offered lots of opportunities in school to use language in authentic ways that are interesting to them and that encourage them to interact with others. Whole language teachers try to provide opportunities for the students in their classroom to use language meaningfully: They read real books full of context; they cook and do science experiements; they go on field trips; students interview guest speakers; they work together investigating topics of mutual interest; and they play games and sing songs.

Another way whole language teachers have helped bilingual students become more proficient at using conventional forms of language is by organizing pen pal letters. Because there is no correction of form and because real communication is the primary goal, students are motivated to invent and use advanced forms and structures they would never use in a controlled grammar-based classroom. At the same time, since students have a real audience with whom they wish to communicate, they are willing to revise their inventions and use conventional spellings and grammar that their pen pal can read.

Sometimes the letters are between classes of students who are the same age and sometimes they are betweeen students of different ages. One model that Yvonne has used is to have teacher education candidates write to children in schools so that they can watch their written language development. Erminda, a first grade Hispanic girl, wrote her first answer to her pen pal, Carolina, a bilingual teacher education student in Yvonne's teaching of reading and writing course (fig. 3–2).

Erminda had a real message she wanted to convey to Carolina. Erminda was not hesitant to use complex conditional structures, though what she wrote would not ordinarily be expected of a first grade child writing in Spanish. She certainly had not been formally taught the conditional tense in her first language.

Another example of students using invention freely when they have a purpose for writing and when they have a real audience comes from Mai, a fourth grade Hmong girl who wrote a series of letters to her student teacher from the year before. Mai has an important story to tell, and she "invents" forms and structures to tell her story in one of her letters to her former teacher:

> On last Thursday I go swimming the teacher that tell us to learn
> how to swimming he was take us to 6 feet tall. When I was

Figure 3.2

Caro ehes buena me gustaria cono
serte megustari leente un cuento
bai

Translation: Caro, you are [a] good [person]. I would like to meet you. I would like to read you a story. Bye.

swimming I fall under the water about 3 or 4 min. Than is nobody can help I was cry the in my class she was cry too. Because I scraed that I dei. I thing that I go in to die and nobody wound care about me.

Despite the unconventional grammar and spelling, Mai's story is dramatic and her message is clear. She is communicating an important event, one that she could not have conveyed if her vocabulary and sentence structure had been carefully controlled by grammar-based teaching. Through language invention, she is moving toward convention.

Notional-Functional Approach

A step beyond a grammar-based approach is a *notional-functional* approach to second language teaching. In this approach, textbook lessons are arranged around functions of language such as asking for directions, apologizing, or making introductions and around notions such as time and space. Though this approach seems more authentic, it is still an artificial one because students are practicing forms for future use. The difference between the notional-functional approach and the grammar approach is that students are practicing how to introduce or apologize instead of how to conjugate verbs or make verbs and subjects agree. A typical lesson includes dialogue repetition—exercises where portions of the dialogue are practiced in pairs—and brief writing activities, such as completing a registration form or creating an ad. These real uses of language take place outside their natural context when included in a structured notional-functional syllabus. As a result, students may be put into unnatural situations where they have to imagine their need to apologize or ask directions.

A typical notional-functional lesson for high school and adult learners might include a dialogue containing introductions. Students would listen to the dialogue, repeat it, and then try out the forms in class by going up to classmates and saying "Nice to meet you." The correct response, "Nice to meet you too," would come back even if the two students knew one another before the practice with introductions. Later students might be asked to perform introductions for the rest of the class using forms such as, "Tony, this is Maria." Again, this becomes an inauthentic exercise when Tony and Maria already know one another.

Although most notional-functional exercises imitate real language use, they are still just exercises, and in doing them students are still simply completing exercises. A listening activity centered around the function of making introductions might have students answer questions after listening to a tape where people meet at a party. Although students often enjoy these kinds of class activities and prefer them to grammar drills, they have difficulty using this language they practice in class when an opportunity arises in a situation outside the classroom. Thus, there seems to be little transfer of learning.

Although functions such as introductions are important for second language learners, especially older learners, to be able to do, they almost always occur naturally as new students meet each other. Notions like numbers are learned when students need to give their own student ID numbers and social security numbers or as they discuss prices of things they need to buy. Functions and notions, then, are best learned when they occur in situations in the students' lives. The key is for the teacher to be aware of these teachable moments and to exploit them fully.

An additional concern about a notional-functional approach to second language learning is that functions of language such as introductions do not prepare students to work with the academic content they need in schools. Instead, in this approach there seems to be an emphasis on vocabulary acquisition and the communicative uses of language only. The classic story is of a second language student of Spanish who shows that even the communicative use is questionable. The student had learned many dialogues and practiced many associated exercises from the dialogue vocabulary and then traveled to Mexico. When he returned, friends asked how he had done with his Spanish. His response can almost be predicted: "I didn't use any Spanish! I waited for two weeks and no one gave me the first line of any of the dialogues!" Though the story is perhaps an exaggeration, the point is clear.

Vocabulary Approaches

Several second language teaching approaches that center around vocabulary learning do attempt to prepare students to communicate and to cope with academic work in schools. The beginning lessons emphasize a "survival" vocabulary of scenes and objects found in the classroom, in the home, at the park, in the store. Several commercial kits are used by school districts, which include picture cards to help students practice vocabulary and to stimulate discussions. Though the vocabulary is important, these lessons are often out of the context of the students' real lives or immediate needs. New immigrants sometimes spend hours with vocabulary pictures and cards identifying household objects they may not need or use, products they never can buy, or places they cannot afford to go. The vocabulary in the lessons is chosen by someone outside the students' world who is not aware of what any particular student needs to succeed in school. Even when the vocabulary does contain objects from the students' school world such as pen, chalk, notebook, or binder, it is not this vocabulary that students have trouble learning or really need to compete academically with their peers. Second langue learners do not need to be practicing isolated vocabulary that they might eventually use. Instead, they need to be offered authentic opportunities to use vocabulary to express their own meanings.

Frances, an adult education ESL teacher, shared a writing sample of student work with us that shows how students can stretch their vocabulary resources in writing. Second language learners can write powerfully and movingly when they are not constrained by a set of vocabulary words or asked to write on a topic they did not choose. Frances explained that one of her students, a Laotian mother, produced a two-page essay because she wanted her children to remember that life was not always as good as they have it now. Although the letter contains unconventional grammar and spelling, the vocabulary is vivid and the message is clear. The mother's voice comes through strongly as she tells of life before the arrival of the Vietnamese Communists and the contrast after:

> I was born in Laos . . . before our country is beautiful country. Many American or French came [to] visit Laos. I have a good family . . . before I was 13 years old my mother she work so hard to get money, for [the] family to bought something. After that in 1975 [the] Vietnamese Communists belong to the Laos They killed other people . . . they kill[ed] [the] king and queen of Laos who did not belong with their side, they did not want people in Laos who did not belong to their side, they did not want people in Laos [to] have [their] own business . . . No T.V. or Video or stereo and nice cloth[es] . . . They did not have an affordable . . . no Lord Judge or government . . . the people who belong to [the] American side, they must kill . . . if they want to killer someone they came to the house at night time . . . they took the people to the Jungle and kill, it make me scare in my life, then I came to Thailand. When I swim the Mekong river I was afraid of many thing snakes, crocodiles leech the communists and water . . . when I were in the camp I did not have clothes or blanket a sweater and food . . . I was hungry, I have gold necklace my grandmother give it to me. before I was in Laos, I sold it and I got a few money. to bought a bamboo tree to built a cabin, one day in the summer. it was very hot I walk out from the camp, 5 mile away to find wood to build a fire for cook, I sat down under the shady tree . . . it was little bit cool, for me. I look up in the sky . . . I pray to the god, please help me I want to came to America to find a freedom land, I met my husband and I marry him in the camp of Thailand, after that I came to America with my husband I got three children they was born in America, in my new life I have a new land to stay and freedom

In this piece, the author included vocabulary from a variety of topics: family, government, war, household items, animals, clothing, and weather. If this student had been given a topic centered around the word list for the week, she would have had little chance to use such a wide range of vocabulary. This mother had an important message to communicate through her new language, and in that situation she found the words she needed. When there is a function and an immediate purpose for the writing, the range of the vocabulary expands.

Future-Oriented Curriculum

One thing that all three approaches to second language teaching—grammar-based, notional-functional, and vocabulary-based—share is a future orientation. Students practice forms and do exercises with language that the teacher believes the students will need at some future time. Whether it is the correct past verb form, the correct phrase for introductions, or the best synonym for *said,* the language students are using is not meeting their present needs. In this respect, the curriculum in traditional ESL classes mirrors traditional curriculum for students who speak English as their first language.

All too often the curriculum in schools is centered on the future rather than the present needs of the students. Students are told to learn because "someday you are going to need to know what is being taught today." Kindergarten content is taught so children will be "ready" for first grade, first grade prepares children for second, and this future orientation continues all the way through high school or even college, where students are prepared to function in society in the future or in graduate school. At times, teachers have such difficulty in providing a rationale for an assignment that they resort to telling students they are to learn something simply because "it's on the test." And there's always a test in the future.

For bilingual students a future-oriented curriculum is particularly problematic. It is essential to get these students involved in regular content instruction as soon as possible. Bilingual students simply cannot wait. If content area instruction is delayed until second language students are fluent in English, until they speak, read, and write English perfectly, they will never catch up.

Cummins (1989a) has shown that immigrants need about two years to develop conversational proficiency in a second language, but it takes five to seven years for students to develop academic language proficiency. These results are not surprising. New arrivals learn the language they need first. They have to be able to communicate messages orally. It takes longer for them to develop school language, particularly the language found on standardized tests. In part this is because they have less immediate need for such language and in part it is because test content often has little real connection to the world outside school. Collier (1989) conducted research that reinforced Cummins's findings. Even students from families with strong academic backgrounds in their first language took four to eight years to acquire the language necessary to score well on standardized tests in schools.

Even if students are not required to take standardized tests, the academic language of content area classes takes time for second language speakers to develop, so it is important for teachers to have reasonable expectations. If students are engaged in academic content and if they see a purpose in studying content areas, they will develop the language they need to serve their purposes. But this language development will take time.

A Whole Language Approach

Whole language teachers attempt to offer second language students opportunities to learn all the kinds of language they need from the start. They know that language that is rich in context and relevant, interesting, and meaningful is likely to be learned naturally. At the same time, whole language teachers realize that they must equip their students with much more than vocabulary and simple sentences. They need to help their students find strategies to read chapter books with no pictures and work with content areas such as social studies and science that require students to understand extended discourse. These teachers realize they have to break down the walls between school and the "real" world and engage students in lessons that serve the students' present purposes as well as involving them in the content they need for academic purposes. Many whole language teachers have found that a thematic approach allows them to contextualize language and teach both language and content by focusing on topics that students choose. Next we describe one way to organize curriculum by using thematic units that are generated by students.

An Organizational Plan for Units — "The Wonderfilled Way of Learning"

Whole language teachers working with second language students try to make the content meaningful and functional. One way they do this is by organizing around a theme. "The Wonderfilled Way of Learning," an idea from Don Howard, a classroom teacher, helps teachers develop themes that focus on student interests. Howard has suggested that teachers involve students in the process of organizing units by following six basic steps:

Wonderfilled Way of Learning
Don Howard

Step 1: Ask the students: "What do we know about_____?"
Step 2: Ask the students: "What do we wonder about_____?"
Step 3: Ask the students: "How can we find out about_____?"
Step 4: With the students, work out a plan of action and at the same time work school/district curriculum requirements into the unit.
Step 5: Plan some kind of celebration of what all of you have learned together.
Step 6: Learning is continuous. From any unit more topics and questions come up . . . Begin the cycle again.

The first step in this process is to choose a topic. The topic may arise naturally from student questions. For example, students concerned with a water shortage might ask where their drinking water comes from. Once the topic is chosen, the teacher and students work together to pool their resources and discover what they already know about the topic. This can be done in a brainstorming session with the teacher writing on the board. Or the teacher can put up butcher paper and ask students to list things they know over several days. As students list what they know, second language students naturally learn key vocabulary. During this time, teachers can also begin to assess students' background knowledge.

Once the students have reviewed what they know about a topic, they can begin to list their wonders. Where does water come from? How much water is produced by melting snow? What would happen if there were no rain next year? Again, these questions can be collected over several days. Students can talk with siblings and parents to find out what their questions are as well.

The third step is extremely important. The teacher does not need to provide all the answers to students' questions. Instead, the teacher works with the students to discover how they can find out the things they want to know. For example, they could read a book, watch a movie, or invite in a guest speaker. During this step, students start to take responsibility for finding ways to answer authentic questions.

When resources have been identified, the students and teacher work together to develop an action plan. What will they do and what will the time line be? If the teacher has certain district objectives to meet, these can be worked into the action plan. Most teachers find that as they explore a topic, students go well beyond minimum district standards, but teachers can be sure to include in the action plan any items the district requires.

Once students and teachers have completed their plan, it is important to have a clear closure, a celebration of learning. This might take the form of a book or a play presented to other classes. One class we observed celebrated their unit on oceanography with a presentation for other classes and for parents. Students constructed models of sea animals to hang around the room. They wrote a book about the animals. And they shared their new knowledge with their parents and with the rest of the school.

As students finish answering one set of questions, they come up with new "wonders" and these are the basis for beginning the cycle of wonderfilled lessons all over again. This method of organizing curriculum is very different from traditional methods because it starts and ends with questions that have meaning for the students right now.

In using the steps of the wonderfilled lessons as a guide, teachers can apply all the principles of whole language (see Introduction): draw upon students' background knowledge and interests; get the students actively involved in the decision making; get them reading and writing about what they are doing; and give them more choice and responsibility. When all of these conditions are met, the content automatically takes on personal meaning and purpose for each individual.

A Whole Language
Content Lesson

The following is a sample lesson consistent with whole language principles. It might be used to introduce a unit of study organized loosely around "The Wonderful Way of Learning." The lesson can be adapted for students of different age levels and different levels of English proficiency and for different content areas. Although we refer to this as a lesson, it actually would span several class periods.

Activity 1
Begin by asking the students to think about a topic. "Today we're going to talk about something we all have some experience with: money. What do you (does your family) spend money on?" Give

the students a minute to jot down a list of ideas and then allow them to share their lists in pairs. Then ask pairs what they wrote and list all the responses on the board. With the students' help, categorize the list using different symbols. A sample of a typical list dictated by adult students demonstrates this step.

△ rice	★ movies	□ dentist
★ swap meet	□ medicine	★ videos
△ groceries	△ tortillas	□ doctor
★ eating out	O gas	+ clothes
+ shoes	O car	□ hospital
O bus fare	O mechanic	△ fish sauce

The categories might include *food* (rice, groceries, tortillas, and fish sauce), *transportation* (bus fare, gas, car, mechanic), *health* (medicine, dentist, doctor, hospital), *entertainment* (swap meet, movies, eating out, videos), and *clothes* (clothes, shoes). This kind of categorization is an important academic skill and also helps students learn vocabulary by grouping similar items.

The vocabulary here is generated by the students and will reflect their ability level. This kind of group language experience approach helps the teacher assess student knowledge. If the class includes students with different ability levels, the more advanced students will come up with vocabulary the beginners may not know, and this is a good chance for students to learn from one another. If the entire class is at a beginning level in their English proficiency, they could select pictures that represent things they spend money for, and the teacher could label the pictures with the English words. Then students could arrange the pictures in categories.

Activity 2
In this step of the lesson, draw on the students' responses to the first question by asking other questions. "Where do you buy_____? Why do you buy_____ at _____?" Choose a category, such as food or clothes, from the first list. Students volunteer names of stores and explain why they shop where they do. List store names and the reasons given on the board or overhead.

Activity 3
After this listing, ask "What are some things that smart shoppers do?" Students discuss this question in small groups and make a list to share with the rest of the class. Put a composite list on the board. Generally, especially in the case of major purchases, students include the idea of comparison shopping and research. This leads naturally into the next activity.

Activity 4

Give each group a copy of the magazine *Zillions*. *Zillions* is a version of *Consumer Reports* that is high-interest and rich in context with lots of pictures appropriate for intermediate through high school classes. (For other topics, other types of high-interest reading material could be used depending on age level and interest, including *World* or *National Geographic* magazine for science and social studies, *Cobblestone* for social studies and history, *Zoobooks* and *Ranger Rick* for science, and *Sports Illustrated* or *Sports Illustrated for Kids* for topics related to sports. See appendix for addresses of magazines.) Ask the students to scan the magazine, pick out one article in which a product was researched, and prepare a brief report for classmates that includes the answers to the following questions: What product did they research?; What method did they use to conduct the research?; and What were the results?

Groups might be encouraged to begin their reports by posing a question to the whole group about their product. For example, a group reading an article rating fast-food hamburgers might ask: What kind of hamburger do you think was rated highest—McDonald's, Burger King's, or Wendy's?

Activity 5

Small groups of students now choose a product or service they wish to investigate. They decide on the method of research, carry out their research, and make an oral and written report to classmates.

This "lesson" can extend over several days or weeks. Each of these activities can be expanded. Since much of the language generated comes from the students, the level of the language will adjust naturally to students' ability level. During the investigations, students not only interview people outside the class in the "real" world, and sample and study real products, but they also read commercial print including ads, pamphlets, and labels. Often the results are useful to the whole class. By beginning with what students already know about spending money and asking them to explore what they might want to know about products of their own choice, the real world is brought into the classroom.

This lesson follows the steps of the wonderfilled lessons previously outlined. The teacher begins by finding out what students already know. This leads to "wonders" about some product. Students consider how they can find the needed information, they carry out their research, and they produce a final report for their classmates.

This same format has been used by teachers at different grade levels for other content areas. An example from a bilingual first grade and a secondary content reading class for second language learners might provide readers with further ideas about using the wonderfilled lessons model.

Country/City Theme

Sam, a first grade bilingual teacher, lives in a city in the Central Valley of California. He decided that because many of his students had come to the city from rural homes, a broad theme, "La Ciudad y El Campo"/"The City and the Country" would be meaningful for all of his students. (Freeman and Nofziger 1991) The theme also incorporated comparison and contrast to help students develop concepts and make connections (Egan 1986). Sam decided that by beginning with brainstorming about what his students knew about the city and the country, he could see what kinds of comparisons the children could make and capitalize on their strengths and interests. Sam trusted that the students would guide him through the unit and provide the direction the unit would take.

Following the first step of "The Wonderfilled Way of Learning," he began with a brainstorming session. He asked the children to tell him everything they could think of that had to do with the city. He wrote their responses on a large sheet of butcher paper as they dictated:

> *The City*
> It's big
> many persons
> more things than in the country
> big buildings
> lots of cars
> raggers fight
> noise
> houses
> sometimes they don't allow pets
> lights
> zoo
> grass

The list showed what the students knew about the city. Sam's first graders drew upon their personal experiences and shared their perceptions. The addition of items like "sometimes they don't allow pets" reflected common experiences of the children at his school, where the transiency rate is high and living in rented homes or apartments is the norm. Sam was especially saddened that his first graders were so aware of the rival ethnic gangs, "the blue raggers" and "the red raggers."

The teacher invited the students to add to the list as they thought of things and left the list hanging low so students could reach it easily. That same day a police car and five big buildings were drawn on the butcher paper. Next to the buildings one child wrote "GOT BIG BIDES" (Got Big Buildings). Over the next few days, more words were added to the list as things related to the city came up in songs, literature, and conversation.

After a week of exploring what the children knew about the city, the class brainstormed what they knew about the country. The children naturally came up with contrasts with the city, suggesting ideas like "little bit of people" and "little bit of houses." They also listed things grown in the country near their city, including grapes and vegetables and animals commonly found on a farm like pigs, goats, and chickens. As with the lists about the city, their personal experiences were again reflected in suggestions such as "little food," "good people," and "old trucks."

During these first few weeks, several students chose to write stories about the city or the country. It seemed that many things that happened in the classroom or that the class read about or discussed had connections to the theme even when Sam hadn't planned them. In fact, the children were constantly telling Sam, "That's in the city" or "That's like in the country."

As Sam and his students explored their theme of the city and the country, he tried to draw upon what the children wondered and include the children in helping to decide how they could find out about the things they wondered about. The children began to compare and contrast naturally, and one project led to another. They made maps of their school, their neighborhood, and their city. They went on field trips. They did art and science projects. All of the activities were related in some way to the theme.

AIDS: A Topic of Interest to Secondary Students

A secondary teacher working with large numbers of Southeast Asian students used the wonderfilled lessons format with her class to study an important topic: AIDS. This topic came up when a local Hmong man committed suicide because he feared he had contracted AIDS. The students began asking questions about the disease, and the teacher saw an opportunity to help her students learn language through meaningful content. She and the students explored this topic together. She began with what they knew and what they wanted to find out. They then read newspaper articles as well as more technical reports on the disease. They listened to a guest speaker and watched an educational video on AIDS. They had small group and whole class discussions. They wrote journal entries that they shared with each other or had the teacher respond to privately. Through this process the students gained a great deal of vocabulary and at the same time learned about an important and timely topic.

The wonderfilled format can be used in many different content areas. In social studies, students might explore school rules or local laws. They could begin with what they already know, list what questions they have, read and interview, share the results, and make some suggestions for change. When studying history, World War II might seem far from students' lives and interests. If the topic is taught in the traditional manner and students read social studies texts, take lecture notes, answer questions, and memorize dates of battles for a test, the topic might not be comprehensible or meaningful, especially if the students are recent immigrants who have trouble reading the texts or understanding teacher lectures. However, if the topic is introduced by asking students what they know about war in general and what they would like to find out about war, immigrant students immediately not only relate but also can be experts on a topic English-speaking peers usually know little about. Through this format, students can choose to answer their individual or small group questions and discuss and learn about important issues such as the causes of war, the results of war, the economics of war, and how to avoid war. Using the "Wonderfilled Way of Learning" model helps teachers relate lessons to their students, which automatically makes lessons meaningful and purposeful

Other Examples of Teaching with Meaning and Purpose

Of course, not all curriculum for second language learners needs to be organized around the wonderfilled lessons format. In a junior high school class, a world studies teacher began the year by reading Peter Spier's book *People* (mentioned in chapter 2). This time the book served not only as a stimulus for study on similarities and differences, but also for study of world population, individual physical characteristics, religion, recreation, housing, means of making a living, and different world languages. Students then chose areas of special interest to them to read about further. They became experts in those areas and shared their expertise with their classmates. Here again, because students had a choice in the areas they studied, they found the study more meaningful.

Other activities that take place in whole language classrooms on a regular basis and are discussed in more detail in other chapters are also meaningful and functional. These activities that focus on literacy development include daily response journals, message boards, student-made bulletin boards, interviews, book writing, peer tutoring, and literature studies. In some cases, teachers who find it easy to follow practices consistent with whole language when doing language arts find whole language more difficult in the content areas. Secondary content-area teachers sometimes regard whole language as an approach for elementary teachers. The "Wonderfilled Way of Learning" provides an organizing strategy that is useful for whole language teachers at all levels when planning content area lessons. Lessons developed following this format make learning easier for all students, but they are especially appropriate for second language learners because they begin with what students already know and develop around students' real interests.

A Final Example

One final example of how language is learned through meaningful and functional content comes from Nancy, a first grade teacher who has many Hispanic and Southeast Asian students in her classroom. Nancy was anxious to make her math time both rich in concepts and rich in language. She decided to incorporate a math journal. As students worked in cooperative groups on different concepts, they also developed language. For example, after discussing different shapes, the students were given play dough to make the different shapes they had talked about. They then wrote about their experience. In figure 3–3, Xe writes about her hands-on learning, "First I made a sphere Then I made the sides flat and thin It turn out with a cube."

Conclusion

In this chapter we have looked at a third principle of whole language: Lessons should have meaning and purpose for students now. As with the other principles, immediate meaning and purpose are important for all students, but especially important for students who speak English as a second language because these students need to

Figure 3.3

be engaged in activities through which they can learn both English and the academic content.

For a lesson to be meaningful, the student must understand it. Students are most likely to understand lessons that build directly on their personal experiences and interests. Whole language teachers, though, attempt to go beyond making the lesson meaningful. Students may understand a lesson and still see no purpose in doing it. When lessons relate to their lives, students are more apt to find a purpose. In addition, when students can make choices, they can set their own purposes. They can take ownership of the learning process, and under these conditions they are more willing to take the risks that are always involved in learning new things.

Students in whole language classes engage in activities in which they find meaning, set purpose, claim ownership, and take risks. However, as we have shown in the examples in this chapter and in the model for wonderfilled lessons, these processes are not generally accomplished by students working alone. Instead, in whole language classes, students are involved in interactions with their peers. They learn from one another as well as from the teacher. In the next chapter we look in more detail at the importance of social interaction for learning.

4

Learning Takes Place
in Social Interaction

David is a student in an ESL class for adults. His teacher, George, arranged for David and his classmates to write pen pal letters to students in a teacher education program at a local college. David's first letter to a college student is a powerful and poignant example of a second language learner developing language through social interaction.

Dear College Student:
Hi!!!
How are you?
I hope you are a good student, no like my!
My name is David, and I come from Mexico City
I work in a company of roofing and I try to learn some English
it's hard to me but I try it, I hope one day I will have the victory
in this matter and then I wish will go to college like you.
What is your name?
What do you study in that place?
It's hard?   do you like it?
Where are you come from?
I will hope are you understand this few lines
If something (word) is incorrect Please don't take care I try to
learn something new for me.
        thanks for be pacient
        I will be waiting for you answer
          be hoping

David got so involved with this pen pal project that he became a pen pal with several different college students. He wrote more letters than any of George's other students. Through these authentic (Edelsky 1986), written social interactions, David improved his reading and writing abilities dramatically. There was also another, perhaps even more important, benefit for him. Because of this letter writing, David really began to see the possibility of becoming a college student himself. Smith (1985) has written about the need for students to see themselves as readers, and thus become part of the "Literacy Club." These letters were one way David was able to consider entering "the club" of college-educated people.

Too often second language classrooms do not offer students the opportunities to interact in authentic ways. Instead, students work alone to practice language skills for future use. George's class differs from those classes. He motivates his students by providing them with real opportunities to use language to communicate.

Pen pal letters are one way that whole language teachers create situations in which their students can develop language in social interactions. In this chapter we review some of the research base that supports the importance of social interaction in learning; we look at how second language teaching has moved toward the promotion of social interaction; we consider ways whole language teachers involve learners in social interaction; and we present a sample unit that engages students in social interaction as they learn both content and language.

Individual Versus Social Learning

The emphasis in American education traditionally has been on individual learning. We can see this individual emphasis in the way classrooms are set up with straight rows facing the teacher. Under the influence of behavioral psychology, materials were developed that further isolated students: programmed texts, mastery learning kits, and dittoed worksheets. Traditional reading instruction, in which one group reads with the teacher while the other two-thirds do seatwork, further reinforces individual learning. Even those students in the reading group are actually giving individual performances. In math classes, students begin with five problems for the day. After the teacher introduces a new type of problem, students often spend the rest of math time working individually to practice the skill that has been presented. Even in social studies, for many lessons, students spend the majority of their time silently reading chapters from the text and answering the end of the chapter questions by themselves.

Advances in technology have, in many instances, only increased this tendency toward individual learning. As Smith (1986) has pointed out, computers have often been turned into electronic worksheets. Smith explains that there are more than ten thousand educational software programs on the market that support this computerized, programmatic approach to instruction. He points out that millions of computerized lessons "claim to teach facts and skills of language, arithmetic, science, social studies, art and every other subject under the academic sun" (p. 3). Students sit in front of computers that have been programmed to give them endless problems in addition and countless variations on the words from their weekly spelling lists. These programs are attractive to educators. The "programs present clearly defined tasks that can be dealt with one at a time. The programs 'remember' how each child has 'progressed' from day to day and can cope with wrong answers" (Smith 1986, p. 8).

Far from being based on our most recent understanding of how learning takes place, the skill-and-drill approach to language learning that these computer programs support comes from *behaviorism*. The behaviorists saw the teacher's role as transmitting the skills and knowledge that individual students should learn through practice. In this view learning occurs when behaviors are reinforced and habits are formed. Skinner's book, *Verbal Behavior*, outlined these principles for language learning. However, as early as 1959 linguist Noam Chomsky "demolished all of Skinner's arguments, insistently asserting that the behavioristic approach trivialized both language and learning" (Smith 1986, p. 23).

Gradually, there was a shift from behaviorist to cognitive psychology. While behaviorists emphasized how the environment acted on the passive learner in shaping learning, *cognitivists* stressed the importance of the learner, who acted on the environment to construct meaning. However, this new view of the learner as active did not mean a change from a focus on the individual to a focus on the social group. In the eyes of many supporting a cognitive view of learning, the meaning that was constructed was the individual's meaning. The teacher's role from a cognitivist's perspective was to facilitate learning by creating situations in which individuals could construct concepts and build schemata. The emphasis was on individual learning rather than on social interaction.

Whole language teachers have supported a view that comes out of cognitive psychology but further recognizes that meaning is constructed in *transactions* between individuals and their learning environments. The individual is changed by the environment even as the environment is changed by the individual. The environment is not simply physical but includes other people. Individuals are shaped by society, and they shape society. An interplay exists between the individual and the social group.

The role of social forces in individual development has not always been recognized. The work of Piaget was influential in support of the view of learning as an individual activity. Piaget recorded in detail how children's understanding of the world developed as they acted on that world. He felt that intellectual development followed a universal pattern determined by biological maturation. Children's conceptual growth could be traced through a series of developmental stages. Students could learn things when they were developmentally "ready" to do so because learning follows development. Language, for Piaget, was a tool that helped children make public what they had learned. As he observed young children, Piaget noted that their play was not cooperative but parallel. Two children might be in the same sandbox, but they were not really interacting with one another. Piaget (1955) believed that at an early stage children's thought was egocentric, and he described egocentric speech as occurring when "the child talks only about himself, takes no interest in his interlocutor, does not try to communicate, expects no answers, and often does not even care whether anyone listens to him" (p. 15).

Piaget believed that social interactions through language help children move away from an egocentric point of view, and in this respect, language is important to development. However, he downplayed the role of language in thinking. He did not believe that egocentric speech served any useful function in development but simply disappeared when children reached school age and became more social.

Other researchers have placed a greater emphasis on the role of shared language in the development of thought and language. Vygotsky stressed the importance of social interaction in the learning process. He saw language as a tool for thought and believed that children use language to solve problems, first in interactions with others, and then, when speech is internalized, by thinking through problems by themselves. Whereas Piaget said that egocentric speech served no function, Vygotsky believed that egocentric speech plays an important role in the development of thought and language. He showed that egocentric speech is social because it actually decreases when children are isolated from others or when it is clear that they cannot be understood by others. Thus, children left alone use less egocentric language as they play by themselves. Vygotsky argued that speech, even speech that seems to lack direction, is influenced by the presence of other people. He believed that language is the key to all development. "Words play a central part not only in the development of thought but in the historical growth of consciousness as a whole. A word is a microcosm of human consciousness" (Goodman et al. 1987, p. 135).

Vygotsky argued that two levels of mental development can be determined. We can look at what children can do alone, and we can look at what they can do when working with others. The difference between these two kinds of development forms what Vygotsky called the "Zone of Proximal Development." He defined this zone as "the distance between the actual developmental level as determined by independent problem solving and the level of potential development as determined through problem solving under adult guidance or in collaboration with more capable peers" (Vygotsky 1978, p. 86).

Children first develop concepts by talking to adults or more capable peers as they solve a problem. Later, they can solve the same problem by themselves because they were able to internalize the concepts needed for the solution. What they could at first only do with the help of others, they can now do alone, but they needed that earlier social interaction to build the inner resources. We talk to ourselves and use those resources whenever we face a difficult problem. Vygotsky noted that even adults may talk aloud when they are by themselves and are faced with a real dilemma.

Views on Social Interaction for Second Language Learners

Second language educators have debated the role social interaction plays in language development. Krashen (1982) has presented a model similar to Piaget's, which emphasizes the active understanding of the individual in order for learning to take place. Krashen argues that language is acquired when students receive comprehensible input (messages they understand) that contains language structures that are slightly in advance of their present ability level. Although Krashen acknowledges the role of social interaction in the development of thinking, he contends that acquisition results from input, and the best sources of input are the teacher, who can make the messages understandable, or an interesting text. According to

Krashen, social interactions help students manage conversations better and help students refine their ideas. Also, these interactions can provide the raw material (comprehensible input) needed for language development.

Other second language educators also believe that social interaction is critical for effective language learning. In two of their four principles of language development, Rigg and Hudelson (1986) refer to the importance of the social aspects of learning:

> 1. People develop their second language when they feel good about themselves and about their relationships with those around them in the second language setting;
> 2. Language develops when the language learner focuses on accomplishing something together with others rather than focusing on the language itself. So group activities . . . are ideal. (p. 117)

In a similar way, Rigg and Allen (1989) comment, "Learning a language means learning to do the things you want to do with people who speak that language" (p. viii). They strongly emphasize the importance of working with others to learn language. These educators believe that other people form a crucial element of the context necessary for language development.

Importance of Social Context: Theory and Research

K. Goodman and his colleagues (1987) have clarified the importance of social context in learning in the classroom by explaining how individual inventions are influenced by social conventions. Students construct their individual understandings of the world, and then they test their conceptualizations against the understandings of others around them. There is always a tension between the individual and the society. Goodman pictures this as the tension between centripetal and centrifugal forces. (These forces keep the water from spilling out of a pail when we swing it in circles and keep a satellite in orbit.) The teacher's job is to keep these two forces in balance in the classroom, being careful not to inhibit individual invention, but, at the same time, to be sure that students check their personal ideas against social reality. Language plays the key role in this process. "Language becomes the social medium for the sharing of thoughts; it creates a social mind from individual minds and thus greatly magnifies the learning ability of any one person" (Goodman et al. 1987, p. 33).

Individual inventions are shaped continuously by social convention in whole language classrooms where students participate in process writing. In these classes, students choose their own topics, create their own stories, and invent spellings to express those stories. But, because their desire is to communicate, they choose topics of interest to others, they read drafts to their classmates, and they revise their stories in response to suggestions from their classmates and teacher. Over time, their spelling and punctuation become more conventional, not because they have worked hard to consciously learn correct spellings, but because they want others to be able to read and understand their work. Children's individual inventions are shaped by their awareness of the social conventions operating around them.

In the same way, when children read, they first construct their individual meanings during transactions with texts (Rosenblatt 1978). Those texts, however, were written by other individuals, and they represent the collected thoughts of the societies that publish and distribute them. Even individual reading is a social act, and for this reason, current approaches to reading are labeled *socio-psycholinguistic* (Weaver 1988).

Responses to reading can be both individual and social. During literature studies, when children talk about the stories they have read, they refine their individual understandings in response to what others have understood. Like writers, readers revise the mental texts they have constructed so that they can talk about the stories with others. When students develop literacy in whole language classrooms, they revise their individual inventions in response to social conventions as they share their reading and writing with others.

Ellen, a graduate student, discovered the importance of social relationships in reading and writing for herself recently when she read a research article written by her teacher, Yvonne, and Sam, a fellow graduate student:

> My first reaction to this article was that it was very easy to read. I read it in one uninterrupted sitting, which is not usually the case for most professional articles I read. The interest level was very high. I know both the authors. Sam and I did a project together in one of our classes. I have observed in Sam's school. . . . Reading this article gave me a better idea of how enjoyable and important it is for students to read "published works" of their peers. They are also curious to hear about their friends' ideas on certain topics. It is one thing to read about a topic of

one's interest. It is another to read a topic of interest written by people you know personally!

Research by Heath (1983) and Cazden (1988) on oral language development also shows the importance of social context in shaping the way children use language. Many children come to school with a well-developed sense of how to use language to do things such as telling stories or reporting experiences. However, what Heath has called these "ways with words" differ from one social group to another. Children may come to school having learned one way to communicate socially and find themselves in a school setting in which a different kind of social interaction is considered appropriate.

Heath studied children in two communities in the Piedmont region of South Carolina. Both groups of children had developed ways of using language that worked well in their home communities but did not work well in school. For example, one group had learned that one should never say things that are not true. These children had difficulty in making up imaginative stories. The other group had difficulty behaving properly in school because in their community even young children were expected to participate in conversations by being verbally aggressive and clever.

Cazden looked at the ways children recounted their experiences during sharing time. Some children used an episodic style of telling stories. Teachers had trouble following these stories and often failed to value them. However, when Cazden presented tapes of these stories to members of the children's own community, these people reported that the stories were well constructed, and they rated the children that told them as highly intelligent.

Because the ways people use language to do things varies from culture to culture, it is crucial that students in schools have a chance for social interactions with people from a variety of social groups. Whole language teachers value the ways with words their students bring with them, but they also strive to make their students aware of the importance of developing forms of oral and written language that will allow them to communicate with other social groups besides their own. These teachers take an additive stance. They celebrate diversity and validate students' languages and cultures. At the same time, they realize the importance of allowing students to interact with others from a variety of backgrounds to increase their language repertoire.

It is for this reason that teachers like George encourage adult ESL students such as David to write letters to college students. In that social interaction, all participants learned. David learned language conventions as he read the letters from the college students and then composed responses, and he learned that he might really consider college education for himself some day. The college students who wrote to David began to examine some previously held stereotypes about immigrants. They learned that adult ESL students have aspirations and a great deal of potential.

Second Language Classrooms and Social Interaction

When students study a new language, they expect to be able to communicate in that language. A variety of teaching methods have been developed to help students reach that goal. Although the methods seem on the surface to be quite different, most of them are based on the assumption that students develop the ability to communicate by first learning language forms or functions. Thus, authentic social interaction is delayed.

Brumfit (1979) has noted that in traditional second language classes, the goal of instruction is to develop grammatical competence. In a typical lesson the teacher presents some grammatical structure, the students then drill on that structure, and finally, they practice it in context. For example students might replace nouns with pronouns, shift verb tenses, or change sentences with singular nouns to the plural forms. Teachers in these classes assume that students must master the grammar before they can really communicate.

Willis (1983) classifies classroom language activities into three types: *citation*, *simulation*, and *replication*. Citation activities involve repeating and transforming sentences. For example, a student might change a statement into a question. Simulations are closer to true communication and include such things as discussion and role-play. In replication activities, the teacher creates situations that require communication to solve a problem or play a game. However, Wilkins (1976) has pointed out that even when teachers have used activities such as role-play that are closer to real communication, the purpose for the role-play often has been to practice some grammatical structure in context.

Teachers who have students engage in simulations and replications have shifted from a focus on developing grammatical competence to the goal of building communicative competence. These teachers often organize their courses around different language functions, such as greeting people or asking for information, rather than around grammatical forms such as verb tenses. However, although the focus has shifted from grammar to communication, real social interaction is absent from the classes.

Widdowson (1978) has captured the difference between grammatical and communicative teaching methodologies with his terms "usage" and "use." For example, a student might develop the grammatical competence needed to produce sentences such as *The rain destroyed the crops*. This sentence shows the student's mastery of usage. We would judge such as sentence in isolation as being formed correctly. On the other hand, if a speaker produced a sentence such as *The rain is destroy the crops*, we would judge this usage to be incorrect.

A mastery of "usage", as Widdowson argues, is not the same as a mastery of "use." If I ask you *Could you tell me the way to the railway station, please?*, it doesn't really matter whether you answer with *The rain destroyed the crops* or *The rain is destroy the crops*. Although the first response contains grammatically correct usage, neither answer shows correct use of the language. Widdowson and others have argued that in classes for second language students, too much time is spent on "usage" and not enough time is devoted to helping students "use" the language to accomplish social purposes. Yet, that should be the goal of any language class.

Larsen-Freeman (1986) points to the need for students to engage in real communication :

> since communication is a process, it is insufficient for students to simply have knowledge of target language forms, meanings, and functions. Students must be able to apply this knowledge in negotiating meaning. It is through the interaction between speaker and listener (or reader and writer) that meaning becomes clear. The listener gives the speaker feedback as to whether or not he understands what the speaker has said. In this way, the speaker can revise what he has said and try to communicate his intended meaning again, if necessary. (p. 123)

However, even classes that involve students in communicative activities lack real social interaction. Whether students are practicing verb forms or ways to introduce one another, the activities are not instances of authentic language. As Willis (1983) explains, in a role-play a store clerk can be downright rude with no risk of losing a customer. In authentic interaction, there are penalties for certain kinds of interactions, but no such penalties hold in a role-play.

Another difference between the kinds of interactions in life outside and inside the classroom is that in the classroom the language forms or functions that are practiced are determined by the teacher or the text, not by the people interacting. Students are using the language to get better at using language. They practice certain functions so that they will be able to use them later. Students are not using the language to accomplish social or academic purposes such as establishing and maintaining relationships with other people or developing their knowledge of some content area. The problems and games in the classroom are not actually part of students' lives outside of the classroom.

Therefore, Widdowson and others have argued that students learning a second language should have a real purpose for the language they are learning. One way to accomplish this is to teach language through some content area such as science or social studies. Classes in which language is taught through content involve students in real communication because the focus is no longer on language forms or functions. Instead, students use language to accomplish academic purposes. If students in these classes collaborate on research projects, discuss class readings together, edit one another's written reports, and critique each other's oral presentations, the classes reflect an approach that is consistent with whole language because the students are using language in authentic social interaction.

Problem Posing: A Method Consistent with Whole Language

One communicative method that leads to social interaction is "Problem Posing," which was developed by Paulo Freire (Wallerstein 1987) to help teach literacy to adults. In this method, the teacher first listens to the students and assesses their situation to help them determine the things that truly concern them. The teacher then chooses a code (a picture, a story, a song, etc.) to present to students to help them take an objective look at their personal experiences and concerns. The code is chosen to help students focus on a particular problem area. For example, the teacher might show students a snapshot that depicts the substandard housing in the neighborhood where the students live. The students meet in small groups that Freire calls culture circles to discuss the picture. In the process, they identify or "pose" what they perceive as a problem. Through their collective dialogue in the culture circles, they plan for social action to improve their situation.

In discussing their situation and planning social action, students learning a second language can use the target language to solve a real problem. Younger students might deal with a problem such as lack of playground space. Somewhat older students might tackle the problems presented by drug dealers on campus. Adult students could consider the effects welfare programs have on members of their community.

The key to Problem Posing is social interaction that leads to social action. There are many similarities between Problem Posing and whole language (Freeman and Freeman 1991c). In fact, of all the methods that have been developed to teach a second language, Problem Posing appears to be the most consistent with the principles of whole language. Below, we show how aspects of Problem Posing correspond to whole language principles.

Whole Language Principles	Problem Posing
1. Learning progresses from whole to part	1. The code is a whole story, picture, or film
2. Classes should be learner centered	2. The code is based on the learners' lives
3. Learning should be meaningful and purposeful	3. Learners identify and solve real-life problems
4. Learning takes place in social interaction	4. Learners work cooperatively to solve community problems
5. Learners need input from all four modes	5. The goal is literacy for the learners
6. Faith in the learner promotes learning	6. The goal is to empower learners—to develop their faith in themselves

At the end of this chapter, we present a sample unit of study based on whole language principles that follows the Problem Posing model. However, before looking at this unit in detail, we would like to describe several activities that we have observed whole language teachers using to promote social interaction with second language students.

Whole Language Activities That Promote Social Interaction

Teachers have found certain activities especially helpful in promoting social interaction: pen pal letters, book exchanges, cross-age tutoring, and cooperative learning projects. Each of these activities can provide students with opportunities to use oral and written languages for real purposes as they interact with others.

Pen Pal Letters

The letters that George's adult ESL students exchanged with college students served a number of purposes. George taught in one community and the college class was in a different community, so letters were an appropriate way of using written language to communicate across space. When students use writing in situations such as this, they develop a better sense of the functions of writing. The pen pal letters gave George's students an audience they didn't have in their own classroom, an audience of fluent English speakers and writers. These ESL students were motivated to use conventional English because they knew that that was what their audience would expect. David expressed this when he wrote, "I will hope are you understand this few lines. If something (word) is incorrect Please don't take care. I try to learn something new for me." David realized that his English was not completely standard, but he also saw this as an opportunity to "learn something new."

The college students also benefited from the exchange of letters. They were in a teacher education class and were studying about ways to work with diverse populations. They were able to see that despite errors in syntax and spelling, George's students were intelligent adults who really wanted to learn. Students like David wanted to "go to college like you," not just work at a fast-food restaurant. The college students also had to think carefully about their own writing. They had to find effective ways to communicate with students whose English proficiency was limited. They had to find things to write about that they had in common with another group of students who were different from themselves in many ways but also, as they began to realize, in many ways, quite similar.

Pen pal letters serve the primary function of helping students develop proficiency in writing, but they also provide many chances for students to talk and read. In George's class, for example, the students first talked about the whole idea of writing the letters. They discussed who would be receiving them and what they might write about. They talked with their teacher and with one another about their ideas for their letters. As they wrote their letters, they read drafts to one another and talked about more effective ways of expressing their ideas. Then, when the college students wrote back, George's students first read the letters addressed to them and then shared these letters with their classmates. In these ways, the pen pal letters involved students in a great deal of writing, reading, talking, and listening.

Figure 4.1

Each of you will have at least two pen pals. Several of you will have three. There are several things you should be doing and plan to do for this activity.

1. Always be sure to have the pen pal letters ready on the day they are collected in our class. Send yours in if you must be absent. There is nothing sadder than a disappointed child.

2. Keep all the letters you receive and make copies to hand in for your study. Also keep copies of the letters you write to see if the students use your letter in their responses. When you do your final analysis, I will want you to turn in Xeroxed copies of the letters you get and you sent.

3. On Thursday, January 25, you will be meeting your pen pals at both Lane and at Aynesworth. For that day you should be prepared to do the following:

1. Read and discuss a short story with the 1st or 2nd grader at Lane.

2. Read and discuss a poem or story with a sixth grader at Aynesworth. For the sixth graders we may decide as a class to do something different like reader's theater as a group or groups. We don't have much time. We'll discuss this.

3. Interview the 1st or 2nd grader using the "Child's Concept of Written Language and Pictorial Representation" interview form. Keep the data for your final analysis. For this interview you will need supplies: different kinds of paper, different writing utensils, etc.

4. Interview the sixth grader using the "Writing Strategies Interview."

5. As we study written language development, use your samples to relate your reading and our class discussions to what you are seeing.

6. When you write up the final reports, be prepared with two sets— one for me and one for the classroom teacher.

Whatever you do, try to take into consideration what you learn from pen pal letters about your pen pals. Draw on your learners' interests and background.

Another group of teacher education students in Yvonne's reading and writing course wrote letters to two classes of elementary students. Although one of the purposes of the assignment was to help these students view writing and spelling development over time, there were other goals for both groups involved. Yvonne hoped her teacher education students would come to know at least two elementary students at different grade levels and come to appreciate those students' interests and strengths. Sam and Jaime, the first and sixth grade teachers, hoped to give their students authentic purposes for writing. In addition, the elementary teachers wanted their students, most of whom were labeled as "limited" because they were second language learners, to begin at an early age to see themselves as having potential and to think about college education for themselves.

Yvonne's handout to her teacher education students gives an idea of the kinds of interactions the college students had with their young pen pals (fig. 4–1).

The project was quite successful. Not only did the college students discover a number of things about their young pen pals' writing development, but they also learned important lessons about how children learn in school. Diane shared a special book her pen pal made just for her and analyzed the spelling following Wilde's (1989) questions about spelling development. Figure 4–2 shows the pages of the book and Diane's analysis of her pen pal's spelling strengths.

At the end of her pen pal analysis, a second college student, Denette, summarized what she had learned from working with Ramiro, a first grader, and Tirza, a sixth grader, "Thank you for this experience. Not only did I enjoy it but my pen pals gained from it. As a teacher I have learned the value of practice in writing, giving choices and bringing real purpose to writing. Kids want to learn."

Steve discovered how important the pen pal letters were to the children when he met his Spanish-speaking first-grade pen pal, Paula, face to face. Steve had not realized that the many letters she had been sending him, which consisted of drawings, bears, and his and her names, were considered by her to each merit individual replies:

> Today the lesson of how far apart I perceive our worlds to be became painfully clear. Paula asked me why I hadn't written her as much as she had written me. I had no answer. Up until now I had felt I was doing my part by keeping up with a reply when she wrote. . . . What I didn't realize was that Paula considered EACH ONE of the papers she sent me, even if two or three were in the same envelope, to be worthy of an answer. What must she be thinking about me? Here she works so hard to put all these letters together and I only reply with one!

Yvonne, the college instructor, and Sam, the teacher in the first grade bilingual classroom, realized the value of this activity during the first meeting of the college students with their first grader pen

Figure 4.2
Diane's
Pen Pal

In her spelling she consistently began and ended with the correct consonant sounds. She wrote "HS" for "house".

Other times she included consonant sounds within the word, as she did in ladybug (LDBg) and Christmas (CMtS). This is a progression in hearing and distinguishing more sounds in words.

When she wrote butterfly (BRLFI) she also heard and recognized the vowel sound "I" on the end. This is another example of "letter name spelling."

Rinette came very close to conventional spelling with "STOR" for "star."

pals at the elementary school. Their description of this meeting highlights the learning that was going on:

> The sounds of both English and Spanish in the classroom create a productive buzz. . . . The adult students and young children are totally engaged in learning from each other. . . . They are seeing children, mostly second language learners from low income backgrounds, reading and writing for real purposes and sharing what they have learned with someone they care about and trust. The interest and enthusiastic support of the college student empowers the young bilingual learners (Freeman and Nofziger 1991).

Later in the semester, the first graders visited the college campus. The two classes met on the green and were treated by the college students to a hamburger lunch. Then pen pals went off together for a campus tour. The afternoon culminated in the college classroom where pen pals read books to each other, sang together, and recited poems for one another. There was little doubt that everyone had learned a lot, not only about reading and writing but also about the importance of social interaction for learning.

In some cases pen pals who exchange letters are about the same age. One year Lonna, who teaches high school ESL classes, worked in two different schools. Often, in her classes, she would talk about things the students in the other school were doing, their games and assemblies, their clubs and dances, and their problems with English. After a short time, the students in each school developed an interest in the students in the other school. As Lonna talked, both classes felt they knew the other students. It was a natural extension, then, for the students to begin to write to one another. They wanted to ask one another questions and to know these other second language students more personally.

Lonna worked with her classes to help them write their letters. This activity included lots of talk about possible topics as well as how to express their ideas in standard English. The students were really interested and put more energy into these letters than they had into any other writing assignment. They were writing to other second language learners, not just for the teacher. When Lonna delivered the letters, the students were very excited. They worked together to help each other read what had been written. They really wanted to know what another student had said, and they were eager to write back. In fact, on days when there were no letters, Lonna reported that the students were very disappointed. The pen pal letters between her two classes helped all her students develop their English proficiency.

When Yvonne taught beginning Spanish at the university level, she initiated pen pal letters between two of her classes. She was a bit hesitant to do this. Would her students think they were too sophisticated for this sort of activity? It turned out that college students also saw a real purpose in communicating with other students. At a large university, they were eager to meet others (especially others of the opposite sex), and they were willing to work very hard to complete that interaction in a second language. Like Lonna, Yvonne found that students spent a great deal more time and effort in composing letters to their peers than they had spent in writing formal compositions for her, the teacher. The pen pal letters served an authentic purpose. Many of the pen pals arranged to meet one another and several became friends.

Linda teaches high school Spanish. She wanted to find an authentic audience for her students' writing, but rather than having them write to another group of high school Spanish students, she started an exchange with Susan's class of bilingual first graders. The high school students wrote to children who already spoke the language they were studying. In the process both groups developed their Spanish writing ability. Each group had different kinds of challenges in writing and reading the letters. The pen pal activity led to many chances for both Linda and Susan to help their students develop their Spanish proficiency.

Long-Distance Book Exchanges

Dan Doorn, a professor at New Mexico State University, has worked with teachers at a local elementary school to start a new kind of writing program in which students share books, rather than pen pal letters. This program, called "The Seed Pod Travelers," began with twenty bilingual students from a local elementary school. Doorn took their writing to the 1990 TESOL (Teachers of English to Speakers of Other Languages) convention in San Francisco. Copies of the stories were picked up by teachers from around the country and taken back to their classrooms, where their own students read the books and then wrote back to the authors.

This program provides real audiences for a variety of types of writing. Students write stories, reports, personal experiences, poems, reader's theater scripts, and songs. Doorn comments that the authors have learned a great deal from the responses they have received: "One story will spark such different types of reader-response feelings. A story can prompt authentic questions not anticipated by the writer. A story may have surprising connections to similar ones re-told by readers" (Doorn 1991, p. 2).

The teachers have reported that their students have gained important insights from the "Author's mail" that they continue to receive as their seed pod books are sent to new audiences. "One girl added specific details to help her readers understand the difficult time she had at a wake for her grandfather. One boy wrote a new account of his farming chores for a California reader who also worked on a farm with his father" (Doorn 1991, p. 2).

Doorn's project has fostered social interaction through writing among second language students around the country and in Canada. He has created a network of teachers who send their students' stories off to one another.

Cross-age Tutoring

A second activity used by many whole language teachers to promote social interaction is cross-age tutoring. Although there are different kinds of tutoring programs, all these programs create situations in which students can develop language as they interact with one another.

Many cross-age tutoring programs link older students with younger students. For example, Charlene, a fourth grade teacher who had many second language learners in her classroom, arranged for her students to read to first graders weekly. The fourth graders chose books they thought were appropriate for the first graders. They practiced reading them to one another in preparation for their visit to the first grade "buddies." Many of Charlene's fourth graders spoke English as a second language. They were very successful with the books written for younger children because the books often followed predictable patterns and had pictures that provided contextual support. Charlene actually used these books to help her second language students develop reading fluency. There was a purpose for her older students to read the picture books. In choosing books, practicing reading, and discussing the best ways to work with their "reading buddies," the fourth graders had many chances to interact with one another and develop their oral skills as well as their reading ability.

Charlotte, a high school teacher, extended this idea with high school students who were in her special reading class because they were considered to be low readers. She had them read picture books so that they could find ideas to help them create their own books. They spent a great deal of time discussing book ideas, writing the texts, and illustrating them. Then students took the books they made home and read them to their younger siblings. The results were exciting for the students and their teacher. The students became much more confident readers and the books they created were so beautifully written and illustrated that Charlotte was asked to share the project with other teachers throughout her school district.

Organizing Cross-age Tutoring

Cross-age tutoring sessions can be conducted in different ways. Sometimes students read to two or three younger children together. More often the reading is one-to-one with the older student reading first and then the younger one reading something he or she has written or has learned to read. The older students may work with the same student each time, or they may meet with different students in subsequent sessions and read the same book to different children.

More than reading is involved in tutoring sessions. Students talk a great deal together as they plan and practice their reading before going to read to their little buddies and then there is more talk when they return to their class to debrief, to discuss the experience of working with the younger students. Labbo and Teale (1990) described a successful cross-age tutoring program they were involved with in Texas. They list the four phases of that program:

1. Preparation: The teacher helps tutors, in this case fifth graders identified as low readers, select appropriate books from the library to read to kindergarten children. The fifth graders practice reading the books, alone and in pairs, to develop fluency. The teacher helps the tutors decide how to introduce the books to their kindergarten partners.
2. Prereading collaboration: Small group collaboration time was established for the fifth graders to set personal goals, try out ideas, and receive and give feedback. They shared their books with other fifth graders and received feedback on the fluency of their oral reading and their expressiveness as well as on their use of questions and comments during discussion of the book. This time helped readers to prepare for successful sharing with the kindergarten students.
3. Cross-age reading with the kindergartners: The reading took place in the kindergarten room. Tutors from fifth grade chose their own partners and read to them. Some tutors read the same book to a different kindergarten child each day for a week while others read a different book during each session.
4. Postreading collaboration: After their reading sessions, the tutors met with their teacher to reflect on the quality of the storybook reading interactions. During this time, the teacher also showed the fifth graders a number of strategies they could use with the kindergartners, such as asking them to predict what the story

would be about or asking them to make connections between the characters or events in the story and their own lives.

The success of this program rested on its careful organization. The older students were well prepared to work with the kindergartners. It is interesting that both groups of students learn through this kind of interaction. In fact, they learn not only reading skills but also social skills. One sixth grade teacher whose students read every morning to younger children commented that her students were at their "most human" during that reading time.

Writing can also be involved in the cross-age tutoring projects. Heath (1990) has described a program that adds a research dimension to this kind of tutoring program. She had the older students take field notes and do a case study of their reading partner. These students who were labeled "at risk" became critical researchers as they analyzed their own work as tutors and their students' progress. In this way, older students became ethnographers.

Kay, a bilingual resource teacher in a small farming community, has also shown that non-English speakers can benefit from a cross-age tutoring project. Seventh and eighth grade Spanish-speaking students read in Spanish to the monolingual Spanish-speaking kindergarten children at her school. The junior high school students who do this tutoring have formed a "Teachers of Tomorrow" club. Several have begun to see themselves as future bilingual teachers. Their interest in doing well in English has increased as these older students have begun to see a need for both their native language and English in the future. The younger children they tutor are supported in their first language and also see the older students as positive role models. All the students benefit from the social interaction of the tutoring.

Morrice and Simmons (1991) reported on an extensive cross-age tutoring program that went beyond reading buddies. These two teachers arranged for their grade five and primary students to meet at regular intervals during the year for various purposes. They made and read big books and giant pop-up books, they celebrated various holidays, and they worked together through a number of science investigations. They found that their students made both social and cognitive gains as they worked with one another over an entire year.

Cooperative Learning

Whereas cross-age tutoring provides social interaction across grade levels, cooperative learning provides for interaction within the classroom. Kagan (1986) has outlined three benefits of cooperative learning for second language students: increased academic achievement, improved ethnic relations, and prosocial development.

Kagan has reviewed studies comparing classrooms that use cooperative learning with those that use competitive and individualistic learning structures. These studies, almost without exception, show greater gains for students in cooperative learning situations. A number of studies have focused on second language students. Kagan reports that "One of the most important findings to emerge from the cooperative learning research is the strong achievement gains among minority pupils in cooperative classrooms" (Kagan 1986, p. 245). In addition, studies comparing high-, medium-, and low-achieving students show that the high achievers do about as well in the cooperative classes as in individualistic classes, but the medium and low achievers make dramatic gains. These results indicate the importance of social interaction in classrooms with high numbers of second language students.

Cooperative classrooms also foster improved ethnic relations and prosocial development. Kagan's research shows that there is ethnic segregation in traditional classrooms, and this segregation increases with student age. However, research in classrooms that used cooperative learning showed that "The very strong ethnic cleavage observed in the traditional classrooms was reduced to insignificance" (Kagan 1986, p. 250). One reason for improved ethnic relations in cooperative classes is that in these classes teachers often teach social skills directly. Students are involved in group activities that develop positive interdependence among group members.

Cooperative Learning and Whole Language

Classes that use cooperative learning follow the whole language principle of promoting social interaction. However, in other ways there are often differences between collaboration in whole language classrooms and cooperative learning. Cooperative learning activities often present material part to whole. For example, students may spend time in their groups memorizing spelling words or practicing math facts. These lessons may also be highly teacher centered, and they seldom begin with student interests. As a result, students may not find meaning and purpose in their group activities. Another important difference between collaboration and cooperative learning is that in whole language, teachers follow the students' lead. Whole language teachers view curriculum as inquiry (Watson, Burke, and Harste 1989). Rather than finding better classroom structures to help students learn prescribed information, whole language teachers explore topics with their students. Teachers are colearners, not just facilitators.

In whole language classrooms, students and teachers collaborate as they investigate subjects of interest to them. They find answers to questions by reading together and talking together, and then they write up their findings and sometimes also present their findings orally to others. In short, although whole language teachers often have students work cooperatively in groups, using cooperative groups does not make someone a whole language teacher. Nevertheless, whole language teachers can learn many useful strategies as they review the different cooperative techniques that have been developed.

Charlene's fourth grade classroom, previously discussed, provides an example of a whole language classroom where children worked in groups collaboratively. The students prepared a unit on oceanography to present to other classes in the school. Groups of children became experts on different sea animals of their choice. They read about the animals, visited an ocean aquarium, wrote about their sea animals for a class book, made models of the animals to scale, decorated their classroom like an ocean, and then presented their knowledge to other classes and to parents who came to visit their student-created ocean aquarium on display.

Charlene's students developed a great deal of written and oral language as they worked on this project. They conducted their research, did their writing, and made their presentations in small groups. As they worked together, both their language ability and their understanding of academic content increased much more rapidly than if they had carried out more typical individual research projects.

One common element among successful activities that promote social interaction is that they are well organized. The key to successful collaborative activities is cooperative planning. Teachers like Charlene spend time with their students helping them understand how to work together effectively. These teachers work in the "Zone of Proximal Development." With their teachers' assistance students can work successfully in pairs or in groups. Later, these students can work collaboratively without their teacher's help.

Using Problem Posing

Whole language teachers have found a number of ways to work with students to organize class projects. In chapter 2, we discussed how many teachers organize their curriculum around big questions. Another model for the cooperative development of class projects comes from the Problem Posing method of language teaching described earlier. Like the wonderfilled lessons described in chapter 3, Problem Posing involves students in researching a topic of interest to them. In addition, it leads them toward some specific social action. Throughout the process, students learn language as they use language to solve problems.

As an example of how the Problem Posing method could be used to teach social studies, we present the steps for a unit centered around the question, How does where we live influence how we live? (Freeman and Freeman 1991c). Throughout this sample unit, a great deal of social interaction takes place as students work together.

A Sample Social Studies Unit: Where We Live Influences How We Live

Teachers using Problem Posing are "kid watchers" who use their knowledge of students' interests and concerns to help them pose and solve problems. In this process, second language students develop language proficiency as they study content areas. In this particular social studies unit, through the critical observation of different kinds of communities, including their own, students are led to view their own living conditions objectively and then to consider ways to improve the quality of life in their community. Six steps are involved in organizing a unit of study such as this using the Problem Posing approach:

1. Begin with the learners' actual experiences. Draw on the students' background knowledge.
2. Develop background concept(s) through actions, visual aids, discussion, and so on.
3. Begin critical observation using pictures, books, personal stories and experiences, community events, and so on.
4. Through comparison and contrast help students to view concept(s) and how those concepts relate to their lives.
5. Research the concepts through reading, writing, interviews, discussions, films, field trips, and so on.
6. Plan appropriate action(s) related to students' own lives and resulting in social change.

Steps One and Two: Introduction of the Lesson

The first activities are designed to help students develop the concept of a community as a group of people who are interdependent or interactive in some way, presumably to serve some purposes. Students might begin by brainstorming answers to the questions: Who are the people with whom you live? play? go to school? This could begin to develop an awareness that they are part of a series of overlapping communities: the family, the neighborhood, and the school. These communities might be represented visually by a series of Venn diagrams, which would show that any individual is part of several communities. Students could also brainstorm and categorize the different roles community members take as they work, study, worship, engage in politics, and participate in recreational activities.

Once students begin to develop the concept of community in general, they can look more closely at a particular community. One kindergarten teacher helped her students understand their school community by taking pictures of the various people around the school: the principal, the bus driver, the cafeteria workers, the nurse. She showed the students the pictures and talked about the roles each of these people played in the school community. Then the class went on a walking tour to see where each of these people worked. Students asked the members of their school community questions about what they did each day. When the class returned to their room, they made a class book. On each page they put a picture of one of the people who worked at the school, and underneath, the teacher helped them write information about that person by taking dictation. The book included their favorite page, the picture of their own class.

As students study particular communities, they can start to focus on how the natural and built environment influences community life. One way to do this is for students to describe their communities for someone living in another place. A fourth grade teacher in a small local farming community arranged for her class to exchange pen pal letters with students of the same age living in a city in another state. In their writing, students were asked to describe their community so that their pen pal would recognize it on a visit. They could limit the description to either the built or natural environment. One of the questions the teacher might have asked to help the students write more detailed description was, If there were no signs, could your pen pal recognize the community?

Students can also compare and contrast communities. Often the students in a single class have had the experience of living in two different communities. Sam, the bilingual teacher mentioned in Chapter 3 had a number of students who had been born in rural areas and whose families had then moved to the city to find work. He developed an extensive unit in which his students examined differences between the city and the country. The activities gave the students who had migrated from rural areas added prestige because they were able to be the country experts (Freeman and Nofziger 1991).

In the study of communities, students with limited English proficiency can begin to build their vocabulary. Certain terms come up repeatedly. When students begin by talking and writing about their own community, they already understand many of the basic concepts and can start to build the vocabulary needed to express those concepts in English. Activities such as writing pen pal letters provide a further purpose for developing the vocabulary and grammatical structures needed to express students' ideas. Since bilingual students are often the ones who have lived in more than one community, they actually have a head start on their classmates when it comes to making comparisons. This can build their self-esteem.

Steps Three and Four: Critical Observation of Communities Using Comparison/Contrast

After students have spent time building the concept of community by examining the communities they have been a part of, they can analyze communities with which they have not had direct, personal experience.

Students work in groups of four or five. The groups are given pictures of different kinds of areas (rural, city, village, ocean, desert) and asked to list characteristics of these areas. Anything that comes to their minds is acceptable, including descriptive words such as *quiet, noisy, isolated, hot, dry,* and *rainy* or nouns such as *sand, water,* or *buildings.* Each group lists their words on the blackboard, on an overhead, or on butcher paper.

This activity serves two purposes. For students with limited English proficiency, it provides important vocabulary, which is supported by the use of the pictures. At the same time, all the students can begin to think about the physical characteristics of different geographic areas.

Next, students list some of the needs of people living in the area they have described. They brainstorm what people would need to (1) survive and (2) live comfortably. This list helps prepare for the next step in the activity in which students are asked to list what they believe would be the advantages and disadvantages of living in each of these areas. A typical list for the picture of the city follows.

Advantages	Disadvantages
easy to shop	crowded
good entertainment	too much crime
live near friends	live alone
more choices of things to do	life is boring
easy to get places	polluted
	noisy

Step Five: Research through Reading

In another activity, the groups work with articles about different communities. We have found that articles from magazines such as *World* are effective because they are short and include pictures to help make the text comprehensible. Some sample articles include "Undersea Adventure," about the world's first underwater hotel (*World*, February 1988); "On Top of the Town," about how New York City residents are converting roof space into recreation and garden areas (*World*, November 1988); and "Cold, Cold Harbin: China's City of Ice," about living in a city in China where the world is frozen during the long winter (*World*, January 1989). These articles could be supplemented by school textbooks or other reference texts or magazines from the library.

In their groups the students read to discover how these various environments strongly influence the way people live. Each group chooses an article to report on. We suggest the following steps to guide the students in this activity.

1. Appoint a recorder.
2. Look over the article in your groups. Think about the needs of the people who live here. How do they meet these needs? What kinds of homes, jobs, clothes, and so on are important? How is this place different from where you live? What would be the hardest/easiest aspect of living in this place?
3. Pick out characteristics of the place described in the article that affect what people do—how people live in that place.
4. List some of the characteristics and some examples of how the characteristics affect what people do and how they live. Put your results on a chart as shown here.

Characteristics	What People Do
_____	_____
_____	_____
_____	_____

5. Be prepared to share your responses with the whole group.

This activity is designed to encourage students to read for a purpose and to help them develop the concept that where we live influences how we live. For example, people build cities to create an environment that serves certain urban and commercial functions. The environment that is created then has a strong effect on how people in the city live. Students using the article "On Top of the Town" might produce a chart like the following one:

Characteristics	**What People Do**
tall buildings with large, flat rooftops	plant rooftop gardens
little space for recreation	make rooftop playgrounds, raise animals on rooftops
high up and dangerous	put up safety fences on the edges

Step Six: Community Research and Action Plan

After having read about other places, and how the environment of those places affects how people live, students can refocus on their own communities. They might begin by brainstorming a list of questions: How did our community develop the way it did? Why do we have the kinds of homes built here? Why do we wear certain kinds of clothes and buy certain products? How does our community use the resources it has? How does the environment relate to the jobs that adults and children have? Answers to these questions can help students determine the advantages and disadvantages of living in their own community.

Students can then think of different ways to find data they could use to answer their questions. Depending on student age and interest, this could include reading, field trips, library research, and guest speakers. In larger cities, students might wish to concentrate on their own section of town. Students could be involved over a period of time in collecting and presenting the data. During this process, they could look for examples of how the environment affects the way people live.

In one class we have seen, students were divided into teams. A map of the city was posted on the bulletin board with sections marked off. Each student team studied a particular area of the city. This involved traveling through that area, taking pictures, interviewing residents, and visiting places of interest as well as areas that were not interesting and areas that provided unsatisfactory environments. Then, each group reported the results of their research to the class. Since many of the students in the class are recent immigrants, this activity helped them to learn valuable information about their new home.

Once students look objectively at their surroundings, they can begin to evaluate the quality of life in their community. They might debate the advantages and disadvantages of living there. From this discussion teachers can encourage students to develop an action plan for community improvement. The following list of questions might lead students to develop projects or suggestions for changing their communities.

Advantages and Disadvantages of Living in Your Community

1. List some advantages and disadvantages of living in

   _____.

2. How can we obtain more information about some of the things we have listed as advantages and disadvantages?
3. How do we affect the quality of life in the place we live? Positively?   Negatively?
4. How can we improve the quality of life in our community?

After students have brainstormed the positive and negative aspects of living in their community and as they begin to formulate their action plan, they often need to do further research to find additional information about the things they have listed. For example, they might list as a benefit the high quality of the recreational facilities available. A group of students could check with public agencies or the chamber of commerce to compile a list of available facilities. If "too much violence" is listed as a negative aspect, students can get statistics from the police department or the newspaper to support their contention. In either case, they may need to compare their community with other communities to make reasonable judgments.

At the same time that students are discovering more about the advantages and disadvantages of living in their community, they can begin to assess their own contribution to the quality of life. What are they doing that is positive or negative for the quality of life in their community? This question could lead to writing assignments, class surveys, and discussions.

Out of this could come a specific plan for action. The class might decide to clean up or repair an area around school or plant a garden. They could write letters to the editor of the local newspaper to support certain city development plans. They could attend city council meetings to raise important issues. There are many possibilities, but it is crucial for social studies to result in social action, in really "doing" social studies. By using a Problem Posing approach to social studies, all students, and especially second language students, engage in authentic social interaction, and through that functional use of language they can develop their knowledge of subject area content and their ability to use language.

Conclusion

In whole language classrooms students frequently engage in social interaction. They may read with a buddy or a cross-age tutor. They write letters for pen pals in other classes. They form teams to investigate topics and answer questions, and by inquiry they explore different content areas. Together, students decide on ways to take the information they have gathered and actually apply it to their lives. They consider how they can use what they learn to solve real world problems.

Whole language classes buzz with a kind of controlled noise. Students, both those who speak English as a first language and those learning English, are constantly talking with their classmates and with their teacher, using the language or languages they possess. They are learning as they engage in authentic social interaction.

5

Lessons Should Include All Four Modes

A Whole Language Content Lesson

As the bell rings, the twenty-eight students in this junior high ESL class settle into their seats. Bill, the teacher, has just pinned a large poster on the front bulletin board. It shows a spotted fawn lying in a meadow surrounded by yellow spring flowers. Bill addresses the class, "I'd like you to do a quickwrite this morning. Look at this picture and write down any words or phrases that describe what you see. I'll write too. You have two minutes."

These students have done *quickwrites* before. They open their notebooks, take out their pencils, and begin to jot down ideas. The teacher also writes on his clipboard, glancing up at the poster. At the end of two minutes, Bill announces, "Your time is up. I'd like you to stop writing now. Then I want you to share your list with someone sitting near you. Circle the things you both put down and talk about the things that are different." The students move their desks together and begin talking quietly, reading through their lists and marking off the items that they have in common and the ones that are different.

131

After a few minutes, as student talk dies down, Bill states, "Now I want to put some of the words and phrases you wrote up here on the overhead. Let's go around, and I'd like each pair to tell me one thing both of you had. If I put up something you don't have written down, you might want to add it to your list." For the next ten minutes Bill writes the words and phrases the students give him on the overhead. He continues until students run out of ideas.

Some of the words the students give are shown in figure 5–1.

Now Bill asks, "Do some of the words on our list go together in any way? For example, what words go with 'big eyes'?" The students call out other words on the list, *soft fur, spots, long legs, four legs,* and *pointed ears.* Bill puts a triangle next to each of these words. Then he asks, "Is there another group of words that go together?" This time, the students start with *yellow flowers* and then add *grass* and *spring.* Bill draws squares next to these words. The teacher and students continue categorizing the items on the list using various symbols. They notice that some items could go in two categories, so the teacher marks them with symbols for both categories. The list now looks like figure 5–2.

Now, Bill puts up a second poster. This one shows a young horse running through tall grass. Again, yellow flowers are in the picture. Bill asks, "Let's think of some things about these two pictures that are the same and some that are different. What are some things that are the same?" As the students volunteer answers, the teacher writes them on the board under the heading, **Same.** The students note that both animals are young, both have four legs, both have brown fur, and both pictures are in the spring with green grass and yellow flowers.

Then Bill asks for differences and again lists them on the board. Students notice that the horse is bigger. The fur is different. The

Figure 5.1

peaceful	fawn	deer
young	grass	spring
big eyes	calm	weak
soft fur	yellow flowers	long legs
spots	pointed ears	lying down
four legs	Bambi	baby

Figure 5.2

# peaceful	* fawn	* deer
Δ* young	□ grass	□ spring
Δ big eyes	# calm	Δ weak
Δ soft fur	□ yellow flowers	Δ long legs
Δ spots	Δ pointed ears	Δ + lying down
Δ four legs	* Bambi	* baby

fawn is lying down, but the horse is running. They even notice a difference in perspective. The picture of the fawn is more of a close-up, so although the two animals look to be about the same size, the horse is really bigger.

After the students have noted the similarities and differences, Bill pulls out a pile of pictures of animals. In an activity the previous week the students had cut these pictures out of different magazines and pasted them on colored paper. They had also labeled their pictures and given a brief report on their animal to the class. Now Bill gives each student one of these pictures. Students can exchange pictures if they get one they don't like. Mai hands back the orangutan picture, explaining amid some laughter that she would rather have the picture of the kitten.

When each student has a picture, Bill says, "I want you to get together with all the other people whose animals have the same outer covering. You're going to have to get up and walk around to do this. When you find the other people whose animals have the same outer covering, you should all stand together." For the next few minutes, there is a babble of voices. As students move around, words like *fur* and *feathers* are repeated many times. Soon students separate into groups. Students with pictures of the elephant and the walrus call José, who has a rhinoceros picture, over to their group away from the dolphin and shark group.

Once the groups have formed, Bill asks each group to hold up their pictures and say what kind of outer covering their animals have. Then he asks the other groups if they agree that all the people should be in that group. Elise, who has a picture of a collie, is told to move from the short hair group (tiger, deer) to the long hair group (lion, fox), and Veronica with a picture of a cow moves from the short hair group to animals with hides (camel, giraffe). Xia with her picture of a porcupine is in a group by herself.

When all the students agree that the groupings are right, the teacher gives a second category, "Now I want you to get together with all the others who live in the same environment." Later, he has students whose animals eat the same things form groups. In some cases, students who are together for one category have to regroup for the new category, and in other cases, they can stay where they are. For each new category, students decide if the groups are properly formed. Sometimes they aren't sure about where certain animals live or what they eat, and the teacher notes those questions on the board for later research. Throughout this activity there is a great deal of meaningful language use. Words like *fur, mountains,* and *plants* are repeated many times as students hold up their pictures and walk around the room to find other students whose animals fall into the same category as their animal.

Next, Bill asks the students to sit with the others in the group they have just formed. He splits the larger groups and has students pull desks together in threes or fours. One student collects the pictures as Bill hands out a copy of *Zoobooks,* a magazine published by the San Diego Zoo, to each group. Each issue of *Zoobooks* features a particular kind of animal. As with the pictures, Bill gives groups a choice of several books. After a quick perusal, one group exchanges their issue on butterflies for one on pandas. The students begin to leaf through the magazines, looking at the many colorful pictures and drawings and reading the captions.

As soon as each group has a magazine, Bill announces, "We only have a few minutes left today. Tomorrow we're going to start some research projects on animals, but in the time we have left I want you to look through your magazine and find a fact about your animal or animal group that you think might be interesting for the class. Make up a question about the information. Be sure your question is clear and that the answer is in your book." For the next few minutes, the students look through their magazines and discuss possible questions.

Bill asks for the students' attention. "Who has a question for us?" Xia raises her hand—"How many hours a day does a panda eat?" she asks. The other students call out their guesses: "Two hours?" "Eight hours?"

"You better tell us, Xia" says the teacher.

"Sixteen hours a day!" says Xia.

"Boy, those pandas must get fat. What do they eat all day?" asks another student.

"Bamboo," says a student from Xia's group, making a face.

Other groups pose their questions. The bell is about to ring. A student collects the magazines and returns them to a stand in the front of the room. Bill reminds the students that they will be starting to do research on animals tomorrow, and they should be thinking about particular questions they would like to explore. They will become experts on certain animals or families of animals and have choices about how to share their knowledge: They might put together information books or newsletters; decorate the room with charts, models, and drawings; and/or prepare a program to be shared with parents or others in the school. The bell rings and the students file out of the classroom joking with each other about the animals they had pictures of or had been reading about in the magazines.

Using All Four Modes

The lesson just described is consistent with the whole language principles outlined so far. It moved from whole to part. Rather than starting with the preteaching of vocabulary and facts about animals, students began with a picture and came up with all the descriptive words the different students knew. They looked at an entire magazine that had not been simplified to find information for questions of interest to them. These aspects of the lesson also made it learner centered. Students had choices and could draw on what they knew as they participated. This helped them find a purpose in what they were studying. They were learning language through meaningful content rather than focusing on the language itself. In addition, there was a good deal of social interaction. Students worked in pairs and small groups during most of the period.

This lesson also followed a fifth important whole language principle. The teacher involved students with both written and oral language throughout the lesson. Rather than assuming, as many second language instructors do, that students must develop an oral language base before learning to read and write, Bill recognized that both oral and written language can develop together. He found ways to foster reading and writing activities in his classroom because he believed that reading and writing are important in every whole language lesson and that it is important to develop both oral and written language proficiency for all students.

From a whole language perspective not only are students involved in the four modes of listening, speaking, reading, and writing as they learn, but all the senses are considered important. Gardner (1984) suggests that there are seven intelligences that should be valued: the traditional *linguistic* and *logical-mathematical* and five others including *spatial, musical, bodily-kinesthetic, interpersonal,* and *intrapersonal.* Harste (Harste & Mikulecky 1984) relates the idea of multiple intelligences to literacy by referring to the *semiotic* systems beyond oral and written language that have communication potential. In Harste's model of communication potential (fig. 5–3), he shows how art, math, music, and language all have their own kind of *syntax*, or ways of organizing information and showing relationships, as well as their own *sign vehicles.* Changing from one sign system to another is called *transmediation.* For example, when students draw pictures to represent part of a story they have read or heard, they are crossing media or transmediating. In the process of transmediation, students also transform language to re-present their knowledge using another sign system. Accessing a variety of sign systems in this way expands students' communication potential.

Harste believes it is critical that schools recognize all ways that learners communicate:

> ... the sum of what is known across communication systems constitutes a "communication potential." By this view, society, and the school curricula which that society creates to further its

Figure 5.3
Communication Potential: Language as Process

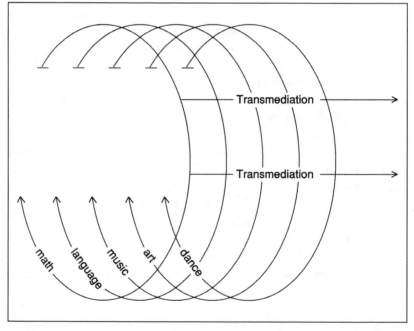

Source: Harste, J.C. (November 1991). *Toward a Theory of Literacy Instruction* (mimeographed). Discussion paper presented at the Literacy Forum, Indiana University.

ends, ought to be concerned with expanding communication potential rather than systematically shutting off certain forms of expression through overemphasizing some, and neglecting others of the humanities. (p. 49)

In his lesson, Bill tried to involve students in many different ways in order for them to learn both language and content. He realized that some of his students might have difficulty with written English so he limited the time of the quickwrite and then had students share in pairs. Not only did students share ideas, but they also moved physically with their pictures as they categorized. Using a language experience approach, Bill wrote words on the overhead and chalkboard for the students to see as they shared their ideas. The reading material was rich in context because there were pictures and drawings. The amount of print was not overwhelming and students could make sense out of the print with the help of others in their groups. After researching different animals, students would be offered the opportunity to share what they had learned through artwork, group-made books, or presentations.

Collier (1989) has shown that although second language students can develop oral proficiency in about two years, it takes at least five years for these students to develop academic proficiency as measured on standardized tests. Although Bill does not accept the value many place on the results of those standardized tests, he realizes that it is important to offer his students many ways to learn content. He knows that his junior high students cannot take the time to perfect their listening and speaking skills in English before starting to read and write. If they do, they will be almost sure to fail academically because they will fall far behind in the content area coursework they need. Bill's students don't have the five years that Collier's research suggests second language learners need to compete with native speakers of English. Like many second language students before them, they will drop (or be pushed) out of school well before that, if they are not offered the opportunity to develop proficiency in both oral language and academic written language.

Written Language in Traditional Second Language Teaching

Although Bill, an ESL teacher, is aware that written language actually can support the development of oral language, many teachers use methods of teaching a second language that emphasize mastery of oral language before the introduction of reading and writing. These methods are based on insights from structural linguists who claimed that "Language is speech, not writing" (Diller 1978). Methods such as the audio–lingual method (ALM) even proclaim the primacy of speech in their title.

Recently developed materials for second language teaching also separate the areas of listening, speaking, reading, and writing to ensure that students learning English master oral language before they begin with literacy, even if they can read and write in their first language. For example, the introductory material in the teacher's guide of Scott Foresman's *I Like English* series states:

> *I Like English* is very carefully structured. Painstaking attention has been paid to the progression from one skill to the next and from one book to the next. Book 1 stresses oral language—listening and speaking. Printed words first appear midway through the book. In Book 2 the students begin to read English; in Book 3 to write. (Gay and Sintetos 1985, p. 5)

A number of publishers produce separate books for each of the skill areas. McGraw-Hill's series, *Interactions and Mosaic*, which is presented as "the whole language approach," contains individual books for listening/speaking, speaking, reading, writing, and grammar. In promotional materials, the editors comment:

> Most ESL books focus on grammar, on one of the four skills (reading, writing, listening, speaking), or on notions and functions. Yet, research has shown that none of these can be learned in isolation. *Interactions/Mosaic* presents the "whole language" as an integrated program where grammar reading, writing, listening, speaking, and notional-functional material are coordinated level by level. While all of the books can function together to provide coherent instruction, **they are carefully designed so that each book can be used separately.** [boldface ours]

The editors use the term "whole language," but by writing separate books for each of the skill areas and then pointing out that these books can by used separately, they seem to follow the more traditional ESL pattern that divides up the skills.

Many ESL programs, especially at the postsecondary level, provide separate classes for each of the skill areas as well. Students might take a class in listening followed by one in speaking or reading. In practice, teachers often ignore these distinctions, but if the class is called "reading" or "speaking," that is what gets emphasized. In professional materials as well as in commercial publications, the four skill areas generally have been treated separately. For example, in his excellent text, *Developing Second Language Skills: Theory to Practice*, Chastain (1976) includes separate chapters on listening comprehension, reading, speaking, and writing. In Valette's (1977) book on language testing, *Modern Language Testing*, chapters 5, 6, 7, and 8 are entitled "The Listening Test," "The Speaking Test," "The Reading Test," and "The Writing Test," respectively. When students in training to teach ESL are presented with professional texts and commercial materials such as these, they naturally come to regard listening, speaking, reading, and writing as distinct skills to be taught separately, and, as a result, that is the way they organize their own courses.

Two popular methods originally based on the idea of the primacy of oral language are Total Physical Response (TPR) developed by Asher (1977) and The Natural Approach, by Krashen and Terrell (1983). In TPR students are given simple commands such as, "Raise your right hand." Students then indicate their comprehension by raising their hands. As students progress through TPR lessons, the commands become more complex. For example, "If you are wearing a blue shirt, scratch your nose" might be one-combination command. Eventually students begin giving the commands to their teachers and classmates. In some adaptations of TPR, students write the commands or follow commands that are written. The sequence that is generally followed, however, is listen and speak, with reading and writing coming after students have developed oral language proficiency.

One popular adaptation of TPR has been developed by Segal. Her book, *Teaching English through Action* (1983), emphasizes the development of oral language. In her rationale for the book, Segal explains that reading and writing "come easily and naturally after considerable exposure to listening and practice in speaking" (p. 1). Although Segal does provide some context for commands by organizing them in series around different topics to develop certain vocabulary, she doesn't specify exactly what constitutes "considerable exposure." In fact, in her book of 102 lessons, there is no reading or writing at all.

Another popular adaptation of TPR, developed by Romijn and Seely (1979), also presents contextualized series of commands. Their book, *Live Action English*, includes reading and writing much sooner. The following is a typical sequence taken from *Live Action English*:

Candle

1. Put the candle in the candle holder.
2. Take out your matches.

3. Tear out a match.
4. Light the match.
5. Light the candle.
6. Blow out the match.
7. Throw it away.
8. Put the matches away.
9. Look at the candle.
10. Smell it.
11. Blow it out.

A *Live Action English* lesson begins by having the teacher set out the props, perhaps talking about them as she or he does so. Then the teacher goes through the steps in the sequence, acting each one out and repeating the words as the students watch. Once students are familiar with the sequence, they perform the actions along with the teacher, but they are still silent. Then the students are shown a written version of the sequence and may be asked to copy it. In the next step, the teacher performs the actions without speaking, and the students provide the dialogue. The teacher may stop at any point to work on students' pronunciation. Once students are able to repeat the sequence, they read the commands and the teacher performs the actions. Finally, students go through the sequence in pairs, one student reading the commands and the other student acting them out.

Live Action English has been used in a modified form by whole language teachers who have beginning second language students. Some of the series are quite useful, and reading and writing are introduced fairly soon. However, these reading and writing activities are generally restricted to copying down the series of commands and then reading them back. Throughout the series, written language is built on the oral language base.

Early lessons in Krashen and Terrell's (1983) Natural Approach are similar to or actually incorporate strategies from TPR. In The Natural Approach students move through four stages, which the authors explain are consistent with the stages children go through as they learn a first language. Lessons are designed to provide large quantities of comprehensible input and to keep the anxiety level low.

The following scenarios come from a promotional booklet from *The Rainbow Collection*, The Natural Approach materials produced to be used in elementary school. Each scenario shows in a series of cartoons how a teacher would conduct a typical lesson and how students would be expected to respond in that stage of The Natural Approach.

Scenario 1: Preproduction—First Stage

In the first scenario for this preproduction stage, the teacher is talking about the color of her eyes as she points to them. She also talks about the color of the students' eyes and has the students point to their eyes as well as other body parts. Students are then asked to point to one of the other students who has brown eyes or to name students who are pointing to different body parts. Finally, the teacher asks some yes/no questions about body parts, such as, "Is this my nose?" In *preproduction*, students do not have to talk except to name other students or answer yes and no. They are encouraged to communicate with gestures and actions. Lessons focus on listening comprehension and build receptive vocabulary. TPR is often used as a strategy during the preproduction stage.

Scenario 2: Early Production—About a Month Later

In the the pictures for the second stage, *early production*, the teacher is holding a flowering plant and talking about the flowers and leaves. When she asks "Do any of you like to smell flowers?", students answer with responses like "I do" and "Yes." As the lesson continues, students answer questions about the color of the leaves (*green*) and what we use our noses for (to *smell*). In this stage students use one or two words or short phrases. The lessons expand the learners' receptive vocabulary and activities are designed to motivate students to produce vocabulary they already understand.

Scenario 3: Speech Emergence—Some Time Later

In the example for the third stage, *speech emergence*, the teacher is holding a picture of a boy smelling a flower. When she asks what the boy is doing, students answer, "smells flower" and "He smelling flower." As the lesson continues the teacher explores the students' understanding of their senses by asking, "What do our eyes and hands tell us about the flower in the picture?" Students answer, "It's white and yellow," "Leaves are green," "It feel smooth." In the speech emergence stage, students are speaking in longer phrases and complete sentences. The lessons continue to expand students' receptive vocabulary. In this stage, activities are designed to develop higher levels of language use.

Scenario 4: Intermediate Fluency—Still Later

In the fourth stage, *intermediate fluency*, the teacher is shown discussing several pictures that are related to the senses. When the teacher asks "How do our senses help us?", one student answers, "We can know if something is hot or cold." When asked how our senses could tell us about the orange in a picture she is holding, students explain "I smell it," "I can see it. It's round and orange," and "You could taste it." At the end of the discussion, the students and teacher write a story together about their senses. At this stage, students engage in conversation and produce connected narrative. They continue to expand their receptive vocabulary. The activities are designed to develop higher levels of language use in content areas, and reading and writing activities are incorporated into the lessons.

Although The Natural Approach follows the traditional sequence of listen, speak, read, and write, there is some recognition of the value of reading and writing. The authors state that "with adults . . . both reading and writing can be profitably begun during the prespeaking and early production stages" (Krashen and Terrell 1983, p. 88). However, the writing generally consists of copying commands into a notebook, and the reading is limited to recognizing key words written on the board. The authors warn of the danger of "supplying written input too soon" (p. 88). The concern with too much writing too soon is that students may be distracted, and their pronunciation may suffer.

It should be noted that methods such as The Natural Approach were developed to counter the emphasis that traditional methods, such as ALM, put on early production. In many second language classes, students were expected to produce the target language (by repeating words or phrases) from the very beginning. By delaying production, methods such as The Natural Approach lower what Krashen calls the affective filter by allowing students to relax and understand what they are hearing, before being forced to produce the new language.

More Recent Research on Using Four Modes

Perhaps part of the de-emphasis on literacy in The Natural Approach relates to the goal of the method, which is to develop basic communicative skills rather than academic skills. Although The Natural Approach delays reading and writing, the authors do note that reading can "serve as an important source of comprehensible input and may make a significant contribution to the development of overall proficiency" (p. 131). In subsequent work, Krashen (1985) has emphasized the need for a great deal of reading for academic school success. In his article "The Power of Reading,"

Krashen argues for lots of "reading exposure," that is, reading done for its own sake. Krashen cites many studies that show that "reading exposure alone has a strong effect on the development of language abilities necessary for school success." He adds that reading "may be the primary means of developing reading comprehension, writing style, and more sophisticated vocabulary and grammar" (Krashen 1985, p. 90).

Many ESL materials still reflect the oral language supremacy assumption, but research in second language acquisition has come to recognize the important contribution written language makes in the development of a new language. As just suggested, rather than focusing only on speech for language acquisition, Krashen (1985) has found that "reading exposure" or "reading for genuine interest with a focus on meaning" provides language learners with reading "comprehensible input" similar to oral "comprehensible input." He argues that reading contributes to second language acquisition in the same way as listening to oral language does and proposes that reading contributes to competence in writing just as listening helps children develop the ability to speak.

Hudelson's (1984, 1989) research supports Krashen's more recent views. Children who speak little or no English can read print in the environment and can write English, using it for various purposes. In fact, Hudelson found that some second language learners can write and read more easily than their oral performance in English might indicate. Along those same lines, Edelsky's (1986) research in bilingual classrooms indicates that written expression in English may precede formal reading instruction and that bilingual learners use knowledge of their first language and of the world and actively apply their knowledge as they write.

The research suggests, then, that functional reading and writing as well as speaking and listening should be integral parts of all language classroom activities because all these processes interact with one another. Harste, Woodward, and Burke (1984) describe each time someone reads, writes, speaks, or listens as a language encounter that feeds into a common "data pool." Subsequent encounters with language can then draw on this pool. Rather than assuming that speaking, listening, reading, and writing are separate and should be kept separate, Burke explains that all expressions of language "support growth and development in literacy" (Harste, Woodward, and Burke 1984, p. 53). This data pool concept suggests that requiring bilingual students to master oral skills before they write and read actually can limit their learning potential by limiting the number and kinds of language encounters they have.

The importance of using all four modes for all learners is also highlighted by California's *English Language Arts Framework*, which states:

> As the human mind seeks unity among the parts for a wholeness of understanding, so do the English-language arts require integrating all the elements of language before students can make sense of the processes of thinking, listening, speaking, reading and writing. In-depth learning of any kind presumes various levels of effort and involvement of all the human senses and faculties. (1987, p. 6)

In comparing effective and ineffective programs, the *Framework* states that effective programs "emphasize the integration of listening, speaking, reading and writing" whereas ineffective programs "focus on only one of the language arts at a time, such as reading without purposeful writing, discussing, and listening" (p. 3). When referring to second language students, the *Framework* comments that "Limited English Proficient students need a rich linguistic environment . . . and frequent opportunities are provided for students to speak, listen, read, and write in meaningful contexts" (p. 23).

Modes and Modalities

At times, the discussion of integrating the four modes—listening, speaking, reading, and writing—into whole language classes has become confused with discussions about cultural differences in learning styles or modalities. When we talk about using all four modes, what we are saying is simply that teachers should not delay the introduction of reading and writing in classes with second language students. These students need to develop all aspects of both their first and second languages, and written language development may be even more important than oral language development for academic success.

The reason we stress the early introduction of reading and writing for second language students is that in traditional programs, methods, and materials designed specifically for teaching English as a second or foreign language, there has been a history of following the strict sequence of listening, speaking, reading, and writing, with literacy delayed until oral language is well developed. This pattern of instruction is beginning to change in ESL classes, but many classroom teachers with some limited or non-English proficient speakers may rely on traditional materials or methods for these students.

In the same way that some teachers may feel that their second language students would benefit from perfecting their oral language before beginning to read and write, other teachers may feel that students from various cultural backgrounds have certain learning styles, and that instruction should be geared specifically to those styles. As Robin Scarcella (1990) puts it:

> Students are entitled to educational experiences tailored to their unique cultural needs. We fail to provide these experiences when we create classroom environments which are incompatible with our students' learning styles. Educators use the term learning style to refer to cognitive and interactional patterns which affect the ways in which students perceive, remember, and think. (p. 114)

Scarcella goes on to consider four different ways that researchers have looked at learning styles: sensory modality strength, global/analytic, field sensitivity/field independence, and cooperative/individual. Before reviewing each of these, however, she comments that there are grave dangers of stereotyping. Not all members of a particular cultural group fall neatly into any one of these categories:

> I do not advocate assessing students' learning styles, labeling them, and employing specific instructional practices with specific students. Rather, I advocate deliberately varying teaching approaches to appeal to a wide variety of learning styles and encouraging students to try out new behaviors. (Scarcella 1990, p. 115)

Scarcella's warning here is appropriate. From a whole language perspective, we do want to center instruction on the learner, and that means being sensitive to the ways of learning that students bring with them to school. We want to celebrate diversity of all kinds, including diverse ways of learning, and help our students develop cognitive flexibility, the ability to learn in different ways in different situations. We can do this by using a variety of teaching methods and giving students choices in what they learn and how they go about learning it. This approach to learning styles is different from an approach that attempts to identify students as having particular learning styles as the result of belonging to certain cultural groups and then designing instruction specifically for that style.

Learning Styles
Probably the best-known distinction among learning styles is the classification of learners as *visual, auditory,* or *kinesthetic*. Individuals (or cultural groups) may be convinced that they learn best in one

of these three ways, and chances are, if that is what they believe, that is how they will learn. But the reasons are more affective than cognitive. As Scarcella (1990) says, "to say that a student prefers one sense does not mean that he or she cannot function effectively using other senses" (p. 115). It may be, for example, that a reader in trouble relies heavily on classroom discussions of the reading to gain understanding. This should not lead us to label the student as an auditory learner. There may be a problem with reading, but there is no problem with vision.

In reality, it is hard to imagine teaching in a way that is entirely visual or auditory, except for a case where a student carries out an independent study that involves reading a book and writing a paper without ever having a chance to discuss the contents of the book. Even in lecture classes, students read books and write notes, and they generally talk to one another before exams. We might ask whether writing is kinesthetic or visual. The distinctions among the modalities sometimes blur, but it does seem that the one area that is used least is the kinesthetic. Math and science classes have moved toward a much more "hands-on" approach, but this is not always true of language arts. However, such language arts activities as role-play, finger-play stories, or story telling with props do involve physical actions.

One of the problems of focusing first on oral language and delaying reading and writing, from the perspective of modalities, is that we are limiting choices and limiting the ways students can learn by making learning primarily auditory. Some adults will remember trying to learn a foreign language in high school or college using a direct method. The introduction of written language was delayed so that pronunciation would not be contaminated by spelling. For these language learners, this was a frustrating experience. Many students in these classes surreptitiously began writing down what they thought the language would look like. An approach that allows students to use all their senses makes the most sense.

Another distinction that has been made in learning styles is between the *global* learner and the *analytic* learner. Global learners like the whole picture and look for patterns in events, whereas analytic learners begin with the parts and piece them together. In many ways the global/analytic distinction is similar to the *field sensitive/field independent* classification. Field sensitive learners deal well with concepts in story format, whereas field independent learners focus on details or parts of things.

We have discussed in some detail the whole language view that learning goes from whole to part rather than part to whole. How, then, can we account for analytic or field independent learners? In most cases the students who are found to be analytic or field independent are the language majority, middle-class, white students. Given certain experimental tasks, they show an ability to find details or parts. On the other hand, language minority students are more apt to be global or field dependent learners who look first at the big picture.

The difference here, we would argue, is that the students who look at the parts know that in many school situations, there are rewards for picking out specific details. They have learned how to play the school game, and they do so in experimental test situations. Many second language learners, on the other hand, are less familiar with part to whole school activities such as worksheets and tests. They focus on the whole first. They need to see the patterns before they can see the parts that make up those patterns. Some of these students may not have learned the rules of the school game yet either, and they may not realize that in many school activities, there are rewards for finding details.

Another distinction between field sensitive and field independent students is that the former are characterized as liking to assist others whereas the latter prefer to work alone. In this respect, this distinction matches the split in learning style between those who are individualistic and those who are more cooperative. The *individual* style is more often found among mainstream language majority students, and the *cooperative* style is frequently attributed to members of linguistic and cultural minority groups.

American culture, with its emphasis on competitive sports and all kinds of contests, certainly would predispose some students toward an individualistic, competitive learning style. In many schools, there is competition for getting the best grades and thus getting into the best colleges. It is not surprising that the students who most often compete in schools are those under the most pressure to succeed and those with the best chance of winning—the mainstream English speakers. Students from minority language and cultural backgrounds may realize that, especially when they are still learning English, they are not in a situation where they can compete successfully. If it takes five to seven years for second language students to score at the 50th percentile on many standardized tests as Cummins (1981) and Collier (1989) suggest, they show wisdom in cooperating with others to learn because cooperation is an effective strategy for learning both language and content.

A number of factors, then, may help account for particular students or groups of students seeming to prefer a certain learning style. Whole language teachers who have studied the area of learning styles are hesitant to attribute differences in students' learning to single causes, either cognitive or cultural. For example, in one well-known study, Au (1980) found that Hawaiian children, who had trouble learning to read using phonics, did much better when teachers used a comprehension-based approach that included "talk stories" of the kind told in the children's communities. Although the more familiar talk stories undoubtedly helped students make sense out of stories because they were culturally appropriate, the change from a phonics approach to one that emphasized comprehension also may have helped.

What much of the research on learning styles actually tells us is how certain groups interact socially. Phillips (1972) found that the native American Indian students she studied had more success in classrooms that fostered cooperative learning than in those that promoted individual competition. In addition, students were reluctant to answer questions about newly learned material. Phillips attributed these results to social practices in the students' communities where cooperative activity was stressed and where it was not considered appropriate to "show off" or look better than others. In addition, in their communities the students could choose to demonstrate knowledge or a skill only when they felt completely proficient in it. For these students, working individually, showing off knowledge in school, and answering before they felt ready were inappropriate cultural responses. When teachers adopt classroom practices congruent with social practices in the community, students have much greater school success.

Suggestopedia: A Second Language Method that Uses Different Modalities

Suggestopedia is one method of teaching a second language that attempts to incorporate different modes and modalities. This method was developed by Bulgarian psychiatrist-educator Lozanov (1982), who wanted to eliminate the psychological barriers that people have to learning. Stevick (1976) summarizes Lozanov's view of learning into three principles: (1) People are able to learn at rates many times greater than what is commonly assumed; (2) learning is a "global" event and involves the entire person; and (3) learners respond to many influences, many of them nonrational and non-conscious. Suggestopedia uses drama, art, physical exercise, and de-suggestive-suggestive communicative psychotherapy as well as the traditional modes of listening, speaking, reading, and writing to teach a second language. The influence of the science of *suggestology* is clear in this method that calls class meetings "sessions." In these sessions instruction is made pleasant and students' aesthetic interests are aroused. Lozanov's (1982) goal is that "new material to be learned will be assimilated and become automatic and creatively processed without strain and fatigue" (p. 157).

Several characteristics of Suggestopedia distinguish it from other second language teaching methods. First, the physical setting is extremely important. Classes are small and students sit in comfortable armchairs in a semicircle. On the walls of the room hang posters of the country of the language to be learned as well as posters with grammatical information such as verb conjugations.

Lessons begin with the teacher speaking in the students' first language. The teacher tells the students about the successful and enjoyable experience they are going to have. Students are told they will choose a new identity and a new name in the language they are learning. Baroque music is played as students close their eyes and do yoga breathing exercises to relax. The students and teacher then read the lesson to the beat of the music. Then students listen to the lesson and music with their eyes closed. In subsequent lessons, students do role-play, sing songs, play different games, and make up skits to work with the material in the lessons. Lozanov (1982) claims that Suggestopedia has had great success because students can assimilate a great deal of vocabulary, they can put the vocabulary to use, they can read, they can communicate and they are not afraid to use their new language. Lozanov attributes the success of Suggestopedia to the use of many modalities. Besides listening, speaking, reading, and writing, students listen to music, relax using techniques based on yoga, and perform role-plays.

Several aspects of Suggestopedia are consistent with whole language principles. Learning takes place in a relaxed setting. The teacher is positive and affirming. The students' first language supports the learning of the second. Language can be learned through the arts including music and drama. The attention of the learner is not focused on linguistic forms but rather on using the language to communicate. Errors are acceptable. Learning can be fun.

However, Suggestopedia is not entirely consistent with the whole language principles we have been presenting. Lessons are not learner centered. The teacher decides which material to present, leads all activities, and is the center of instruction. The emphasis is on the acquisition of vocabulary for future communication rather than for meeting immediate needs. Although students work with long dialogues, role-plays, and skits, they are not given choices in what they do or how they do it and the emphasis is on the parts, the individual vocabulary items that they are to learn. Although certain aspects of Suggestopedia are not consistent with whole language, a number of the techniques that Lozanov has developed would be useful in any classroom.

Whole Language and Learning through the Modalities

Whole language teachers recognize that their students have multiple intelligences so these teachers use different modes and modalities in teaching. They are also aware that too much emphasis on differences in learning styles can have negative effects on students. In particular, whole language teachers are careful not to assume that certain students have certain styles or learn better with certain modalities. These teachers don't wish to label their students, and thus limit their learning potential. Labelling can be especially harmful when students from diverse language and cultural backgrounds are being considered.

Whole language teachers avoid labels such as "visual learner" because they are aware that when it comes to research on the brain, little has been learned that relates in any direct way to learning styles. Cognitive scientists have made great strides in understanding more about the physiology of the brain, but almost nothing is known about what really happens when we think or about the relationship between thought and language. Frank Smith (1990) puts it well when he says:

> Thought is not accessible to direct inspection or introspection. . . . Attempts to explore thought by examining its physiological substructure have proved remarkably unrevealing. Dramatic discoveries have been made about how the parts of the human brain are put together and about the kinds of chemical and bioelectrical processes that take place within the millions of bundles of nerve fibers of which it is comprised, but they tell us nothing about the nature of thought that was not known before. The operations of thought remain as unpredictable from the wiring inside the skull as the operations of computers, refrigerators,

toasters, vacuum cleaners, and a multitude of other appliances are unpredictable from the wiring system of a house. (p. 120)

Smith comments that it is common sense to say that "some people prefer looking at pictures to listening to music, or would rather read a book than watch a movie, but that does not mean that they can only learn through specific modalities" (p. 121). As Smith points out, it doesn't matter whether the sensory input comes through the eyes, the ears, or the skin; the brain doesn't recognize the difference because all the input is changed into chemical and electrical impulses.

Individuals might have preferences about how they accomplish certain things, including learning, which might reflect what is generally done in their social communities, but there is no reason to believe that instruction must somehow match students' learning styles. Whole language teachers find a number of different ways to support students' learning. They are kid watchers and follow the students' lead. They are aware that for many second language students, long lectures or extensive textbook reading assignments may be particularly difficult. These teachers ensure that all students have chances to talk and listen, read and write every day by embedding all learning in a rich verbal and nonverbal context. They provide opportunities for students to learn through drama, art, music, and dance. In the section that follows we provide examples of lessons our students have shared with us. These lessons are good illustrations of how all the modes and modalities of learning can be used with second language students.

Lessons that Use All Four Modes—and More

The first three lessons we describe were projects from teachers taking a graduate course in linguistics. All three teachers have large numbers of second language students in their classes. The teachers had been asked to taperecord and transcribe one of their lessons. Then they were to analyze the classroom discourse. This procedure has been advocated by Paley (1981), who suggests that teachers gain insights into how they interact with their students and how their students interact with one another by looking closely at lesson transcripts. The three teachers reported on lessons that combined speaking, listening, reading, and writing. Two lessons also included drama.

By transcribing the lessons and reflecting on them, the teachers were able to improve the teaching and learning that went on.

Cyn

Cyn teaches British literature at a high school. Her students were beginning a study of Victorian literature. Cyn divided the class into six teams. Each team was asked to read a different section from their anthology, which provided background on the historical period, information about one of the authors they were to read, and a short excerpt from a novel by that author. Then each group presented a report to the class.

Cyn analyzed one presentation in detail. She found that the girls who made the report presented the details of the period as a kind of grocery list. She attributed this style to the fact that their textbook also presented the information as a list of facts and dates. The students had simply repeated this information in the same format rather than reorganizing it to make it more understandable.

She also found that though the two girls had worked together on their report in some respects, they had really worked separately in that they didn't coordinate the data they had collected. Some of the same facts appeared in each girl's talk. In addition, at times the girls spoke quite rapidly, and the other students had trouble taking notes.

After listening to the tape of the lesson, Cyn decided to try "Say Something," a reading strategy activity developed by Harste, Watson, and Burke. For this activity, pairs of students read a text together. They scan the text and decide how far they will read. They both read the agreed-upon section and then "say something." Then they choose the next section to read. This activity emphasizes co-operative reading and lets each reader check his or her understanding with a partner. Cyn decided to expand on this strategy and

> have the two students continue with the previously mentioned exercise and not only verbalize but also write down their inter-pretation. Then following the reading, together the students co-ordinate their notes into subtopics to support the overall thesis of the reading into an essay. It is hoped that this might help develop coordination and organizational skills for reading, writ-ing, and speaking.

Cyn also plans to have students listen to tapes of future presentations so that they can hear themselves and evaluate their effectiveness. Students in Cyn's classes are improving their reading, writing, speaking, and listening. All four modes are involved as they prepare and present their oral reports.

Barbara

Barbara teaches middle school ESL classes. She taped a class session where students were working on a project in small groups. The students in each group chose a story to read from a book containing cliff hangers. The stories in this book are left unfinished at an exciting point, so the students wrote their own ending. In addition, they divided the whole story into parts, decided who would take each part, and prepared a reader's theater presentation for the class.

Barbara taped and transcribed one group. They worked together very effectively during the entire time they had, about half an hour. During that time Barbara only came by twice to check on them. Even without close supervision, they focused on their reading, writing, and preparation for the class presentation.

Barbara was impressed at how these students, as well as those working in other groups, negotiated meaning. She found that shy students spoke up more in the small group situation, that the students were able to clarify ideas without teacher intervention, and that they could handle disagreements and still stay on task. In addition, she noted that second language students could communicate effectively in this situation. Barbara wrote in her paper, "It is also obvious that students do not need to speak in formal English dialect to be understood by their peers. The groups studied in this discourse included three Hispanics, one Southeast Asian, and one Black American. Each uses a different form of English dialect, but there was no communication breakdown."

The project Barbara invited her students to complete clearly contained all four modes as well as drama. Students read the story, wrote an ending, chose roles, and presented the story to classmates in reader's theater. The group Barbara taped showed creativity by adding sound effects. They became so involved that they even took their scripts home to practice that night.

As a final step, Barbara asked the students to evaluate how well they had worked together. They concluded that things had gone pretty well but that they would be more serious and stay out of arguments next time. Carlos felt the planning "helped us get our parts together and it was even fun!" Doua commented, "It didn't really all come out the way we wanted it to, but it worked kind of OK." And Mario said, "I liked it 'cause I didn't have to do all the work myself."

Mary

Mary teaches fourth grade in a rural community with a large percentage of Hispanic students. She decided to have her students collaborate on writing and acting out a fairy tale. She had read many fairy tales to the class, and in writer's workshop each student had written a fairy tale and read it to the class. When Mary suggested the idea of a collaborative play, the students were very enthusiastic. They began by brainstorming the characters who would be in the play. Then they named the characters, and students volunteered for the different parts.

Next, the class brainstormed the plot for their tale. Mary wrote the plot out on butcher paper and taped it up around the room. The whole class read the plot aloud and discussed what each of the characters might say in carrying out the action. They cleared a space in the middle of the room and the actors walked through their parts without dialogue. After this Mary gave the students time to create the dialogue for the play. Then she videotaped the performance.

The experience was positive for many of the second language students. One boy who had done poorly in other activities performed very well. Hugo had been given the part of the king in the play, and perhaps that important role helped raise his self-esteem. Another student, Gildardo, found a clever solution to a problem in the play. All the students enjoyed the activity, and Mary shared the videotape with parents at open house.

Although the activity was generally positive, Mary was not entirely satisfied with the results. To improve future performances, Mary plans to have students walk through their parts once without speaking and then a second time with dialogue, stopping after each scene for discussion before the videotaping. She also plans to have her students view the tape and revise their performance.

Like Cyn and Barbara, Mary created a series of lessons that incorporated speaking, listening, reading, and writing as well as other sign systems. Her students wrote a fairy tale, read it, and then performed it. They also got to see and hear themselves on the videotape. By involving students in lessons such as these, Mary, Barbara, and Cyn help all their students develop their language proficiency and expand their communication potential.

Two additional examples show the importance of incorporating multiple sign systems in lessons for learners of all ages. Research has shown that second language learners can often read and write before they develop fluency in oral language: (Ferreiro and Teberosky, 1982; Hudelson, 1984, 1989; Urzúa, 1989; Rigg, 1986; Edelsky, 1986). The following examples, which come from a primary class and an adult ESL class, illustrate the benefits of including music and art as well as speaking, listening, reading, and writing to help students develop both concepts and ways of expressing those concepts.

Katie

In Katie's pre-first classroom, students discuss ideas and activities, read, draw, sing, and write stories. They also write in their interactive journals daily.

Children for whom English is a second language read and write from the start in Katie's classroom. This is demonstrated clearly by a story written by Dang Vue, a Hmong child. The children had talked and read about Valentine's Day. They made valentines and exchanged them, and they had their party. The next day, Dang chose to write and illustrate a story about the experience. His sophisticated illustrations and his story show that he is well on his way to being literate in his second language, English (fig. 5–4).

Sometimes teachers of younger children feel that they should not introduce reading and writing too soon. This is particularly true for teachers of young second language students. This example from Dang shows the value of introducing reading and writing from the beginning. There is no need to insist on perfect pronunciation and lots of vocabulary drill before allowing a student to read or write at any age.

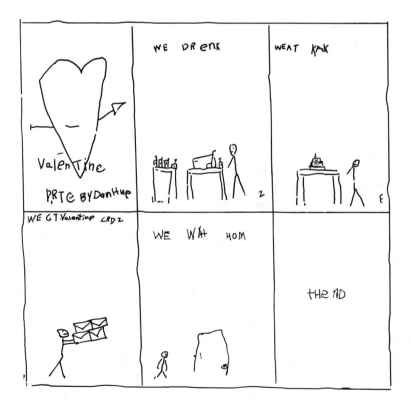

Figure 5.4
Valentine Story

Figure 5.5

Miriam

Miriam shared some examples from her adult ESL students that show that students, when allowed to express themselves in different modalities, can show their strengths. Most of her adult students from different parts of Southeast Asia had no previous schooling before they began attending adult school. They spoke very little English and were extremely shy about sharing orally in class. Miriam also felt their frustration when they tried to write in their journals because most of the students were embarrassed about their limited writing skills.

During one discussion, the students and Miriam began talking about the differences in houses and yards in the United States and their native counties. The students tried to explain to their teacher what their homes in Thailand and Laos were like, but neither the students nor the teacher felt that important points were being com-

Figure 5.6

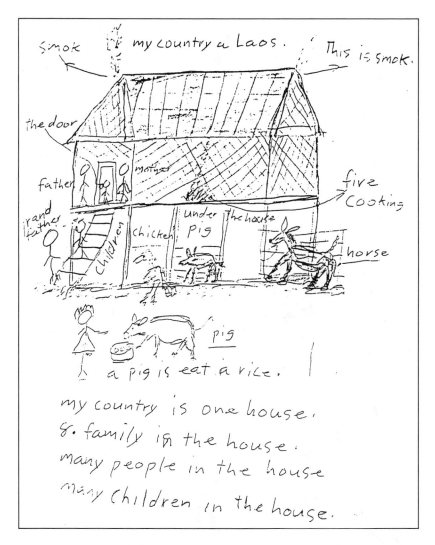

municated. Since the topic was one that everyone seemed very interested in, the class decided to draw pictures of their homes in their native lands as a homework assignment and that the discussion of differences in houses would be continued at the next class.

The following class meeting began with Miriam asking for the drawings. There was silence in the room. At first Miriam thought that no one had done the drawing, but she soon realized that the students were all hiding their work and were hesitant about showing their pictures. "No good draw," "Very bad," and "So sorry, teacher" were phrases that filled the room. After much coaxing, Miriam was finally able to get the students to reluctantly pull out their pictures.

What Miriam saw brought tears to her eyes. Her students had spent a great deal of time painstakingly drawing their homes and yards, often in colored pencil with great detail. One woman had drawn and labeled the house, the storage house, crops, animals, and important family members (fig. 5–5). Another student had labeled the house in detail and added a descriptive paragraph (fig. 5–6). One student had drawn in detail four homes he had had in Laos and Thailand and two in the United States (fig. 5–7). Others included details of villages and village life similar to the pandau tapestry that

Figure 5.7

is embroidered by Southeast Asians (figs. 5–8 and 5–9). Miriam realized that she would never again limit her students' communication to only listening, speaking, reading, and writing.

Conclusion

We've pointed out in this chapter that oral and written language can develop together and that students can learn and communicate through many different modalities. Often, second language students find that reading, writing, music, drama, and art can help them develop the language they are learning. Listening, speaking, reading, and writing can be supported by other ways of communicating as well.

Figure 5.8

Figure 5.9

Traditionally, oral language has been stressed over written language for students learning a second language. However, it is important that students have opportunities to read and write from the beginning as they learn a new language. Since oral language passes by rapidly, bilingual students have more control over written language. They can reread passages, they can look at individual words, and they can take their time to express in writing what they want to say. In addition, whole language teachers include reading and writing from the start because they know that their students need to develop academic competence as well as communicative competence.

The same factors that help students develop oral language help them to develop written language. According to Cochrane and colleagues (1984), writing develops when students are immersed in a literate environment, when they find that written language is meaningful and purposeful, when they see people who are important to them using written language, when they get support in their attempts to read and write, and when they are given time to read and write daily.

We'd like to end this chapter by describing one more lesson that is specifically designed for second language learners and uses reading, writing, speaking, and listening to help them learn language through content.

Fast-Food

Karen teaches fifth grade. Her class of twenty-seven is comprised of twelve students whose English is limited and fifteen who speak English as their first language. Karen has found that the techniques she uses to make lessons comprehensible for her second language students are helpful for all her students. Today her lesson is an introduction to a unit on health and nutrition. Karen wants her students to identify questions of interest that they will explore over the next few weeks. At the same time, she wishes to assess what they already know about this topic. In particular, she wants to find out what her second language speakers have learned about American food customs.

Karen starts the lesson by announcing, "Today we're going to talk about a special kind of food, fast-food. Do any of you know the names of some fast-food restaurants? As the students call out names of restaurants, "McDonald's," "Wendy's," Kentucky Fried," Karen writes the names on the board. After a few minutes she has compiled a list of fourteen different restaurants. Then she asks, "What kinds of food can you buy in these restaurants?" She works down the list with the class, writing in the kinds of food each restaurant serves. The students know that they can get hamburgers and fries at McDonald's, and that Domino's has pizza and salad.

When the students have named all the kinds of foods they can think of for each restaurant, Karen asks them to do a quickwrite, "In the next two minutes, write down what you like and what you dislike about fast-food." The students work busily for the next two minutes, often glancing up at the board where the names of the restaurants and foods are listed. At the end of the time, Karen asks students to get together in groups of three and make one composite list. The students push their desks together and start on this activity. Karen circulates around the room, noting what the students are writing and answering questions. After a few minutes, she asks the students to stop. "I'm going to start with what you like about fast-food. I'll ask each group to give me one thing you wrote down, and I'll write it here on the overhead."

Karen elicits first the likes and then the dislikes from the groups, writing their responses on a transparency on the overhead. Several of the likes and dislikes relate to health matters. One group comments that they dislike fast-food because it is high in fat. Another group claims that fast-food is too salty. Karen asks, "You've said that in some ways fast-food is not very healthy. Why don't you talk in your groups for a couple of minutes and try to decide what makes a healthy meal? Have somebody in your group write down your ideas, and I will ask you to report back." Again, as the students discuss this question, Karen circulates around the room.

The students come up with a list of factors that make a healthy meal. They mention low fat, low sugar, and a balance of all the food groups. Karen writes their responses on another transparency. Then she hands out a pamphlet for each group. These have come from the National Dairy Council (1989) and are a sample of the kind of nutrition information that can be collected from different organizations, restaurants, and companies. She asks the students not to open the pamphlets yet. On the colorful cover are pictures of a shake, a hamburger, and fries. At the top is written "Fast-Food" and below that title "Junk? Gems? or Just OK?" Karen asks, "Do you see some things on the cover that we have been talking about?" The students nod in agreement. "Is there anything on the cover we didn't mention?" The students note that they had forgotten shakes, so Karen adds that word to their food list.

"What do you think 'Junk' and 'Gems' refers to?" asks Karen.

The students respond, "Bad things and good things."

"Something worthless and something valuable."

Karen lists the responses on the board in two columns. "Are there other ways to talk about good and bad things?" she asks. One student mentions "pros" and "cons" while another calls out "likes" and "dislikes." Karen adds these pairs to the list.

"OK, now open the pamphlet once." Inside is a series of columns printed in different colors. The first lists fast-food items by restaurant. For example, under Burger King, the Whopper is listed and under Arby's comes Ham 'n Cheese. Beside each food item is the number of calories it contains. The Whopper has 628 calories; the Ham 'n Cheese has 353. The remaining five columns are color coded. They are labeled milk group (blue), meat group (red), fruit-vegetable group (green), grain group (yellow) and others (gray). For each food group, the chart lists the number of recommended daily servings according to the Dairy Council and the important nutrients. Then, across from each food item, such as the Whopper, the ingredients included in each food group is indicated. The Whopper has cheese for the milk group; hamburger for meat; onion and lettuce for fruit/vegetable; the bun for grain; and catsup, pickles, and mayonnaise under others.

Karen asks a few questions to be sure her students understand how to read the chart. "How many calories would I get if I ate a Long John Silver's Fish and More?"

Quickly, one student answers "978."

"How many food groups are included in Wendy's chili?"

Another student answers, "Two."

"Which ones are missing?" asks Karen, and the student explains that chili lacks the milk, grain, and others groups. After a few more questions, Karen is satisfied that the students can read the chart.

"There's lots of fast-food listed here, isn't there?" Karen asks. "I'd like you to imagine that this chart is really a menu for a super fast-food restaurant. I'm going to be the waitress, and you'll be the customers. You can order anything you like that's on the chart. I want everyone to write down what people order. Now who would like to go first?"

Abel raises his hand. "I'll have a Taco Bell beef taco and a Dairy Queen ice cream cone."

"Would you care for something to drink?" asks Karen.

"Sure, I'll have a glass of milk."

Karen takes orders from three other students. Everyone writes down what they order, often reading the chart to get the spelling right. Then Karen says, "We've been talking about what makes a healthy meal. Who do you think ordered the healthiest meal? I want you to talk about this in your groups. Then we'll vote. Each group gets one vote, and you have to be able to justify your choice."

The students talk animatedly. They discuss which meals cover all the food groups, which have the most calories, and which ones contain the most nutrients. When they have decided, they vote and discuss their choices. Karen distributes additional pamphlets so each student has one. "If you open up the pamphlets completely, you'll see that there is information about the question we've been asking, 'Is fast food good for you?' You'll also see some meals like the ones you just ordered, and each meal is analyzed. There's also a section called, 'So what should a fast-food eater do?' I want you to read over this information tonight and decide whether or not you made a good choice when you voted on the healthiest meal. You might discuss this with your family. Then, we can talk about it tomorrow."

This introductory lesson is followed up the next day with a re-analysis of the votes for the healthiest meal. As the students continue to look at the topic of American food customs and as they continue to formulate questions about good eating habits, Karen involves them in other activities as well. Together, they look at *You* magazine (1986). This is also a publication of the National Dairy Council and has articles such as "It's Time You Faced the Fats," "Are You In—or Out of Shape?" and "Look Before You Eat." The articles are on topics of high interest to Karen's students, and they are supplemented by pictures and charts that make the content comprehensible for second language learners. In addition, there are separate versions of the publication, one for girls and a different one for boys. Girls feel it's unfair when they learn it takes them 45 minutes of swimming to burn off the calories from one cheeseburger, but it takes a boy only 37 minutes. These differences lead to lively discussions.

Other activities include visiting local fast-food restaurants, which give tours and free materials, interviewing parents and friends about their eating habits, and surveying other students about how often they eat fast-food and which restaurants are their favorites. A discussion about the bias the National Dairy Council or other companies might have in putting together a chart for distribution is discussed. The students also talk about cultural differences in conceptions about healthy meals. For example, in some cultures, it is considered unhealthy to combine hot and cold food during a meal. Many cultures have very little meat in the diet. Some cultures use a lot of lard in cooking their food.

During these different activities, all students develop the vocabulary and concepts associated with food and health through reading, writing, speaking, and listening. They can then use this base as they begin to investigate their own questions about food and health. Second language students may choose to look at the food customs of their own culture and contrast those with American food, or they might try to investigate whether or not immigrants to the United States retain their own eating habits or adopt U.S. customs. What is important is that as they explore these questions, all students, including second language students, are increasing their content area knowledge as they develop their oral and written language proficiency.

Chapter 6

———

Learning Should Take Place in the First Language

———

> Well, I'am born in Thailand, but I don't know how to speak Thai at all. You may find it amusing but I really don't know how to read or write, or speak Thai at all. Even though I'm Hmong, I don't even know how to read and write in Hmong. The only language I really know how to read and write is English. In my high school year, I'm planning to take French for my foreign language. (14-year-old Hmong girl)

This sample came from a journal exchange between Julie, a student teacher, and a Hmong junior high school student, but it could easily have come from any one of the many second language students in our schools. Unfortunately, these students often lose their first language so completely that by the time they reach high school, they need to study a foreign language!

The sixth principle of whole language stresses the importance of supporting students' primary languages and cultures to build concepts and facilitate the acquisition of English. Sometimes, as in the example of the Hmong teenager above, children are not literate in their first language, and it is difficult to know how to support them. We have found that when we do show students the importance of their first language, they become empowered. This empowerment helps them to see their own potential as learners in English as well as in their first language.

Katie and Teresa support their students' first languages even though these whole language teachers are not able to speak those languages. They recognize that if they wish to teach the whole child and build on the strengths each child brings to school, they can not ignore the language the child speaks or the culture in which the child has been raised.

Mo, a Hmong boy in Katie's pre-first classroom, proved that he could not only learn but also teach. Since Katie had several Hmong children in her class, she asked that a Hmong storyteller come to tell the story "Three Billy Goats Gruff." Before the storyteller came, Katie read several versions of the folktale to her class. When the storyteller arrived, ready to take the Hmong students off to a corner to tell his tale, Katie insisted that he tell the story to the entire class in Hmong. She reasoned that the children knew the story so well that they would be able to follow along. She was correct. When the storyteller arrived at the part of the story where the goats cross the bridge, the students shouted in delight at the "Trip trap, trip trap" spoken in Hmong. All the children, no matter what their language background, enjoyed the story.

The real benefit for Mo of having the story told to the whole class in Hmong became more obvious in the days that followed the storytelling. First, Mo wrote and drew in his journal about his favorite story, "Three Billy Goats Gruff" (fig. 6-1). Then Mo became a "teacher" of Hmong to his own teacher. Figure 6-2 shows how Mo drew and labeled pictures to demonstrate what he had written. Below the pictures, he wrote in English "theys are mog log wich theys are the thine to me" (These are Hmong language. These are the thing to me.) Katie responded by telling him how much she liked reading his Hmong. Katie reported that from the time of the visit from the Hmong storyteller, Mo showed not only a pride in his first language and culture but also an enthusiasm for school not evident before.

Teresa, a second grade teacher, also found a way to support the first language of her students. After a class discussion on the importance of being bilingual, Navy, a Khmer student, took recess and lunch time for several days to produce a book of letters, numbers, and words that would teach her classmates and the teacher Khmer. Teresa had the book laminated and put in the class library (see fig. 6-3).

Neither Katie nor Teresa are bilingual teachers, and their students are not in bilingual programs, but both teachers have found ways for their students to use their first language as they are acquiring English. Although neither Katie nor Teresa can provide primary language instruction themselves, they understand the importance of celebrating and expanding the language and culture of all of their students.

Mo and Navy are fortunate to have such excellent teachers. However, even under these good conditions, they will not be able

Figure 6.1

to develop their first languages fully and may exit school as monolinguals in English. For students like Mo and Navy, the best education would come through a bilingual program that follows

Figure 6.2

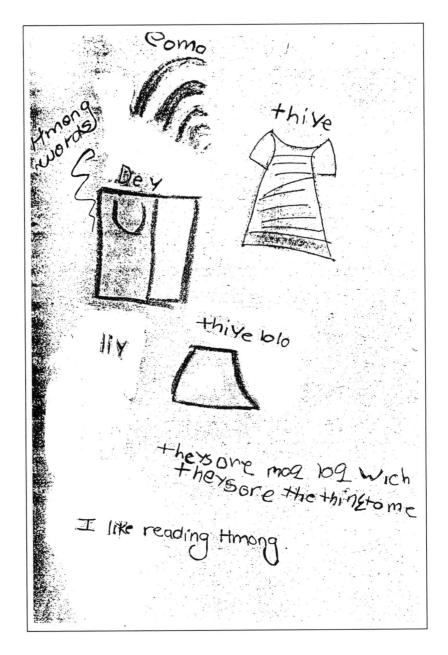

whole language principles. It is important that whole language teachers understand the rationale for bilingual education so that they can support their students in every way possible.

Figure 6.3

Teacher: Teresa Calderón Parker

2nd grade

9 year old

Khmer lang.

Whole Language and Bilingual Education

Whole language and bilingual education have several things in common. Both have received a tremendous amount of bad press based on insufficient or incorrect information. The research that supports both is often ignored whereas research that opposes either is broadly publicized, especially in the popular press. In the introduction, we explained that there are many misconceptions about whole language, including who it is good for and how best to implement it.

Similar misconceptions surround bilingual education. Since both whole language and bilingual education have the goal of empowering all students, public acceptance or rejection often is based more on politics or emotions than on what we know about learning and teaching. However, when we examine the research on bilingual education, and when we look carefully at the progress of individual students, it becomes clear that whole language teachers support first language development because they know that students learn concepts best in their primary language and that the development of the first language leads to faster acquisition of English as well. Moreover, programs that support a student's first language and culture help the student gain self-confidence and a positive attitude toward school.

Probably no other principle that we propose for second language learners is more controversial than this one. The debate over bilingual education has continually confused both the public and educators. Since 1968, when the Bilingual Education Act was added as an amendment to the 1965 Elementary and Secondary Education Act, there has been misunderstanding about the purpose and effectiveness of bilingual education for language minority students. Opponents of bilingual education argue that students should be taught in English to become fluent in English and compete in our society. Bilingual education was attacked by former President Reagan (Crawford 1989) and former Secretary of Education Bennett (Bennett 1985) in the past and continues to be attacked today by U.S. English advocates (Imhoff 1990).

Bilingual education is a political and emotional issue that is seldom evaluated from a pedagogical perspective as it should be. Even among whole language advocates, who recognize the importance of building on the language and culture students bring with them to school, some do not fully understand the importance of first language support for second language learners. This has become clear to us over the past few years as we have worked with experienced teachers who are studying how to use whole language with bilingual learners.

One of the courses teachers in our graduate program take is "Methods, Theory and Materials of Bilingual Education." Yvonne decided two years ago to teach this course bilingually in Spanish and English even though only one-fourth to one-third of the students speak or have studied any Spanish. Yvonne felt it was critical to try to "practice" what she was "preaching." She wanted to challenge herself to make the course content comprehensible to non-Spanish-speaking teachers, and she wanted the teachers in this class to experience what it was like to have to learn in a second language. Yvonne employs strategies and techniques consistent with whole language and good bilingual education to help her students understand the research and reading they are doing on bilingual education. Although the teachers have sometimes resisted taking the class and begin the class with reservations or even fear, their weekly responses and self-evaluations show that their attitudes change and that they see the value of first language support for their own students. Responses from two of the teachers illustrate how they changed their attitudes toward bilingual education as a result of their reading and research and also because of their experience of being second language learners themselves in this class. Rose Marie wrote:

> I know I've been a little obnoxious about this class (OK, a lot obnoxious). You were absolutely right about teaching this class in Spanish. I think I have a greater understanding about bilingual education because of the Spanish. As a whole language person I am conflicted about having to take this class. Yet, if there was a choice I would not have chosen this class.

Nancy reflected on her past experience and could see how her attitude had changed:

> When I was a student teacher in the teacher education program, almost every day I would walk by the office of bilingual education. I would think, "What is this program needed for? We don't need bilingual education. It is the parent's fault that the minority students are failing in school—not the teacher's fault!" Now it is embarrassing to me to realize how prejudiced I felt about the bilingual education program. Even worse my opinions were completely unfounded. I knew nothing about the bilingual education program. . . . I now realize that my prejudice arose from ignorance and fear.

Teachers like Rose Marie and Nancy have come to understand bilingual education and have joined us in our concern over the misunderstandings some educators and the public have developed concerning bilingual education.

In this chapter we present the historical background of bilingual education, describe the pedagogical rationale for bilingual education, contrast several bilingual programs and alternatives to bilingual education, and propose an approach to bilingual education that is consistent with whole language principles. Our hope is that, even if they are not bilingual, whole language teachers will support the concept of bilingual education. In addition, we offer suggestions for both bilingual teachers and monolingual teachers who want to support their students' first language and culture by using whole language.

Historical Background of Bilingual Education

The perception of the general public is that English has been the official language of the United States since the early settlers arrived in the 1600s. Yet, in 1664 at least eighteen different languages were spoken on Manhattan Island (Crawford 1989). During the 1700s bilingualism was quite common. In 1750, for example, when Benjamin Franklin tried to force schooling in English because he could not reach the German-speaking electorate, he was voted out of office. By the mid-1800s bilingual schools in different languages were operating across the United States: German/English schools in twelve states, French/English schools in Louisiana, and Spanish/English schools in the Territory of New Mexico. To give an idea of the extent of bilingual education, in 1900 more than 4 percent of the elementary school population was receiving instruction partly or exclusively in the German language.

In the early 1900s, with the threat of war against Germany, Theodore Roosevelt (1917) led a campaign against bilingualism, giving immigrants five years to learn English or be deported. Letters to the editor in various newspapers today are similar to Roosevelt's sentiments:

> . . . any man who comes here must adopt the institutions of the United States, and therefore he must adopt the language which is now the native tongue of our people. It would be not merely a matter of misfortune but a crime to perpetuate differences of language in this country. (reported in Trueba (1979), p. 3)

This attitude toward immigrants led to the view that the United States should be a great melting pot and that the goal for all immigrants should be to melt into the rest of society. Some still hold this belief today: "The idea of teaching children in other languages is an affront to sacred traditions" (Crawford 1989, p. 18). The battle between the "English Only" advocates who oppose bilingual education and the pro-bilingual "English Plus" followers has never been merely a language issue. A review of the research supporting bilingual education suggests that there are other, more disturbing reasons that bilingual education receives the opposition it does. JoAnne, another graduate student, reflected on this phenomenon:

> I began this semester wondering why, when there seemed to be such a sound rationale for bilingual education, there could be such controversy surrounding it. I did not realize that bilingual education is more than an educational issue, that it is part of a societal context involving the power struggle between ethnic and racial groups.

We will explore some of the concerns with the power struggles involved in bilingual education, but first it is important to establish the rationale for bilingual education by briefly reviewing bilingual research and theory.

Rationale for Bilingual Education

Recent research-based theory in second language acquisition has strongly supported bilingual education (Collier 1989; Crawford 1989; Cummins 1984; Cummins 1989a; Edelsky 1986; Edelsky, Altwerger, and Flores 1991; Freeman 1988b; Freeman and Freeman 1991b; Hakuta 1986; Krashen 1985; Krashen and Biber 1988). When we support students' first language, we are building on their strengths and validating them as individuals. We are teaching the whole person. Using a second language learner's first language in school is important for several reasons: (1) Bilingual students build important background knowledge and concepts when they receive comprehensible input in their first language, and this helps them succeed academically later in English; (2) when students have a well-developed first language, they can learn a second language more rapidly; and (3) bilingual students come to value their own language and culture and maintain important family ties. The potential for a clash between school and home values is lessened. They can become valuable bilingual members of the larger community.

Considerable research shows that students who speak, read, and write their first language well are more apt to succeed academically in English (Collier 1989; Cummins 1989a; Krashen and Biber 1988). A key to this success is that students who receive instruction in their first language can keep up academically while they are learning English. In contrast, programs that focus exclusively on teaching English may do so at the expense of academic achievement. If students' school time is spent learning English, they fall behind in math, social studies, science, and other subjects. It is very difficult for students who lag two or three years behind in academic subjects ever to catch up with their English-speaking peers.

By providing instruction in the students' first language, it is possible to build on their strengths. Cummins (1989a) has argued that concepts are most readily developed in the first language and, once developed, are accessible through the second language. In other words, what we learn in one language transfers into the new language. Cummins compares the languages that bilinguals speak with two tips of a large iceberg. That's all we can see, but the main part of the iceberg, which is below the surface, contains all the concepts developed in the two languages. The languages are simply channels that allow bilinguals to take in or express the concepts.

Cummins argues that the concepts a bilingual person builds form a Common Underlying Proficiency (CUP), which is available for expression in any language the person speaks or writes. Once a child knows how to read in one language, for example, the child can transfer that knowledge about the reading process to the second language. The child does not have to learn to read all over again any more than Einstein needed to learn physics all over again when he came to the United States. If high school students come to this country having studied algebra in their first language, they don't need to learn algebraic concepts a second time. What they need is the ability to express their mathematical understandings in English.

It is easier to learn something in one's first language. However, there may be other reasons for learning basic skills in the first language. Swain and colleagues (1990) report on an interesting study that compared bilingual students who had learned to read in their first language with other bilinguals who had learned to read in their second language. When both groups of students studied a third language in school, the bilinguals who had developed literacy in their first language learned to read the third language faster than the other bilinguals who had learned to read only in their second language. This study suggests that there may be cognitive benefits involved in developing the first language as fully as possible.

The commonsense assumption for second language learners in schools, then, that "more English equals more English" does not hold true. Cummins (1981) explains that those who insist on using only English to teach English do not understand how building concepts in the first language supports second language learning. A person who insists that instruction be given in English only must believe that the different language systems are totally separate and that what one knows in one language cannot be transferred to a second language. This idea is what Cummins has labeled SUP or Separate Underlying Proficiency.

Both research and personal experience discredit the idea of SUP. For example, we have a close bilingual friend who lives in Mexico City. When we visit Lucy, she encourages conversation in English so she can practice. Lucy's husband, however, does not speak English. When he joins us, Lucy is able to recount the gist of our conversation in Spanish even though the conversation was in English. The ideas we discussed in English can be easily explained in Spanish. The things we learn are not restricted to one language or another and are not kept in separate parts of the brain.

Research by Kolers (1973) makes the same point in a different way. In one experiment he asked English/French bilinguals to read passages that contained words in both English and French. He found that bilinguals could read passages that mixed the two languages as rapidly as they could read passages that were written entirely in either French or English. This led him to conclude that these bilinguals read directly for meaning. They did not have to convert words in a mixed passage all to one language to understand them. "If the readers had had to make all of the words of a mixed passage conform to a single language before they could understand them, they would have had less time to work out the meaning of a mixed passage than of a unilingual one; and having less time, their comprehension would have been poorer. But it was not" (p. 47). Kolers concluded that "when a reader knows the words of a language, he perceives them directly in terms of their meanings" (p. 47).

Words are the surface-level elements of language. Meaning occurs at a deeper level, and it was this deeper level that the bilinguals in Kolers's experiments worked on when they perceived the meanings of the words. When people read for meaning, they access what Cummins describes as the common underlying proficiency they have developed. In the first experiment described, the bilinguals read silently. In another, they read aloud, and when they did, they often substituted French words for English words or English words for French words. They might say *door* when *porte* was printed, or the reverse. These substitutions occurred at points in the text where there was a switch from one language to the other. The substitutions of the equivalent words were translations that showed again that the readers were focusing on the meaning of the passage and not on the surface elements, the words.

Proficient readers focus on meaning, not on the surface forms of the language. Proficient bilingual readers, as Kolers's experiments have shown, are not even concerned with the language the text is printed in because they have developed a proficiency common to the languages they speak or read. The language input is comprehensible for them in either language. However, for students beginning to read or beginning to cope with academic content, input in English may not be comprehensible. In chapter 1 we discussed Krashen's idea of the importance of teachers providing second language learners with lots of comprehensible input. In his research and writing on bilingual education, Krashen explains that the best way to make input comprehensible is to use the students' first language (Krashen 1985). Frank Smith (1985) expresses the same idea when he argues that, although learning is natural and happens all the time, we cannot learn what we do not understand. Learning involves *demonstrations* (we see people doing things), *engagement* (we decide we want to do those things), and *sensitivity* (nothing is done or said that convinces us we can't do those things). When the demonstration is given in English to non-native speakers, they may not understand what they are seeing or hearing. If they don't understand the demonstration, they probably won't choose to engage in the activity. And if they don't understand what the teacher says, they may become convinced that they can't learn. At all three stages, instruction in English simply may not be comprehensible enough for learning to take place.

Skutnabb-Kangas (1983) provides another reason that instruction in a second language may not result in learning in the same way that primary language instruction does. She begins by asking what happens when "The child sits in a submersion classroom (where many of the students have L2, the language of instruction, as their mother tongue), listening to the teacher explaining something that the child is then supposed to use for problem solving" (p. 116). In this situation the results are predictable: "The first result of the input or part of it being incomprehensible is that the child gets less information than a child listening to her mother tongue" (p. 116). If a child fails to understand even a few words, she may lose the meaning of an explanation.

Second, "Listening to a second or foreign language is more tiring than listening to L1" (p. 116). All children have limits on their attention spans, but second language learners need even more frequent and longer pauses to maintain concentration. If adult students are put in situations where they do not understand instruction, they will use one of two strategies. They may simply decide that the class is not worth their effort and leave. This is one factor that helps explain irregular attendance in adult ESL classes. Or, they may try to change the situation by asking for more explanation or for a translation. In Yvonne's bilingually taught graduate class, the adult teachers did, in fact, often ask questions and were relieved when Yvonne had them work with partners who could understand and speak both English and Spanish fluently. Children, in most cases, don't have or take these options. State laws require them to attend school, and they are usually not in a position to request a change in the way the class is conducted. What may happen, though, is that students simply drop out mentally until they are old enough to leave school.

In the California Tomorrow research report *Crossing the Schoolhouse Border*, Olsen (1988) interviewed a number of second language students who expressed their frustration at not being able to understand instruction in English. A ninth grade Mexican girl reported:

> I just sat in my classes and didn't understand anything. Sometimes I would try to look like I knew what was going on, sometimes I would just try to think about a happy time when I didn't feel stupid. My teachers never called on me or talked to me. I think they either forgot I was there or else wish I wasn't. I waited and I waited, thinking someday I will know English. (p. 62)

An eleventh grade Cambodian boy commented, "My first school I didn't want to go, just to stay home. When I went I just sat there and didn't understand anything" (p. 62). The failure to understand can undermine a student's self-confidence. As a tenth grade Mexican girl put it:

> It's very frustrating. I didn't feel good. I couldn't really adjust to life here. I felt really dumb. I would sit in class and not understand anything. I went home and tried to read but had to look up every word in my dictionary. I spent hours reading each page. Sometimes I just gave up. The teacher didn't expect me to do anything. I was most fearful to get my report card. (p. 64)

When students like these, who are not proficient in English, are submerged in a mainstream class, they present a problem for their teachers, who are under pressure to keep up with the curriculum and cover the content. Teachers don't want to ignore these students, but they may simply not know what to do. In addition, parents of the English-speaking students may be putting pressure on the school not to slow down or water down the content for the second language students. We say more about what mainstream teachers can do with second language students toward the end of this chapter, but a schoolwide program is necessary to meet the needs of all students, and, as Krashen and Biber (1988) have shown, the most effective programs are those which provide students with instruction in their first language.

When concepts are taught in the first language, second language learners are able to grasp those ideas more easily. If they are receiving content instruction in comprehensible English at the same time, they also can learn the language associated with those same concepts in English and thus learn both concepts and language (Cummins 1989a; Krashen 1985). To make this process clearer, it might be helpful to provide an example. Imagine a kindergarten classroom at the beginning of the school year. Several children in the class speak only Spanish. Their teacher and the other students speak only English. The teacher has a camera. She explains to the class that they are all going to go on a tour of the school to take pictures of people and places around the school. The class visits the attendance office, the principal and vice-principal's offices, the school cafeteria, the school custodian's office, and the library. At each place the teacher and the children take pictures and ask questions. When the class returns, the teacher explains that when the pictures are developed the class will write stories together about the people in the pictures and make a big book about their school.

It is quite possible that the non-English speakers in the classroom might have been thoroughly confused by this activity. Though the teacher provided context by actually taking the children to see the places and talk to the people, the purpose of the activity was probably lost on the Spanish-speaking children. They might not have made the connections between the tour of the school, the pictures, and the class book until the pictures arrived and the class began to assemble the book. Even when the class started to make the book, the Spanish-speaking children might not have been able to fully participate because the brainstorming about what should be written in the book and the actual writing took place in a language they did not understand. The learning the teacher hoped would take place may have been minimal for the non-English speakers.

If we change the scenario, there is great potential for learning through this activity for both the native English speakers and the second language learners. Before introducing the activity to the class, the teacher has her Spanish-speaking aide, a Spanish-speaking parent, or an older bilingual child give her Spanish-speaking kindergartners a preview in their first language of what is going to happen. The non-English-speaking children, therefore, understand the purpose of the tour, and as they move from place to place, they can make predictions about what is being talked about in English. The activity, then, not only has a purpose for them, but, because the students understand what is happening, they can make more sense of the English being spoken and begin to pick up English words.

It is important, however, that the learning not be restricted to the learning of language. The teacher did the activity with her English-speaking students so that they would be comfortable in their school and understand their school community. The goals should be the same for the Spanish speakers. Because these students did understand the purpose of the tour and could make predictions, they had much to say about what they saw and learned. Even though they could not yet explain their understanding to their teacher in English, the children could be encouraged to work with a Spanish-speaking classroom helper to brainstorm and make pages for a big book in Spanish. Thus, they have the same kind of learning experience their English-speaking peers have. In addition, they build more background, and they are more likely to understand the English being used when the big book is read in English.

Use of the primary language, then, can help students develop academic concepts and can also help lead them into English. When students have a good understanding of a subject area, that background can help them comprehend a discussion in English about that subject. Their knowledge of the content helps them make predictions about what the English words mean.

It is also important that students develop one language fully in both oral and written form. Children come to school with a language that has served their needs up until that time. If the language is English, the school will continue its development. Although six-year-olds have a good control of the phonology of their first language, their syntactic competence doesn't fully develop for at least another six years, and their vocabulary continues to develop throughout their lives.

Children who come to school speaking a language other than English may not learn to read and write in their first language. They may continue to develop their primary language at home, but their academic development may be entirely in English. Collier (1989) found that even when there was support for first language, it took students five to seven years to catch up with their peers in a new language. Without first language support, students may never catch up. It's not that they lack language—they are not *alingual* or *semilingual*—they just don't speak the language that counts in school, and they fall behind academically while they are trying to learn it.

If, on the other hand, language minority students can develop their first language fully in school, their knowledge of language forms and functions transfers to English in the same way as their knowledge of any other subject matter. In other words, the more students know about their native languages, the more background they have to help them understand the English language. Research on language universals shows that even unrelated languages share many common features of both structure and function. People who speak several languages often comment that the third language was easier to learn than the second, and the fourth easier than the third. These people have a rich linguistic background that makes learning new languages easier. Second language learners retain this same advantage if they are allowed to develop their first language fully.

Although the key component of any bilingual program is primary language instruction, successful bilingual programs, which we describe in the next section, always include effective ESL instruction as well. Often, people think that in bilingual programs, students spend the whole day receiving instruction in their first language. In fact, they also receive instruction in English. Effective English instruction is meaningful, functional, and context-rich so that it meets the needs of bilingual students. In other words, it contains large amounts of comprehensible input. Krashen (1985) has shown that it is comprehensible input that counts in language acquisition, not just exposure to a second language. That is the reason that students receiving only one or two hours of English a day may actually acquire English more rapidly than students who are in an English environment all day long. The students in the bilingual program with good English instruction are receiving greater amounts of comprehensible input.

Valuing the First Language and Culture: A Key to Success

Acquisition of English and knowledge of the content gained through primary language instruction can help students build self-confidence. Students with high self-confidence have what Krashen calls a *low affective filter*. They are open to new concepts and new language. On the other hand, as Skutnabb-Kangas (1983) points out, "A person who does not understand the language of instruction is bound to perform worse than the one who understands, and poor performance often leads to poor self-concept, making the affective filter high" (p. 118). Under those conditions, it is difficult for the student to learn either English or subject area content.

Development of a positive self-image, then, is another benefit of bilingual education. There is more to bilingual education than developing concepts for academic success. Since bilingual education values the language of non-English speakers, it can help students value themselves and their culture. They know that others see them as intelligent and not just "dumb" like the Mexican girl quoted earlier. Further, they are not put in a position where they have to choose between the culture and language of the school and the culture and language of the home. Lucas (1981) found that the students who dropped out of high school were not the least proficient students in English but the ones who rejected their native cultures and lacked confidence in themselves.

Michael teaches junior and senior English in a high school with a large Hispanic population. He asked his students to write about their bilingualism and what it meant to them. The following responses show their struggles in schools where their language and culture were not valued. A twelfth grade Hispanic girl wrote:

> I have grown up in a Hispanic community since I can remember. But ironically the important thing in our classrooms was and is not how well you spoke your own language, unless that language was English. In fact the stress was on how "American" one was and is. But it wasn't until I got into the working force that I realized what people meant by the youth losing their culture. . . . It is extremely difficult for me to effectively communicate with my own people in Spanish. That is what I regret the most about "losing my culture" is losing my language.

An eleventh grade boy expressed his concerns:

> Our language at home is Spanish and English as our second. My youngest sister is only four. She speaks only Spanish. We want to teach her all the Spanish she can get before entering the schools. If she doesn't learn the Spanish language now, we're afraid she never will.

Another twelfth grade Hispanic girl also shows the tension that results from being in a situation where one language is used at home and another in school.

> In our household Spanish is a first language but is often overshadowed by English. My mom and dad only speak Spanish but are accustomed to hearing English from us . . . so while they speak Spanish to us, we speak English to them.

It has been made clear to these students that English and the culture of those who speak English is all that really counts. When schools do not help students feel pride in their primary language and culture, those students may lose confidence in themselves. Their parents are also put in a difficult situation. Lorna, a graduate student originally from the Philippines, describes the conflicts that early elementary schooling may create for bilingual children and parents:

> My husband and I decided to bring up our first born as bilingual. We were very proud of him when he first started to talk because he communicated with us in our native language. We thought he was very smart because he was fluent in Tagalog and learned also to speak some English. When he entered kindergarten, I filled out the form on the home language survey. I proudly wrote down that he speaks English and Tagalog. He was pretested and classified Limited English Proficient. My son whom we thought was very smart before entering kindergarten was not that smart anymore. Sometimes he would tell me that he was dumb. . . . I felt we were a failure as parents. I began blaming myself because I was the one who wanted to raise him as bilingual.

When schools do value students' languages and cultures, second language learners succeed in school more often. Lucas and colleagues (1990) conducted a comprehensive study of six high school programs that had achieved high rates of academic success with language minority students. The first of the eight features those schools had in common was "Value is placed on the students' languages and culture." The researchers listed eight specific ways these schools placed value on the students' language and culture:

- Treating students as individuals, not as members of a group
- Learning about students' cultures
- Learning students' languages
- Hiring bilingual staff with similar cultural backgrounds to the students
- Encouraging students to develop their primary language skills
- Allowing students to speak their primary languages except when English development is the focus of instruction or interactions
- Offering advanced as well as lower division content courses in the students' primary languages
- Instituting extracurricular activities that will attract students (p. 324)

In his high school English classes, Michael is trying to show students that he values their language and culture. Michael himself has a Hispanic heritage that was lost in his own schooling. He does not want that to happen to his students. Michael's encouragement and support helps his students develop pride in their backgrounds. One of his twelfth graders wrote:

> Spanish is important to me because it is part of my history. To me being bilingual is an important part of my life because my parents have always influenced me to know Spanish and also to speak fluent Spanish and among all things never to be ashamed of my heritage. I believe that I should be proud of my heritage and I was taught to be proud and to let everyone know of my Hispanic background and my Spanish-speaking family and people.

By showing a respect for diverse cultures and by providing bilingual support, schools and teachers can help students take pride in themselves and realize their potential. This lessens the tension that many second language learners feel when the school culture and language differs from the home culture and language, forcing them to choose between the two. An effective bilingual program allows students to succeed in both arenas. Their bilingualism is seen as a benefit, not a deficit.

Both home and school communities would profit if more second language students became proficient bilinguals. When bilingualism is not valued in schools, many students who enter schools monolingual in a language other than English leave school monolingual in English. They look for success in their new culture rather than returning to enrich their home communities. The students who do return are often those who have not assimilated, who have rejected English and the culture of those who speak English. However, they return to their communities without the education they need to contribute positively to that community. If students' first language and culture were valued, there would be less tension between home and school, between parent and child. Bilingual graduates could return as contributing, educated members to their bilingual communities.

Schools would benefit as well from effective bilingual programs. The United States is one of the few countries in the world where bilingualism is not highly valued. While people often think of Switzerland as the prototype of a bilingual country, people from other countries also value bilingualism. When we taught in Mexico, our students were adults who wished to learn English to advance in their work. They attended early morning or late night classes over a period of years to become bilingual. Many middle class Mexican parents make considerable financial sacrifices so that their children can attend private bilingual schools. In Japan, ESL classes for adults are highly valued by students and businessmen who realize the advantages of being bilingual. Good bilingual programs in the U.S. would allow all students to acquire a second language. Students who enter the school with a language other than English could learn English, and students who come to school monolingual in English could learn a second language. They could also learn about a new culture. And they could learn how to deal with the diversity that exists in the larger communities they will be part of when they leave school.

The biggest obstacle to establishing bilingual programs is that schools lack bilingual teachers. However, until schools develop proficient bilinguals who value education, the shortage of bilingual teachers will continue. Thus, a cycle develops. There are not enough bilingual teachers, so schools don't adopt bilingual programs. Schools that do not have bilingual programs do not produce the students who become bilingual teachers.

Even when schools are able to hire bilingual teachers, they still must decide on the kind of bilingual program they wish to institute. In the next section, we review the types of bilingual programs that have been successful.

Bilingual Education Programs: What Really Works?

Bilingual education programs have received a great deal of negative press over the past two decades. The Epstein (1977), American Institutes for Research (Danoff, Coles, McLaughlin, and Reynolds 1977, 1978) and Baker and de Kanter reports (Baker and de Kanter 1981) all challenged the effectiveness of bilingual education. Critiques of these reports by Crawford (1989), Cummins (1989a), and Krashen (1990) have shown them to be incomplete and inappropriately interpreted. School programs evaluated by these reports often did not have any bilingual teachers or materials. In contrast, programs that provide first language instruction have had positive results (Cummins 1989a; Krashen and Biber 1988; Willig 1985). Cummins (1989a) calls the publicity against bilingual education "disinformation." He believes a deliberate attempt has been made to misinform the public about bilingual education:

> . . . proponents of efforts to make English the official language of the United States have consistently argued that bilingual education hinders children's acquisition of English and other

academic skills, despite the overwhelming research evidence that this is not the case. (p. 87)

Articles and books, such as Rosalie Porter's *Forked Tongue* (1990), continue to stir the debate. Part of the controversy that surrounds bilingual education stems from confusion about programs that have been called *immersion* and those called *submersion*.

Immersion versus submersion

Advocates of the English Only movement, including Imhoff (1990), propose an immersion program for language minority students similar to the successful French Immersion programs in Canada. The reasoning used is that French Immersion worked in Canada, so why can't it work here in the United States? Because so many public schools misunderstand immersion education, this suggestion has often been followed. However, because of key differences between U.S. and Canadian programs, the immersion education many language minority students in the United States have received really amounts to "sink-or-swim" or submersion education.

The goals and results of the French Immersion programs in Canada are very different from the immersion programs offered to language minority students in the United States (Hernández-Chávez 1984). In the original St. Lambert French Immersion program, middle-class, educated parents of English-speaking Canadian children requested French Immersion so that their children would become bilingual and bicultural. In kindergarten the children in these programs were put in an all-French classroom with other English-speaking peers. There were no native speakers of French to compete with them. Teachers were bilingual and allowed the children to ask questions and give answers in English. Instruction was provided for teachers to help them with techniques of how to make the content of the classes comprehensible to the children. As students progressed through school, their native English was added to the curriculum, until in the sixth grade 40 percent of the curriculum was in French and 60 percent in English (Genesee 1984). At the end of fifteen years of study, it was clear that French immersion students achieved on a par with English Only program students except that the French immersion students achieved in both French and English.

The success of the Canadian programs can be attributed to several factors. Parents initiated and supported the programs. Teachers were carefully prepared to work with the children. All the children in a class were at about the same level of French ability. They did not have to compete with native speakers of French. At the same time, there was no danger of losing their English, since that was the language spoken in the home, and it was the prestige language of the larger community. The Canadian programs are additive. Their goal is to produce students who are bilingual and bicultural in both French and English.

In the United States, language minority students face a very different situation when they are put into a "submersion" program. In the first place, they are minority, not majority, students, and they are in direct competition from the beginning with native English-speaking peers. Their parents have not chosen the immersion program to make them bilingual and bicultural. In fact, since their parents are often from a disempowered segment of society, they have little voice in what happens in the school program. The first language and culture of the language minority students is not valued by the larger community, and it is clear from the beginning that the goal is not to produce bilingual, bicultural students but to produce students who are monolingual English speakers.

Immersion programs in the United States are really submersion programs, where students are more likely to "drown" in the English they receive. Since no first language support is given and teachers are seldom prepared to be sensitive to the needs of second language learners, students do not receive comprehensible input and soon fall behind academically. Unlike the Canadian program, which is additive in that students come out of the programs with proficiency in two languages, immersion programs in the United States are subtractive because students lose their first language at the expense of their second; that is, students rarely come out of programs achieving at the same level as the native English speakers.

Few educators who propose immersion for second language students understand the differences between the Canadian and U.S. versions of immersion education. This is doubly unfortunate because when language minority students fail in immersion programs in the United States, the perception is that it is because something is wrong with the second language learners. The students or the students' background and culture is criticized because, "After all, immersion worked so well in Canada."

Features of Programs that Work

Immersion education is not the answer for language minority students in the United States. However, many different models of schooling for language minority students have proven successful.

Crawford (1989) reports on the two-way bilingual Case Studies Model that has been used in California and duplicated in other areas of the United States. In the two-way programs, students who enter school speaking a language other than English continue to develop that language as they learn English. Monolingual English speakers begin immediately to learn a second language. The goal of the two-way programs is for all students to become bilingual and bicultural. Krashen and Biber (1988) reviewed a number of programs in California in which bilingual students achieved academic success as measured by standardized tests in English.

An important longitudinal study (Ramírez 1991) contracted by the United States Department of Education was watched carefully over several years by both proponents and opponents of bilingual education. In this study comparison was made of 750 classrooms with 2,000 students in three kinds of bilingual programs: Structured English Immersion, Early-exit and Late-exit Bilingual Education Programs. Students in Structured English Immersion were taught only in English. In the Early-exit programs students were supported in their first language for two to three years and then exited into all English programs. In the late-exit programs, students received some support in their first language for up to six years, even after their English became proficient. The study offered seven important conclusions for educators working with second language students:

1. When second language students receive substantial primary language support, their English is not delayed.
2. Developing proficiency in English takes more than 6 years regardless of which of the three approaches is used.
3. When students receive primary language support, they also progress in content instruction. However, they fall behind when they are too quickly switched to all English instruction.
4. Students who receive either early-exit (3 years) or late-exit (6 years) primary language instruction show more growth in English language, reading, and math than students in all English programs.
5. When primary language instruction is part of a program, minority language parents are more involved in their children's schooling.
6. Minority language parents would like to see their children become bilingual.
7. There is a need for preparing teachers to work effectively with second language learners. This preparation should emphasize a more active learning environment for language and cognitive development.

Although it is problematic to try to identify features of successful programs and then try to plug those elements into a new school situation, it is helpful to look at a broad range of successful programs to discover the features they share. California Tomorrow, an organization that has studied immigrant schooling in California, has reported on successful programs and their characteristics in *Crossing the Schoolhouse Border* (Olsen 1988), *Bridges* (Olsen 1989), and *Embracing Diversity* (Olsen and Mullen 1990). Cummins (1989a) has proposed "A Framework for Intervention" that is meant to empower language minority students in school. The programs reviewed by California Tomorrow all have the features that Cummins suggests are important for student success: Schools must have an intercultural orientation; the view toward students' culture and language should be additive, not subtractive; the community must be encouraged to participate; and schools must be advocates for students.

In their study of secondary schools mentioned earlier, Lucas and colleagues (1990) identified eight features that appeared to be necessary for language minority students' success, which are consistent with Cummins's suggestions:

- Value is placed on students' languages and cultures.
- There are high expectations of language minority students.
- School learners make the education of language minority students a priority.
- Staff development is explicitly designed to help teachers and other staff serve language minority students more effectively.
- A variety of courses and programs for language minority students is offered.
- A counseling program that includes bilingual counselors gives special attention to language minority students.
- Parents of language minority students are encouraged to become involved in their children's education.
- School staff members share a strong commitment to empower language minority students through education.

When schools make an effort to include these features in the education of their language minority students, everyone seems to benefit: the students, the teachers, the administrators, the parents, the community, and, ultimately, society as a whole. Although individual teachers can make a real difference for bilingual students, the best results come from programs that are carefully thought out and that are supported by all the people involved in the education of the second language students.

A Whole Language Approach to Curriculum for Bilingual Students

The features of successful schools just discussed are critical building blocks for an empowering curriculum. However, though it is essential to devise an effective schoolwide program, the education that second language students receive is only as good as the teaching that goes on in individual classrooms. Using the students' first language and being positive about their culture do not automatically guarantee school achievement. Effective education for language minority students requires a curriculum that is consistent with the principles of whole language.

The kinds of changes in curriculum that whole language teachers are making differ from the reforms advocated by a number of national reports, such as *A Nation at Risk: The Imperative for Educational Reform* (National Commission on Excellence in Education 1983), which call for a return to the "basics" to raise alarmingly low standardized test scores. Schools that attempt to raise scores are often reorganized from the top down, teachers are disempowered because they are directed to teach certain facts and skills that commonly appear on tests, and the principal method of teaching is transmission. Cummins (1989b) warns against "The Sanitized Curriculum" that would result from following the guidelines established in these reports:

> ... a careful analysis of the data suggests that the "crisis" has been fabricated to rationalize a conservative educational agenda that is already having a seriously damaging effect on the development of children's minds (p. 21).

Cummins calls for an *interactive/experiential* approach to pedagogy. This model supports the idea that active involvement of students is necessary and that talking and writing are a means to learning. Students actively construct meaning; they don't passively receive information. Cummins's ideas are consistent with the principles of whole language, since whole language teachers organize curriculum to allow students to work together and develop reading, writing, speaking, and listening abilities as they actively explore topics of interest.

Across the country many teachers working with second language students are using an approach consistent with whole language. The California Tomorrow report *Embracing Diversity: Teachers' Voices from California Classrooms* (Olsen and Mullen 1990) summarizes the characteristics of thirty-six teachers working with diverse student populations. Through interviews and visitations, the authors of the report, Olsen and Mullen, identified the core elements of the classroom approaches of these teachers. These teachers:

- Teach to and from the experiences of the students;
- Provide a strong academic context and basis for exploring and understanding issues students face in their own lives;
- Emphasize the development of language and communication including a rigorous integration of oral language and writing;
- Emphasize critical thinking;
- Validate the child's experiences and culture, including the use of language, dialect, literature, music, and the fine arts from the child's culture;
- Use curriculum to explore cultural and national differences, and also emphasize similarities and universals in human experience;
- Create a student-centered classroom in which students learn from each other, with group work and interactive techniques;
- Choose materials and design curriculum specifically to provide all students with exposure to the rich contributions of many cultures and peoples;
- Bring the world into the classroom and the classroom to the world;
- Actively use supplementary materials, and teacher-created curriculum;
- Use visuals and emphasize concept development; and
- Integrate the curriculum.

Each of these core elements is either explicitly or implicitly supported by whole language principles. In its section on teacher education, the report calls specifically for "whole language approaches to integrating oral language development with writing, reading, and listening" (p. 75). Not all of the teachers highlighted in *Embracing Diversity* are bilingual teachers, but they all respect their students' first language and culture, and they have adopted an approach consistent with whole language.

The Importance of Reading and Writing in the First Language

Many teachers have asked us if it is not better to teach second language children who do not already know how to read in their first language to read in English first. After all, they reason, if they do not already read, why waste time teaching them to read in their first language? We believe that if we want to build on the student's strengths, it is important to consider the language the student has been using for communication and for learning about the world before coming to school. Many second language students have seen writing in their own language and have begun to build many concepts about print before starting school. It is important to base instruction on this previous experience and capitalize on the strengths of these students.

When students are given opportunities for meaningful reading in their first language, they also are given an important message by schools: "Your first language is important. It is worthy and has value. It also has books that have stories that teach us something and that we can enjoy." That message about their language also applies to the people who speak it. If their first language is worthy, they also have some worth.

Since all four modes of language are keys to learning, it is critical that teachers understand why they should use their students' first language for reading and writing as well as for speaking and listening. If teachers do not provide students opportunities to learn to read and write in their first language, they are not drawing on student strengths nor are they teaching the whole child. Research shows that knowledge of literacy transfers from the first language to the second. Psycholinguistic research using miscue analysis with readers of different languages has shown that the reading process is the same regardless of the language (Barrera 1983; Goodman, Goodman, and Flores 1979; Hudelson 1981-82, 1987). In miscue analysis teacher/researchers ask students to read stories that are slightly difficult for them. They record the students' unexpected responses or miscues. For example, in a sentence that included the phrase "over the rice house" one boy read, "over the ranch house." The substitution of "ranch" for "rice" is a miscue. Analysis of students' miscues shows that readers from a variety of languages all use cues from the graphophonic, syntactic, semantic, and pragmatic cueing systems to construct meaning during reading. Even when the surface features of two languages are different, readers apply visual, linguistic, and cognitive strategies that they use in first language reading to reading in a second language (Ovando and Collier 1985).

Marilyn, a teacher of high school ESL students, has been instrumental in important changes in her school's curriculum. In a position paper she wrote for a class on bilingual education, she described changes in her curriculum, including the teaching of reading in the first language:

I have seen firsthand how successful a bilingual program can be. This year in our Newcomers School we decided to have a bilingual Spanish/English class for the students from ages 12 to 17 and who have had very little if any education in their first language. We put low level Spanish/English students in one class for two periods with a bilingual teacher. The bilingual Spanish teacher has had remarkable success. The confidence and competence levels of her students have increased greatly over the past eight months. They are coming along in their reading and writing in *both* English and Spanish.

First language reading instruction, even for older bilingual students, is an essential part of schooling. To help second language learners develop literacy in their first language, the materials and methods used to teach reading in other languages should be based on current socio-psycholinguistic research and theory on the process of reading. Unfortunately, this is not always what happens in schools with bilingual reading programs. For example, Spanish/English bilingual programs often use methods and materials that are not consistent with current reading research (Freeman 1988a; Freeman 1988b; Freeman 1988c).

Spanish Reading Programs: What Materials Are Best?

In the bilingual programs for elementary schools that we have observed, Spanish language basal readers often are used to teach reading even in those schools that have whole language literature programs in English. A study of Spanish reading methods and current Spanish basal reading programs (Freeman 1987) showed that Spanish basal reading materials do not reflect current research on the reading process. The reading materials for Spanish emphasize decoding and take a part-to-whole approach to reading. They deemphasize reading as a process of meaning construction. Since socio-psycholinguistic research on reading tells us that reading is a process of constructing meaning that draws on our own background and experiences (Goodman 1984; Weaver 1988; Weaver 1990), it is important to use materials that are whole, authentic, and meaningful to students. Although the advertisements for Spanish basal reading programs claim to reflect recent research and theory and to include many examples of children's literature in Spanish, the materials include decontextualized skill exercises and simplified and adapted examples of real literature (Freeman 1988a; Freeman 1988b; Freeman 1988c).

When teaching Spanish-speaking students to read, it is essential to provide quality children's literature for them in their primary language. Quality literature in Spanish helps Hispanic students celebrate their first language and culture. It promotes self-esteem and pride and encourages language minority students to become empowered learners.

Although children's literature in Spanish may have been hard to find in the past, many quality books are now readily available for students of all ages. Freeman and Cervantes (1991) have compiled an annotated bibliography of more than 350 literature books in Spanish, including big books, content area books, and books of special interest—cookbooks, plays, counting books, and alphabet books. All the books are available in the United States and are published in the United States, Mexico, South America, and Spain.

Books in other languages, especially Southeast Asian languages, are more difficult to find. However, more literature in these languages is being produced (for information on resources, write to Asian Books Resources, Greenshower Corp., P.O. Box 9118, S. El Monte, CA 91733). In addition, if students are encouraged to write in their first language, student-published books can become a valuable classroom resource. When teachers have books available in students' first as well as second language, they can plan whole language lessons that draw on student strengths and support literacy in both languages.

A Sample Whole Language Bilingual Reading Lesson

To support the reading and writing of students in a bilingual kindergarten, Kay, a bilingual/reading resource teacher, used fairy tales. First, Kay read two different versions of *Goldilocks* in Spanish: *Los Tres Osos y Bucles de Oro* and *Los Tres Osos y Ricitos de Oro*. Kay and the students then developed a chart comparing the two stories. The kindergarten children showed a good understanding of how the stories were the same yet different. The charting done with the teacher as the scribe is shown in figure 6–4.

After doing this exercise in Spanish with her students, Kay had the children draw their favorite part of the story. The children shared their pictures and described the pictures in English as Kay wrote

Figure 6.4

Los Tres Osos y Ricitos de Oro		Los Tres Osos y Bucles de Oro
Differente	*El Mismo*	*Differente*
Ricitos se perdió en el bosque	Ambos tienen ricitos de oro	Ricitos estaba paseándose en el bosque
Un conejo le ayudó	Ambos tiene tres osos	Estaba traviesa
Los osos tenían chocolate	Están en el bosque	
No había una silla que se quebró	Hay camas	La silla pequeña se quebró
Los dibujos eran hechos con lápiz.	Comían sopa	Los dibujos eran hechos de pintura
Ricitos tiene pelo chino.		Ricitos tiene pelo largo
Todos se ponen amigos		
Ricitos, en el fin, piensa que ve a los tres osos diciendo "adios"		Ricitos se fue corriendo

Translation in English

Different	*Same*	*Different*
Goldilocks got lost in the woods	Both have Goldilocks	Goldilocks was taking a walk in the woods
A bunny helped her	Both have three bears	She was naughty
The bears had hot chocolate	They were in the woods	
There was not a chair that broke	There are beds	The small chair broke
The drawings are done in pencil	They ate soup	The pictures are painted
Goldilocks has short, curly hair		Goldilocks has long hair
Everyone ended up friends		
Goldilocks thinks she sees the bears saying "Goodbye" at the end		Goldilocks left running

their descriptions down. She then led a discussion in English about words that described the two books. The children came up with the words *exciting, interesting* and *calm,* which Kay wrote on a large chart. The whole class decided together if the portion of the story each child had chosen was exciting, interesting, or calm. The children's pictures and the phrases Kay had written in English were put up on a large chart next to the words that best described the scenes.

Exciting: She wakes up! The bears are staring at her.
             She runs away!
             Bears find leftover soup.
             Bears find chairs.
Interesting: Goldilocks goes into the bears' house.
             Goldilocks breaks baby bear's chair.
Calm: Bears go on walk in woods.
             Goldilocks eats soup.

By teaching lessons such as this one, using primary language literature, and beginning with the children's first language, Kay leads her students toward future academic success in English and, at the same time, allows them to develop their first language.

Monolingual Teachers Can Also Support Bilingual Students

Many teachers working with bilingual students do not speak their students' first language. Or they may be in a class where students speak a variety of different languages. Nevertheless, teachers can support the development of the first language even when they do not speak the first language of all their students.

Marilyn, the ESL high school teacher who helped support bilingual Spanish/English classes as previously described, also explained how she, as a monolingual English-speaking teacher, has supported Southeast Asian students. She has Hmong and Laotian students for two periods a day, and although she doesn't speak their languages, she has an aide who does. In a preview and view model, Marilyn has her aide present a lesson to students in their native languages first. Then they ask questions. The next day she gives a follow-up lesson on the same content in English. Her testimony to the success of the program is important: "It is remarkable how much the students understand because it has been presented in their first language the day before. We use less English but I feel the students are learning more English."

Marilyn's Laotian and Hmong students are separated from other second language learners and from native English speakers for two hours each day to "help them feel their first language is important" and so they "can find comfort in a mostly uncomfortable environment." Marilyn and her colleagues "recognize that Laotians and Hmongs are very different. However, when these Southeast Asian students are with other language groups all the time, "they are very reserved and reluctant to participate in class." Her Hmong and Laotian class is "alive and animated." Marilyn summarizes her conclusions for the success of these two periods daily with Hmong and Laotian students:

> I feel their confidence comes from three things. First, the students know there is someone in class who can speak L1 (first language) and if they have a *really* important message to get across, it will be understood. Second, these students are in a foreign environment. These students are only separated from other students for two hours. It's a much needed break for them. Third, I think they feel pride and self-esteem when they can use their first language to acquire L2 (second language).

Marilyn not only has tried this different approach, but she is also presently taking a class in Hmong. This adds to her ability to work with her students. "The students are so pleased when I attempt to speak to them in their native language and they enjoy helping me acquire language. I let them know English is easy for me but Hmong is very difficult."

Teachers like Marilyn make extra efforts to prepare themselves to meet the needs of all their students. They read current research, take college classes, talk with other professionals, and experiment with different techniques. As these teachers plan activities to expand the range of language uses for their students, they provide consistent opportunities for their bilingual students to develop listening, speaking, reading, and writing in two languages.

An example comes from Vince, who discovered how important it is for bilingual children to be able to work in school in their first language. After reading and discussing research on the importance of first language support for second language learners, Vince shared an experience he had with one of his students:

> Chai came into my fourth grade classroom directly from the camps in Southeast Asia. She was the first second language student I was to come in contact with who felt good enough about

her native language writing skills to employ them in class. I have to give the students in my class a lot of credit too, as they strongly supported and encouraged Chai in all her efforts. When she was finished writing a piece, she would read it to other Laotian-speaking students in my class who would give suggestions on the content and share their ideas with her in Laotian.

Vince described his doubts about letting Chai work in Laotian because he somehow felt he wasn't "doing his job." She remained in his classroom for the rest of the year and seemed to be understanding some English, but she never spoke or wrote in English. The next year Vince met Chai's best friend who proudly explained that Chai was now speaking English and writing it too. Vince wrote his reaction to the news:

> My first reaction was not one of achievement. It was rather a question as to what the fifth grade teacher had done that I hadn't done to get Chai to come this far along. Only later did it dawn on me that those early opportunities that empowered Chai were a big part of why she was comfortable speaking and writing English so soon after her arrival.

Vince had empowered Chai and allowed her to continue to develop her first language.

Vince encouraged Chai to use her first language even though he didn't understand it. Often, teachers are not able to comprehend the first language of some of their students. However, if they allow the students to use their primary language, they may come to realize that the students are more competent than they may appear to be if they are limited to English. Teachers can read stories that have themes that all students enjoy and then allow students to respond in ways that are meaningful to them. For example, Jill read *The Hundred Dresses* by Estes to second language students. Afterward the students were invited to respond to the reading in writing using either English or their first language, Spanish. Manuel not only wrote more than one full page, but he also drew pictures to illustrate the points he had made (fig. 6–5).

Jane, the language arts mentor teacher who had students write to get out of punishment (discussed in an earlier chapter), developed and taught a unit on Martin Luther King, Jr., to a fifth grade class. Jane is a monolingual English teacher working in a school district that is 98 percent Hispanic. Jane and the students read books about Martin Luther King, Jr., saw a movie about him, learned his "I Have

Figure 6.5
Manuel's
Response

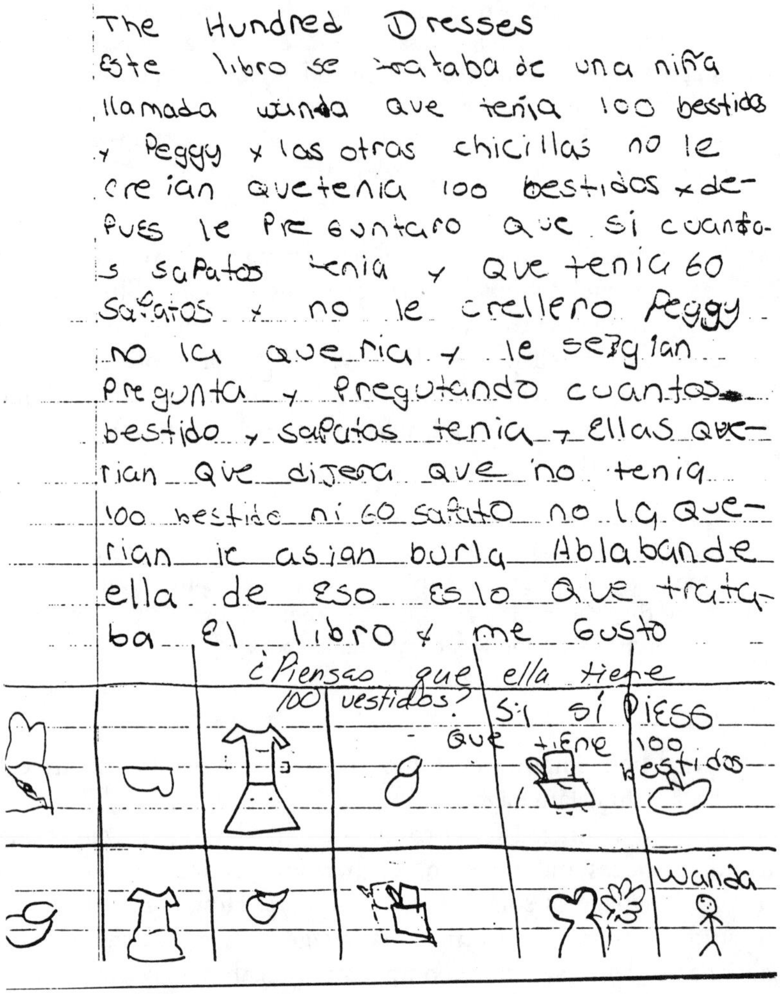

The Hundred Dresses
Este libro se trataba de una niña
llamada wanda que tenía 100 bestidos
y Peggy y las otras chicillas no le
creían quetenía 100 bestidos xde-
pues le preguntaro que si cuanto-
s sapatos tenía y que tenía 60
sapatos y no le crellero Peggy
no la quería y le serg1an
pregunta y pregutando cuantos
bestido y sapatos tenía y ellas que-
rian que dijera que no tenía
100 bestido ni 60 sapato no la que-
rian le asian burla Ablabande
ella de eso eslo que trataba el libro y me Gusto

¿Piensas que ella tiene
100 vestidos? Si sí Piess
Que tiene 100
bestidos

Wanda

Translation in English:

The Hundred Dresses

This book was about a girl named Wanda who had 100 dresses and Peggy and the
other (mean) little girls didn't believe that she had 100 dresses and then they asked
her how many shoes she had and she said she had 60 and they didn't believe her
Peggy didn't like her and they kept asking her how many dresses and shoes she
had and they wanted her to say that she didn't have 100 dresses or 60 shoes.
They didn't like her and they made fun of her. Talking about her and this is what
the book was about and I liked it.

Teacher's question written on top of drawings:
"Do you think she has 100 dresses?"

Student's written response:
"Yes I think she has 100 dresses."

A Dream" speech, and discussed his importance. When it came time to write about him, she told students they could write in either Spanish or English. Lucinda, who had recently arrived from Mexico and spoke little or no English, wrote the summary in figure 6–6, showing clearly that she understood what the class had been studying.

Both of these examples show clearly the way that the first language can help support the acquisition of the second. These students, who were not yet confident to produce English, were able to organize their understanding of lessons presented in English and present their responses in their first language. It is clear that the students who wrote these two pieces understood a lot more than their English production could ever have shown. By encouraging the use of their first language, their teachers helped them become successful learners.

Cross-age reading has been another excellent way to encourage students to read, write, and interact in their first language even when the teacher only speaks English (Labbo and Teale 1990; Urzúa 1990). When upper grade bilingual students prepare to read to younger children and are matched with younger children who speak the same first language, both age groups benefit. Urzúa has worked

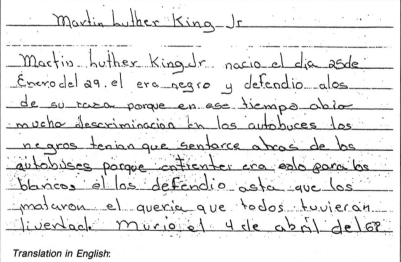

Figure 6.6
Lucinda's Summary

Translation in English:

Martin Luther King Jr was born on the 25th of January in (19)29. He was a Black man and defended those of his race because in that time there was much discrimination on the buses the Black people had to sit down in the back of the buses because in front was only for the white people he defended them until they killed him he wanted everyone to have freedom He died the fourth of April of (19)68

with teachers whose Southeast Asian sixth graders read to kindergartners who speak the same first language. Even when they read
books in English, the sixth graders support the first language of the
younger children by building background knowledge in their shared
first language. As the children interact in both languages, both age
groups improve their oral language and reading ability. Sometimes
the sixth graders take notes on the lessons they prepare and evaluate
their teaching, thus developing more reading and writing skills.

When it is impossible to arrange for children to go from one
classroom to another, pen pal letters can support the development
of the first language. Sam's bilingual first graders write to pen pals
in the fifth grade as well as to students in the teacher education
program at a nearby college. Whenever possible, Spanish-speaking
students in Sam's Spanish/English bilingual classroom are matched
with pen pals who can write in Spanish. Sam has noticed that when
his students correspond with fluent Spanish writers, his first graders
write meaningfully. A series of letters between Elena, a first grader,
and Carolina, a college student, show that writing in a student's
first language encourages real communication. In one letter Carolina
asked Elena, "¿Qué vas a hacer para el día de San Valentín? ¿Van
a tener una fiesta en tu salón de clase?" (What are you going to do
on Valentine's Day? Are you going to have a party in your classroom?) Elena's next letter responded directly to Carolina's questions: "Mi ma es tro si ba aser una fiesta en valentin y ba mos a
comer pastel y stigurs tu a mi ga Elena" (My teacher yes is going
to have a party on Valentine's Day and we are going to eat cake
and [have] stickers your friend Elena).

Children, like Elena and Chai, who are encouraged to use their
first language meaningfully, learn to feel good about their first language and culture and about themselves. Their teachers build background knowledge in their first language that transfers to English
instruction. We have taken the experiences these teachers and others
have had with second language learners and developed a list of "Ten
Tips for Monolingual Teachers of Bilingual Students" (Freeman
and Freeman 1991a) for teachers who are not bilingual but want
to support their students' first language.

1. Arrange for bilingual aides or parent volunteers to read literature
    written in the primary language to the students and then to
    discuss what they have read.
2. Plan for older students who speak the first language of the
    children to come to the class regularly to read to or with the
    younger students and to act as cross age tutors. For example,

sixth grade students might come to a first grade class two or three mornings a week to share reading. This often proves beneficial to the older students as well as the younger students. Younger students can choose books to read to older students on certain days.

3. Set up a system of pen pal letters written in the primary language between students of different classes or different schools.

4. Have students who are bilingual pair up with classmates who share the same primary language but are more proficient in English. This buddy system is particularly helpful for introducing new students to class routines.

5. Invite bilingual storytellers to come to the class and tell stories that would be familiar to all the students. Using context clues, these storytellers can convey familiar stories in languages other than English. Well-known stories such as *Cinderella* have counterparts (and origins) in non-English languages.

6. Build a classroom library of books in languages other than English. This is essential for primary language literacy development. At times, teachers within a school may want to pool these resources.

7. Encourage journal writing in the first language. A bilingual aide or parent volunteer can read and respond to journal entries. Give students a choice of language in which to read and write.

8. To increase the primary language resources in classrooms, publish books in languages other than English. Allow bilingual students to share their stories with classmates.

9. Look around the room at the environmental print. Include signs in the first language as well as articles and stories in English about the countries the students come from. One teacher made bookmarks that were laminated and left in a basket for visitors. On one side was a proverb in English, and on the other, the equivalent proverb written in a language other than English.

10. Have students engage in oral activities such as show and tell, using their first language as they explain objects, games, or customs from their homelands.

Conclusion

Teachers who support their students' bilingualism are teaching to the strengths of the whole child. They know that their students are future bilingual citizens who can contribute positively to a world where more and more bilingual people will be needed in the work force. Perhaps even more important, however, is the fact that second language students need to develop a positive self-image to share with their own children in the future. Nancy, a teacher of Portuguese descent who did not maintain her own language and culture, writes painfully of her loss. She does not want her Southeast Asian and Hispanic students to feel as she does when they are adults:

> My grandmother went into a coma last week. She came to this country as a young bride and in all the years here, she never became a fluent English speaker. When my parents were in the school environment they were made to feel inferior to their English-speaking peers (They both dropped out early on in high school). These feelings of inferiority are carried with them today. When I entered school, I was encouraged by both the people at school and parents at home to act "more American" and stop using Portuguese (Pride in my culture was likewise discouraged).
>
> I just came home from the hospital. As I stroked my grandmother's arm and forehead, I spoke to her (I really believe she could hear me), but I spoke to her in a language she doesn't really understand. She might know who was speaking, but she won't ever know what I really wanted to say to her. I don't ever want this situation to happen to my students. Yes, I do want them to become fluent in English and be able to compete with other students academically, but it is imperative to me that they retain pride in their culture and their bilingual abilities.

Nancy's story has been repeated too often in this country. We began this chapter with an example of a Southeast Asian girl who, like Nancy, has lost her language. If we hope to have successful second language learners in schools, we must not repeat these mistakes of the past. It is important to look at the assumptions we have made about bilingual learners and turn to alternatives based on our best knowledge of current research. Whole language principles, including the principle that supports development of the first language, offer a chance for bilingual learners to succeed academically and to become whole members of our complex, multicultural society.

7

Faith in the Learner Expands Student Potential

Mt. Rushmore Rap

My name is George Washington
Being the first president was lots of fun.
I chopped down Dad's old cherry tree
I could've used it later for my wooden teeth.

Thomas Jefferson is my name.
There's a school in Fresno named the same.
The Declaration of Independence was my letter
Mr. King we want our country to be better.

My last name is Lincoln. My first name is Abraham
I freed the slaves, that's the kind of man I am.
I dreamed so much that I got ill
Went to see a play and I got killed.

I'm Theodore Roosevelt, but you can call me Teddy,
I freed a baby bear that was tied to a tree,
They wanted to kill it, but I said, "No way!"
That's why they named teddy bears today.

—Toua Xiong
7th Grade

205

This creative rap was published in a collection of student writing from Tehipite Middle School in Fresno, California, entitled *Drumbeats*. The rap was written by Toua Xiong, a Hmong teenager, who had spent eight years of his life in a refugee camp in Thailand. He had had no schooling in Southeast Asia before arriving in the United States two years previously.

In his rap, Toua pictures himself as a series of our greatest presidents. These sketches differ dramatically from the description of himself he included in an earlier journal entry he wrote to Alan, an education student: "Before I came to America I was very dumb like a pig. We usually use to talk in Mong because my parent can't talk in English." Although the negative comments in the journal might be attributed to a cultural tendency toward humility, and although Toua's past schooling and traumatic life experiences before coming to the United States would be predictors of school failure, the rap shows Toua's positive spirit as well as his knowledge of U.S. history. Several factors have contributed to Toua's faith in himself and in his future.

Further journal entries as well as personal interaction with Toua helped Alan understand Toua's school success. During his first six months in elementary school in Wisconsin, Toua was given a peer tutor who helped him with reading, writing, and content area explanations in class. In addition, an elderly volunteer would take Toua downtown to the zoo, circus, park, or McDonald's on weekends. These different experiences provided Toua with both written and oral comprehensible input and gave him many opportunities to use English in meaningful and functional ways. Although these experiences showed Toua that he was important as an individual, pride and self-confidence are fragile. Alan was student teaching in math when he began his case study with Toua. An early journal entry shows how important their relationship was to Toua:

> Mr. Hollman I am very happy that you came to me and ask if we can write note back and forth. I'm not very good doing everything wrong and have a lot of trouble in math. How are you doing in college everything is OK? How do you like to go to college? Which college do you go to? How many year you been there? I am sorry I would ask a bad question for you. Can I have a picture of you? And you address too, so I can send you some letter. How do you like to be friend with a Hmong student? I like the America very much I like to live close to them. Thank Mr. Hollman.

Toua was proud of his rapid acquisition of English, and Alan's interest gave him enough faith in himself to brag in one of his later journal entries:

> I don't know how to talk in English before I came it United
> State I learn it only 1 ½ year in Wisconsin so now I only come
> to 2 years in United State. Some teacher they didn't think that
> I only got to United State only 2 year, they said How come I
> speak very well.

This entry shows that Toua is adjusting well to this country. Despite his early journal entry in which he appears to be embarrassed about his heritage, he is also proud of his first culture and language as well. Alan noted this in his case study of Toua:

> His culture is Hmong and he seems to be proud of his heritage.
> In fact when I inquired about his past, he brought me a book
> containing six Hmong folk tales and a brief history of his an-
> cestry.

In addition to his pride in his culture, Toua is also proud of his ability to read and write Hmong, a language few are literate in because it has only recently been transcribed into a written language by linguists. Toua took advantage of the journal exchange to teach Alan some Hmong and indirectly display his bilingual abilities:

> I will write in mong to you, but I will explain it in English. . . .
> Kuv hlub koj = I Love you. Kuv nyiam koj = I Like you. Koj
> yog ib tug nais khu zoo heev = You're a good teacher.

Toua has pride in himself and in his abilities, including his knowledge of his first language and culture. Toua's experiences with Alan obviously are very important. His early journal entries show that he is not always sure about his background and his ability to succeed in his new culture and a new educational system. However, the individual attention Alan gave Toua helped him regain a positive outlook. All second language learners should be shown they are valued in these kinds of ways. When teachers show faith in their students, the students develop faith in themselves.

Toua was fortunate enough to have interested adults who would read and write with him, giving him the attention he needed. Most second language students do not have that luxury. Teachers of bi-linguals want to support their students, but they may be locked into a teaching system that prevents them from providing that support. Unfortunately, in many of our schools for a variety of reasons, the full potential of bilingual learners is not tapped. These students may come to believe that they cannot learn, that their first culture and language are not valuable, and that there is no place for them in American society. This may occur if the curriculum centers on content that is presented part to whole rather than on students. It may also result from a simplified curriculum that contains little real content. In either case, the message that many second language learners get is that they cannot learn or that there is nothing worthwhile to learn in school. To use Ken Goodman's terms (Goodman 1991), these students need to "revalue" themselves as learners, and they need to revalue school as a place where important things can be learned.

Many second language learners drop out of school. Others, in desperate attempts to belong, take on negative behavior patterns in school or join gangs. What these students need is someone within the school system like Alan who will show faith in them so that they can build faith in themselves. Rather than labeling such students as Limited English Proficient or learning disabled, teachers need to help students develop their potential by showing unwavering faith in their ability to succeed. Instead of subjecting these students to standardized tests that confirm they are below the norm, teachers need to become kid watchers and document the amazing progress second language learners often make. Even when students appear to be confused or seem slow to catch on or respond, teachers need to continue to engage them in meaningful activities; they need to keep issuing invitations to be part of a community of learners. We're convinced that if teachers can show students that they can learn and that there are things in school worth learning, there is no limit to bilingual students' potential.

In *Lives on the Boundary*, Mike Rose (1989) tells the stories of a number of students who have struggled to succeed academically. One of these students, Lilia, came to the Los Angeles area from Mexico. She failed first grade and then was put in classes for slow learners. As Lilia puts it, "I guess there was a pattern where they put me in those really basic classes and then decided I would go through my elementary school years in those classes. I didn't learn to read or write" (Rose 1989, p. 39). Fortunately, Lilia's parents decided to break this cycle. They moved to another community where "the schools were good." As Lilia recalls, "The teachers really liked me and I did very well" (Rose 1989, p. 39).

Lilia attended a six-week summer program on the UCLA campus after finishing eighth grade. This program, designed for children of migrant workers, opened Lilia's eyes to new possibilities. "I made it my goal to come here." Lilia did attend UCLA. The new school her parents enrolled her in and her visit to the college campus had helped her build faith in her own potential. She was supported by teachers who "really liked me." What is exciting is that Lilia and a number of other freshmen at UCLA, who began in a remedial writing course, were shifted to a special composition course. In this new course, Lilia and the other students tutored low-achievers in Los Angeles area schools and then wrote papers about their tutorial work and about issues of schooling. Lilia and her UCLA classmates are creating a new cycle. They are expanding their own potential and are, at the same time, creating possibilities for success for younger students who have had similar background experiences in schools.

Stories of students like Lilia and Toua have convinced us that of all the seven principles of whole language we have proposed, this "faith in the learner" principle is the most critical. When teachers show they believe in their students, the other principles follow naturally. When teachers have faith in the learner, they show students the big picture, not just bits and pieces of information. They understand that students learn when they are engaged in meaningful activities that relate to their own experiences. They realize that all four modes can provide important sources for learning and it is not necessary to limit learners to one mode at a time. They recognize that during social interaction students learn from each other, from teachers, and from the community. They know that building on students' strengths, including their first languages and cultures, expands the students' potential. In short, teachers who show faith in their students organize teaching and learning in ways that are consistent with all the principles of whole language.

As we work with students who are just entering the teaching profession, we find people who may have doubts about their ability to teach, but they seldom have doubts about students' ability to learn. They start out with faith in the learner and with a strong desire to develop the full potential of every student. Their experiences in schools, though, may dim that enthusiasm and that belief in students. In this chapter we look at some of the factors that may lead teachers to doubt that their second language students will succeed. First, we look at some of the ways that labeling of second language learners has limited them, and we also consider how the attitudes held toward culturally diverse people can affect instruction. Then we raise the concerns we have with assessment and evaluation and suggest alternatives for evaluating bilingual students. Next, we review methods that have been used to teach content instruction to second language learners and discuss the importance of providing solid academic content for all students. We conclude by describing several teachers whose students, like Toua, have developed faith in themselves. We highlight key features of classrooms and programs that have expanded the potential of bilingual students.

Labeling Second
Language Learners

The following journal entry comes from Irene, the only ESL/bilingual teacher in a school where 80 percent of the students are from Hispanic migrant families.

> It has disturbed me greatly to sit in the teachers' lounge and be approached by other teachers with the proposition that I take some of their "below grade level" Hispanic students for reading because they "just don't know how to motivate them." Furthermore, I have actually seen teachers look at their class lists, count the Hispanic, Portuguese and Hmong surnames and begin to formulate the high, middle and low reading groups.

The teachers Irene observed may simply be reacting in frustration. Many mainstream teachers have never had courses in language acquisition, cross-cultural education, or ESL methods. They probably are not sure what to do with their second language students. They may lack faith in their own ability to teach these students. Or, they may simply decide that these students can't learn, so they put them in the low groups. Whatever the case, their attitudes will not help them create classrooms where students develop faith in themselves. We believe that the attitudes expressed in the teachers' lounge toward language minority students are, at least partially, responsible for the failure of second language learners in schools. Unless educators take a new look at the diverse students in our schools and give them meaningful learning experiences using authentic materials, the already alarmingly high drop-out rate for students will continue to rise, leaving education serving only the needs of a small elite group (Shannon 1990).

Crossing the Schoolhouse Border (Olsen 1988), the extensive statewide report from California that includes interviews with California's immigrant students, immigrant parents, educators, and politicians, brings out beliefs of teachers and concerns of students. A quote from Rosario Anaya, a member of the San Francisco School Board, effectively highlights a key question about working with the state's diversity:

> Immigrant children in our schools enter an educational system that is foreign, where the language is incomprehensible, where the faces of classmates are of many colors, and where parents feel unconnected and frustrated. It is alarming but not surprising that so many fail and drop out of school. While we talk democracy and equal opportunity, in reality many of our students

are barely given a chance to get out of the gate. The basic question is not how can we teach these students, but whether we really want to. (Olsen 1988, p. 40)

It is critical that attitudes toward bilingual students change, because, unless they do, these students will not be given the kind of instruction that will help them to learn. Students with a home language other than English must be given a test of language proficiency. Because of these tests, many bilingual students are labeled LEP, which stands for Limited English Proficient. This label conveys the attitude that second language learners are "limited" and have a deficit simply because they do not speak English fluently. The label LEP focuses on students' weaknesses and denies the value of what students know and can do in their first language. Labels, established by narrowly designed tests, lump together people who vary considerably from each other and suggest that there is something basically wrong with all of them. "They [Labels] deny the notion that diversity is a major quality of American society and suggest that diversity in and of itself is something to be expunged from American classrooms" (Freeman and Goodman in press).

Labels like LEP often keep ESL students from developing a positive self-image. A quote from an immigrant student in *Crossing the Schoolhouse Border* (Olsen 1988) demonstrates how the reactions of others reinforce the negative attitude toward second language learners that the LEP label already establishes:

> I was two years in ESL and I didn't like it. My English level was not that low, but they treat you like your level is so low and you are stupid. (12th grade Salvadoran girl, p. 63)

Suggestions have been made for changing the LEP label for second language learners to something more positive. Hamayan (1989) has suggested PEP, Potentially English Proficient, which emphasizes the potential of diverse students. Rigg and Allen (1989) have suggested REAL, Readers and writers of English as Another Language. PEP and REAL are still labels, but these terms offer a more positive way of describing our second language population. Of course, those who use these terms are not simply suggesting substituting new labels for old and still continuing to use the same tests to determine who gets labeled. If that were to happen, the attempts to make the labels positive would fail. The real point is that PEP and REAL students have potential, the potential to be proficient in *two languages*. And, rather than being a problem, these students offer our nation the potential for an enriching diversity.

Labels such as LEP are used to determine the number of second language students so that a school district can qualify for state and federal funding. State and federal agencies have always tried to find ways to evaluate the English proficiency of bilinguals, and even though whole language teachers realize the inadequacies of these measures, they know that the tests are not apt to disappear soon. To provide a context for an analysis of the current tests, we next briefly review the history of testing bilingual people in this country—a history of looking at weaknesses, not strengths. We also look at the attitudes toward cultural diversity that support the use of certain kinds of tests.

Bilingualism: A History of Misunderstanding

When teachers believe in the learning potential of all students and see bilingualism as an asset, the curriculum is enriched. Unfortunately, the general assumption has been that students who do not speak English fluently have some kind of learning disability. This is not a new phenomenon. Immigrants have been labeled as deficient in this country since the 1800s. Early immigrants to this country were given I.Q. tests as they got off the boats at Ellis Island. When they did poorly on those tests, they were often labeled "Feeble-minded" (Hakuta 1986). In 1910, Goddard, director of the Vineland School for Feeble-Minded Girls and Boys, gave the English language version of the Binet test to thirty adult Jews through an interpreter and assessed twenty-five of them as "feeble-minded." He described the results of that testing:

> What shall we say of the fact that only 45 percent can give sixty words in three minutes, when normal children of eleven years sometimes give 200 words in that time! It is hard to find an explanation except lack of intelligence or lack of vocabulary and such a lack of vocabulary in an adult would probably mean lack of intelligence. How could a person live even fifteen years in any environment without learning hundreds of names of which he could certainly think of 60 in three minutes? (Hakuta 1986, p. 19)

In this and similar types of experiments, the validity of the tests was never questioned, despite the circumstances under which the tests were administered, the problems of translation, or the improbability of the results.

Over the years, educators opposed to bilingualism have debated whether bilingualism leads to language delay or even retardation and whether learning two languages confuses the child. Flores (1982) identified several kinds of deficits educators and the general public have used over the years to explain the academic failure of Hispanics in schools in the United States:

- 1920s—Spanish-speaking children were considered mentally retarded due to language difficulty.
- 1930s—Bilingualism and its effects upon the reading aspects of language were considered a problem.
- 1940s—Because of their "language problem," it was thought that Mexican children should be segregated.
- 1950s—Schools were called upon to provide for deficiencies by providing "a rich and satisfying program."
- 1960s—The child's home and language were viewed as the primary cause of school failure.
- 1970s—It was thought that when bilingual children *code switch*, mix their languages, it was an indication that they knew neither well.

Formal tests provide labels that reflect an underlying belief that something is wrong with people who speak a language other than English. This deficit view leads to misconceptions about bilingualism. After reading about how bilingual students have often been labeled, Sofía, a Hispanic teacher education candidate, wrote of her own painful experiences with the false assumptions conveyed by the school's labeling process:

> In fourth grade, I could not read, write or multiply. My teacher asked my parents to come in for a meeting to discuss my progress. I accompanied my mother so that I could translate into Spanish for her. My teacher told my mother that I was a very slow learner and that perhaps I needed professional help. She suggested several tests so that I may be transferred to a "special class." My teacher said I was mentally retarded. At that age I understood well what my teacher thought of me. I hated school with a passion. The next year I had a different teacher. He recognized my shyness and insecurity. By the end of fifth grade I discovered that I could multiply, read, dance and sing.

Often this kind of labeling occurs because a lack of fluency in English is interpreted as lack of understanding. In reality, although Sofía may not have been fully proficient in English, she was an interpreter for her family. Because she understood a great deal about this and other social situations, she was able to bridge the gap between cultures. Sofía's knowledge of her first language and culture was a real strength, but if her fifth grade teacher had not found her strengths and shown his faith in her, she might never have developed the faith in herself that resulted in her becoming a bilingual teacher.

If school psychologists, teachers, and others who evaluate students do not recognize that knowledge of a language other than English is valuable and that learning a second language takes time, they may underestimate the potential of bilingual learners (Cummins 1984). School officials often are unaware of the second language acquisition research that shows that it takes four to nine years for second language students, even those from well-educated families, to compete academically with native English speakers (Collier 1989). One school administrator interviewed about bilingual education by Susan, a graduate student expressed a common view that students need to get to English as quickly as possible:

> They (bilingual students) need to learn to speak English as fast as they can. They should not have to be in a bilingual program for more than three years, at the maximum. Any child having to stay in a bilingual program longer than three probably has some type of learning disability.

Rather than seeing bilingualism as a special ability and valuing both the language and the culture of bilingual students, this educator views bilingualism as a hindrance. This type of attitude leads to the belief that students in bilingual classrooms are remedial. The goal, then, is to mainstream students as quickly as possible into all-English classrooms. Children in countries all over the rest of the world learn two or three languages as a matter of course, but students in the United States who are bilingual are encouraged to suppress their first language in favor of English. Ironically, when those students reach middle or secondary school, we often require them to take a foreign language.

Second language students are aware of the negative attitudes toward languages and cultures other than English and struggle to fit into American culture. Immigrant parents encourage their children to "speak English" and to "act American" because they see those goals as keys to future success. It is often not until it is too late that their children realize they want to be bilingual and bicultural. The same Sofía who wrote of her own struggles with school tells of the tragedy of her cousins:

> Our cousins from Los Angeles were encouraged to forget Spanish because it just wasn't cool. My brothers and sisters and I used to get teased by our cousins because we sometimes reverted back

to Spanish. Now my cousins that look so Mexican don't speak a word of Spanish. I have sympathy for them because they do not understand who or what they really are.

Recent studies have shown that bilingual children, rather than being confused by learning two languages, are actually more flexible in their thinking (Hakuta 1986). Teachers who are informed about second language acquisition value their second language students' first language and draw on their culture to help students view themselves positively. Studies of several successful programs for bilingual students show that features of those programs include respect for the students' first language and culture (Bird and Alvarez 1987; Lucas, Henze, and Donato 1990; Olsen and Mullen 1990).

The United States has long been considered a "melting pot," where the advertised goal to be achieved by all diverse people is to blend in and be homogenized into the mainstream. In schools, those who currently experience the most difficulty are those who stand out physically, who traditionally have been exploited by the Anglo populations in power, and who have formed communities within the larger American society. Those groups include African Americans, Hispanics, and Native Americans (Cummins 1989). In the last ten years, the Southeast Asian immigrant students, especially those most recently arrived from the refugee camps, have also begun to experience problems because they do not fit into the expected norm (Olsen 1988).

In our schools it is made clear to students, even those who speak little or no English, that it is very important to "melt," that being different is not good. Stories from immigrant students support this perception (Olsen 1988). An eighth grade Vietnamese girl new to schools in the United States explained how the other students responded to her: "The day I started school all the kids stared at me like I was from a different planet" (Olsen 1988, p. 71). A Chinese immigrant student is much more graphic as she describes her introduction to America:

> Before I came to America I had a beautiful dream about this country. At that time, I didn't know that the first word I learned in this country would be a dirty word. American students always picked on us, frighted us, made fun of us and laughed at our English. They broke our lockers, threw food on us in the cafeteria, said dirty words to us, pushed us on campus. Many times they shouted at me, "Get out of here, you chink, go back to your country." (Olsen 1988, p. 34)

With the growing numbers of immigrants, adult members of the community, including professional educators, sometimes also respond negatively to bilingual students. When a bilingual graduate student took a poll about bilingual education, she was disturbed at the responses from the community: "Mexicans are taking over the country as it is now, they don't need any special programs" and "Those Hmongs are taking over the country. We give them houses, welfare, they keep having kids, and then we want to hire Hmong teachers to teach them in Hmong. What kind of programs are these? They just let these people take over the country!"

Although less outspoken, there are also teachers who admit that they feel it is unfair that they have to work with immigrant students. They often insist that ESL pull-out teachers take students out of their classrooms or that they need paraprofessionals and special materials. These teachers say they have enough problems to deal with in their teaching and that also having to deal with a diverse student population is asking too much of them. They believe they are neglecting their English-speaking students by giving too much attention to students needing special help. To encourage second language students to build faith in themselves, teachers need to begin to see diversity as enriching.

Diversity Is Enriching

Embracing Diversity (Olsen and Mullen 1990) is a report that highlights thirty-six teachers who have been successfully working with immigrant students. A key to the success of many of those teachers, according to the report, is an emphasis on international and multicultural studies in the curriculum, which "provides a backdrop for exploration of basic human experience and human rights" (p. 28). As one of the teachers, Amelia Ramirez, explained, "The world is becoming smaller and smaller, and we need to understand each other, or we'll be in big trouble" (p. 29). In Amelia's classroom and the classrooms of the other teachers described in *Embracing Diversity*, this positive approach toward diversity allows students who represent cultures, languages, abilities, ages, or socioeconomic status different from the dominant culture to contribute to a true democratization of American society.

An alternative to seeing immigrants as a "problem" is understanding that diversity is an asset and remembering that much of this country's strength has come from its immigrants. In a recent newspaper article, "America as Seen through Daddy's Eyes" (Blum 1991), the author describes a walk with his 85-year-old father down

Devon Avenue on Chicago's North Side, an exciting multi-ethnic section of Chicago, where signs and displays on shops are in Russian, Yiddish, Farsi, Urdu, Greek, Arabic, Polish, Spanish, Korean, and other languages. "Daddy," who arrived in America in 1924 from Poland with no education and described himself as a "wet back" with no legal status, explains to his son why immigrants are so crucial to America's greatness:

> The dead hand of oppression, bad governments and stifling institutions can keep even the most talented people poor and underdeveloped. . . . But in a democracy, there is always hope of redemption. (p. H4)

Many classrooms in the United States are not true democracies. Children who are put in the low reading group in first grade are still there when they finish elementary school. However, in whole language classrooms there is both democracy and the hope of redemption. Whole language teachers look at ethnicity positively. Instead of subscribing to the melting pot image, these teachers see their students as a great patchwork quilt. Each piece of the quilt is unique and adds beauty to the entire effect. The diverse languages and cultures that bilingual students bring to the classroom can provide that beauty in classes where teachers celebrate diversity. One of the teachers featured in *Embracing Diversity* (Olsen and Mullen 1990), Moyra Contreras, does just this. She describes her approach to bilingual students, "My role is to respect the kids as they come into the classroom as opposed to trying to change them into something they are not" (p. 28). When educators have this alternative view, bilingual students are seen as valuable, important, contributing members of every classroom community.

Assessment for
Second Language Learners

Unfortunately, many types of assessment used with bilingual learners cover rather than uncover their strengths. It is extremely difficult for school educators and administrators to change their view of bilingual learners and for bilingual learners to value themselves when they are labeled by inappropriate evaluation instruments. Standardized tests of all kinds tell educators what students *cannot* do but give very little indication of what they *can* do. Standardized testing is especially harmful to language minority students. When they are required to take nationally normed exams, they are at a disadvantage because they are competing with native English speakers. When language minority students take tests to determine their ability to use English, they are often misplaced. A look at three widely used tests to determine language proficiency might give an idea of the kinds of problems that come up when these types of instruments are used.

The Bilingual Syntax Measure (BSM) was developed by Burt and Dulay, researchers with a strong background in second language acquisition. They note that although vocabulary and pronunciation vary with regional dialect, syntax is quite stable. The BSM is used to determine two things: language dominance and language proficiency. Students are asked to look at cartoon pictures and answer questions such as "What's he doing?" Responses are rated for grammatical correctness, based on conversational norms. Students are not expected to produce complete sentences, and pronunciation is not rated.

The BSM gives only a rough indication of language dominance or English proficiency. It is fairly easy to administer. However, the test has many problems. Younger students are often confused and older students are sometimes offended by being tested with cartoon-type materials that include nonhuman characters. Further, students are rated low for ungrammatical responses, even when those responses show comprehension of the question. For example, when asked, "What's he doing?" in reference to a picture test item of a sailor mopping a ship's deck, a student must use a progressive verb form to receive credit. Thus, "He's mopping" is fine, but "He mopped the deck" is not. The sense of the answer is not taken into consideration. Another test item pictures a girl dancing in a field of flowers with her eyes closed. The student is asked, "What's she doing?" Among the possible correct answers suggested by the test writers is, "She's sleeping." Even though her eyes are closed, she is obviously not sleeping, but the verb form is grammatically correct. On the other hand, a logical answer such as "She dance" would be marked as incorrect because it is ungrammatical.

Perhaps a greater concern, though, and one that extends to the other tests used to determine English proficiency, is that although school success depends crucially on the ability to read and write about academic content, the tests do not attempt to measure literacy, only oral language ability. Students who score high on the BSM may be mainstreamed and then do poorly academically because they have been inadequately evaluated or because their ability to read and write in the content areas is limited.

Two other tests commonly used to measure English proficiency are the Language Assessment Scales (LAS) and the Idea Oral Language Proficiency Test (IPT). The LAS assesses pronunciation, vocabulary, syntax, and pragmatics or functional language use. The IPT measures the same four areas. These tests include activities such as having students distinguish between minimal pairs (*pot* and *dot*), naming objects in pictures, and having them listen to a (very short) story and then answer questions about it. In the IPT, the questions are arranged in sequential order, and the tester stops as soon as the student reaches a level where he or she can't answer. Thus, for many students, this test is quite short. The LAS and IPT claim to measure both conversational and academic proficiency.

All three tests give only rough measures of what students can do. Generally, tests are first administered when students enter a new school system. The students may be confused. They are often undergoing some degree of culture shock, and they may not understand the purpose of the test. The test tasks they are asked to do are not meaningful and students may not see their purpose. Further, these language proficiency tests are fairly expensive, and they are directly tied to specific instructional materials. The tests serve as placement measures for the ESL programs the test makers have also published.

Language proficiency tests such as the BSM, LAS, and IPT violate the principles of learning in which whole language educators believe. They test parts of language; they test language out of context; they have no meaning or function for the students; they are individual and competitive; they fail to draw on background knowledge and strengths of the students; and they are used to label students. The tests don't provide the kinds of information that whole language teachers need to make decisions about how to integrate second language students into their classrooms.

Not only are second language students subjected to language proficiency tests, but also they often are required to take all the other kinds of standardized tests that native English speakers take. During the 1980s children in the United States became the most overtested students in the world. More than 200 million standardized exams are given each year, and yet these tests do not improve education. In 1991, *Rethinking Schools*, a journal dedicated to improving schools, published a position paper entitled "Educators Criticize National Tests." It was endorsed by more than sixty educators and educational organizations and was written in response to a recent presidental call for more national tests as part of educational reform. Organizations supporting the position paper included the American Association of School Administrators, the National Association for the Advancement of Colored People, the National Association of Elementary School Principals, the National PTA, and the Whole Language Umbrella among others. These educators expressed their concern about standardized testing: "Adding more testing is clearly not the way to improve education any more than taking the temperature of a patient more often will reduce his or her fever." The authors of this critique point out that multiple-choice standardized tests pressure teachers to teach to the test and "reduce schooling to test coaching" that "will not include learning to think and create and use knowledge in real-world settings" (p. 5). These educators call instead for performance-based assessment "which can be used to help student learning, guide educational improvement, provide information for accountability, and assist the goal of equity, but not block progress or harm students" (p. 5).

In *Tests: Marked for Life?*, Cohen (1988) suggests the very real possibility that the results of standardized tests may harm students by marking them as failures. Once students are adversely labeled, they may receive instruction geared to their supposed inabilities. Taylor (1990) has recorded a moving account of the struggles of one mislabeled child and his parents in *Learning Denied*. Cohen also points out that although the scores from standardized tests are valid and reliable for characterizing groups of students (at least for those similar to the groups the test was normed on), scores are not reliable for individuals. Nevertheless, norm-referenced tests are often used to make decisions about individuals.

The concern about the effects of standardized tests is especially pertinent to minority populations, including bilingual students. The Ford Foundation has issued a report that charges that the "American testing system has become a 'hostile gatekeeper' that has limited opportunities for many, particularly women and minorities" (Rothman 1990a). Rothman proposes that instead of viewing assessment as a means of finding out what students do not know, educators should explore ways to assess what all students, including those whose first language is not English, do know and can do.

Portfolios: An Alternative to Traditional Assessment?

One alternative assessment tool is a portfolio. In the professional world portfolios are often used: artists gather a variety of their work to display; financial counselors make up a portfolio of information to suggest investments to clients. In schools portfolios give more complete views of students. Although portfolios are perhaps most commonly thought of as a collection of students' writing, they may also contain information about students' reading, science and math projects, social studies reports, and interests outside school.

Because portfolios contain products of work done as part of the regular curriculum, they do not take the time from the teaching and learning process that traditional testing does. Instead, they become part of the process itself. A major difference between traditional testing and portfolios is that portfolios involve students in their own evaluation. In portfolio assessments, students can evaluate the products of their classroom work with their teachers and set immediate goals for further study. Teachers using portfolio assessment involve students because they believe, as Y. Goodman (1989) put it, that the goal of evaluation is self-evaluation.

Portfolio assessment can provide school administrators, teachers, and students with a new view of achievement. Since portfolios contain information about students over time, a more complete picture of student capabilities is evident. Those involved with bilingual students know that these students learn much more than standardized tests show. Their learning is often phenomenal; yet teachers, administrators, and students become discouraged when this is not reflected by traditional tests. In addition, whereas standardized tests are given in English, portfolios can contain work students do in their first language as well as English. For example, writing samples of students who are non-English-speaking at the beginning of the year show their ability to express themselves in their first language. As the year progresses, a collection of writing in both English and in their first language can show how their ability to express themselves in both languages improves.

Portfolio assessment is being used widely. In some provinces in Canada, for example, beginning the first year of school, teachers and students choose representative work to be put in a large-sized portfolio that accompanies students through all their school years. In New Hampshire, educators have shown how much teachers and students learn when they keep folders with information on the reading and writing students do (Graves 1983; Taylor 1990). In New York, the commissioner of education has called for a "results-oriented" student assessment including portfolios (Rothman 1990b). In Florida, more than 2,000 elementary teachers are using portfolio assessment with more than 45,000 students (Matthews 1990). During the 1990-91 school year, fourth and eighth grade teachers in Vermont attended staff development workshops provided by the state department of education to help them implement math and writing portfolios. This project will extend to all fourth and eighth grade teachers in Vermont by 1991–92. According to the project director, Geof Hewitt, the portfolio project "promotes new teaching approaches emphasizing coaching" (Allen, p. 4) Additional ways that teachers have used portfolio assessment across the country and around the world are described in *The Whole Language Evaluation Book* (Goodman, Goodman, and Hood 1989) and *The Whole Language Catalog* (Goodman, Bird, and Goodman 1991).

Perhaps the most detailed and most widely used model for portfolios was developed in England. This assessment tool, *The Primary Language Record* (Barrs 1990; Barrs et al. 1988) was used in the 1989-90 school year by more than five hundred schools in and around London for evaluating student progress in the language arts. The Primary Language Record includes forms for interviews with students and parents, observation of reading and writing, and recommendations that teachers, students, and parents do together.

The use of portfolio assessment can inform educators as well as evaluate students. According to Farr, teachers develop "valuable insights" about their students by using portfolios (Jongsma 1989). The Primary Language Record's two simple interviews, which ask bilingual parents and students to assess reading and writing activities and interests, have radically changed the views of teachers and administrators about their second language students. For example, teachers in England discovered that many of their bilingual students could read in their first language, that bilinguals had more literacy in the home than ever before suspected, and that siblings did a great deal of the literacy instruction at home.

Portfolio assessment not only informs teachers about their students, but also helps them as they plan curriculum. In their research Garcia and colleagues (1990) gave two different groups of teachers information about students they did not know. To the first group, the researchers gave traditional assessment information including standardized test scores, the results of the BSM, a writing assessment, a report on a reading conference and anecdotal records from the previous teacher. To the second group of teachers, the researchers gave all the above traditional assessment information as well as the portfolios of each student. The portfolios included a miscue analysis of oral reading, story retellings, entries from a personal reading journal, and interactive written journals. The results showed how important portfolio assessment can be.

> Teachers receiving the portfolio data were able to design specific
> instructional strategies for the students: strategies that, in fact,

matched the plans made by the teachers of these students who had worked with them for a year. Teachers receiving only the traditional assessment data requested additional information and were unable to recommend specific instructional plans. (p. 431)

In Dos Palos, California, teachers have been working over the past two years on developing a system of portfolio assessment. They studied language development and then created their own model for portfolio assessment. These teachers collected writing samples, conducted interviews, and recorded observations of bilingual students.

After reading and discussing parts of The Primary Language Record, the teachers in Dos Palos decided they, too, might find out more about their students if they listened to the parents during the parent-teacher interview, rather than telling the parents about their own child. Though there was some concern that bilingual parents might not want to or be able to answer, the teachers decided to give the interview a try. They devised a simple short series of questions including the following:

- What does your child like to read at home?
- What does your child write at home?
- Who does your child read and write with?
- What does your child like to do at home?
- What does he/she like to play with?
- How does he/she spend a lot of time?

The results of the interviews were exciting. The teachers could not believe how much more they enjoyed the parent-teacher conference time and how much they, the teachers, had learned about the children in their classrooms. The enthusiasm of the parents as they told about their children moved the teachers and helped them understand the parents' commitment to their children. The interviews were so successful that the teachers continued them in the second parent-teacher conference, altering the questions only slightly to further probe the same areas:

- What has your child read at home since our last conference?
- What has your child written at home?
- Does your child read and write more this year?
- Whom does your child read and write with?
- What does your child like to do at home?
- What does he/she like to play with?
- How does he/she spend a lot of time?
- Have any of these changed this year?

For the portfolios the teachers collected writing samples, tape recordings, and lists of books the students read. They created and revised Spanish/English writing and observation checksheets. Using portfolios helped these teachers to see their bilingual students' strengths and growth and also informed their teaching by showing them the kinds of activities that were most effective with their bilingual learners. At the end of the 1991 school year, Linda, a first grade teacher, gave the following recommendation in her summary case study on seven-year-old Francisco:

> Francisco is the type of child that it would be easy to overlook. It is important that Francisco be encouraged to continue writing and reading and that his work be praised. Because of observations of his responses to different activities, it is recommended that he be looked at seriously for a bilingual placement next year. Strong support in his first language would give Frankie the support he needs to progress even more quickly in English.

Portfolios made a difference in how Dos Palos teachers viewed their students, especially their second language students. In going through their students' portfolios, Linda and the other teachers involved in the portfolio project found that they had more complete information on their students than they had ever had before using report cards and standardized test scores. They felt confident about making recommendations and were amazed at how much they had also learned about their own teaching.

Portfolio assessment is a valuable tool for all students but especially for bilingual students. The following guidelines for portfolios for second language learners might be helpful to teachers considering portfolio assessment.

Portfolio Assessment with Second Language Students

- **What is a portfolio?** A portfolio is a box, folder, or other container that contains various kinds of information that has been gathered over time about one student.
- **What goes into a portfolio?** A portfolio is most commonly considered a collection of students' formal and informal writing. However, portfolios might also contain audio- and videotaped recordings of students' projects, science and math projects, art projects, programs from music and drama events, social studies reports, teacher/parent observation notes, lists of books read with dates and notes, and lists of activities the students are involved in outside the school. For second language students, samples are collected in the students' first as well as second languages.

- **Who is a portfolio for?** A portfolio is for teachers, all support personnel who work with the students, the students themselves, parents, and administrators.
- **Why is portfolio assessment important for second language students?** Research shows that it takes four to nine years for second language learners to achieve on a par with native speakers of English when growth is measured by norm-referenced standardized tests (Collier 1989). However, bilingual students learn much more than standardized tests show. Portfolios provide examples of students' abilities and growth over time in their first language as well as their second language
- **Who decides what goes into a portfolio?** Students, their parents, and all teachers working with the students make choices.
- **How often do things get put into a portfolio?** This varies, but at least once a month. Some teachers and students put things into a portfolio weekly and then, at the end of each month, choose things to be left in.
- **What does a portfolio show teachers and administrators?** It shows student growth over time, student interests, student strengths in the first as well as second languages, and the effectiveness of the present curriculum for the student.
- **What does a portfolio show students?** It shows them what they have learned, what they spend time and energy on, and what they need to work on more.
- **What does a portfolio show parents?** It shows parents what their children are learning, what they are doing in school, what kinds of activities are valued in school, and what kinds of activities parents can do at home to support learning.
- **What are the advantages of a portfolio over other types of evaluation?** Portfolios involve students and allow them to both show and see progress over time. Instead of highlighting what students cannot do, portfolios allow students to show what they can do without time restraints. Portfolios allow students to evaluate what they have learned, to set goals for future learning, and to monitor their progress toward their own goals.

Portfolio assessment has benefits for everyone. In Dos Palos, portfolios helped the teachers see their bilingual students' strengths and growth and also helped them to improve their teaching by revealing the activities most effective with their second language learners. Portfolio assessment offers the kind of evaluation that can form, inform, and reform curricula and programs rather than fragment learning into isolated elements (Barrs 1990).

Content Area Instruction: A Key to Academic Success

Using portfolio assessment can help both teachers and students reflect on which classroom activities are really worthwhile and lead to growth in both language development and knowledge of academic content. Although mainstream teachers have always had the goal of facilitating cognitive growth for all their students, ESL teachers have traditionally focused on helping students develop a new language. As increasing numbers of second language students enter mainstream classes, teachers often are faced with the task of building the academic content knowledge of students who are not yet fully proficient in English. Whole language teachers of second language students understand that the best way for all students to develop language is to use language for a variety of purposes, including using language to explore content areas. Language is learned in the functional context of use. However, if students are not fully proficient in English, teachers need to find ways to make content comprehensible. Insights from mainstream whole language teachers of second language students is beginning to have a profound influence on how ESL teachers approach their students.

The rationalist view of second language learning, based on cognitive psychology and generative linguistics, influenced second language teaching methodology. The main shift for ESL teachers was from a method that emphasized memorization and the repetition of pattern drills to exercises that would lead to real language use. The goal became communicative competence in the target language. This move toward a more authentic use of language really does not meet the needs of students in public schools who not only have to communicate socially in English but also need to be able use the language for academic purposes.

Learning content material in English has not been part of the communicative ESL curriculum. Even today most ESL textbooks used in schools concentrate on developing communicative competence by teaching students basic vocabulary words (color, clothes, transportation, food) and basic functions of conversational English such as making introductions and asking for directions. Total Physical Response (TPR), The Natural Approach, and the Notional-Functional Approach (see chapters 3 and 5) form the basis for these commercially produced ESL materials.

Two major problems arise when the focus is on the development of communicative competence. When the content of classes is everyday conversation, students may not feel they are learning anything worthwhile. This is particularly true for older students who have already learned a good deal of academic content in their first language. Instead of spending valuable time rehearsing vocabulary and dialogues for the kind of artificially set up communication found in most ESL textbooks, second language learners should be learning language through the study of the content that their native English-speaking peers are studying. In addition, second language students fall behind their peers academically if all their class time is spent in acquiring basic communication skills. Their lack of content knowledge may cause their teachers to lose faith in their bilingual students' academic abilities, especially if the teachers value the results of the standardized tests that all their students take.

First and second language acquisition theorists have proposed that language is best learned when there is a functional need and use for it (Edelsky 1986; Goodman 1986b; Halliday 1984; Harste, Woodward, and Burke 1984; Hudelson 1984; Rigg and Hudelson 1986). Halliday (1984) has delineated the difference between *learning* language, learning *about* language and learning *through* language as children learn their first language. Young children *learn* language as they need it to do things and to understand their world. They also learn *about* language as they use language and discover how different words and forms can change meaning. Finally, *through* language they come to understand the world around them, and in the process they learn more language.

This is true also for second language learners. Toua, who was described at the beginning of this chapter, learned language as he attended school and as he interacted with his tutor, his volunteer friend, and the college student. In these different situations he learned about language: how to use written language to interact with his tutor in a journal; how to use oral language to interact socially with the volunteer friend; how words in Hmong and English can express the same ideas. Toua also learned through written and oral language. He explored differences between his culture and that of the United States as shown by his journal entry, which included a picture of him in native dress—"Hi!! It me Toua Xiong these clothes is for everyday use but it because we are living in America we have to wear like they do." But the cultural differences were not all easy for Toua to write about, so he added, "I remember a little about Laos, but I can not explain to you in the note have to talk together." He also learned facts about U.S. history. Through the details in Toua's "Mt Rushmore Rap" (fig. 7–1), it is clear that Toua has learned not only U.S. history but also something of the subtleties of the personalities of the American presidents.

It is this idea of learning language through meaningful language use that is the basis for content area instruction methods for second language learners. Since people learn language as they use it, and second language students need to learn both language and academic school content, it is logical to have them learn English as they study meaningful content rather than have them study the English language as a separate subject apart from meaningful content. Arnie, a foreign language teacher who has studied language acquisition from a whole language perspective, discovered that one of the main problems with his foreign language curriculum was that he really had no content to teach!

Arnie realized that instead of having his students practice language forms on topics that were unrelated to social studies, science, or math content, it would be more effective to create situations in which they could learn a new language as they learned the content of their school subjects. Many ESL teachers as well as mainstream teachers with second language students have begun to follow the same approach as Arnie. Two well-known methods for teaching language through content are CALLA, the Cognitive Academic Language Learning Approach (Chamot and O'Malley 1989), and Sheltered English. Although we believe that bilingual programs that fully develop students' first language are superior to sheltered programs, we realize that bilingual programs may not always be possible. The teacher may not be bilingual, or the students may represent a number of different primary languages. In these cases, sheltered approaches are an alternative to bilingual education.

CALLA

The Cognitive Academic Language Learning Approach (CALLA) was developed to teach content to second language learners. It is an "instructional system designed to develop academic language skills in English for students in upper elementary and secondary schools" (Chamot and O'Malley 1989, p. 111). The rationale behind the approach is that "learning a language has more in common with learning complex cognitive skills than it does with learning facts, isolated pieces of information, or even meaningful texts" (p. 112). The idea, then, is that ESL students will learn English through an organized approach to the content area materials they need to study in the regular classroom.

Three components comprise CALLA: grade-appropriate content, academic language development, and instruction in learning strategies. With CALLA, students first study content materials in science and mathematics because these subjects are least language dependent. In science, students receive comprehensible input through hands-on activities. Mathematics has an international sign system and somewhat restricted vocabulary. Later, students begin to work in social studies, which involves more language. However, teachers are given a number of ways to provide context for the content.

As students explore various content areas, they also develop the academic language they need. Since much of the academic language used in the content areas is context-reduced, particularly the language of textbooks and lectures, the input is made comprehensible through the use of maps, models, manipulatives, demonstrations, written responses, and discussions. As students become actively involved in the content, they learn the academic language they need.

The third component of CALLA, learning strategy instruction, is meant to help students consciously develop techniques for working with content area materials. In the CALLA model, teachers first find out what learning strategies students already use by interviewing them and having them "think aloud" as they do a task. Once strategies are identified, teachers provide students opportunities to practice other strategies. Chamot and O'Malley have identified three major types of strategies, and they have developed activities for each type. *Metacognitive strategies* include such activities as advance organization, selective attention, and self-evaluation. These strategies are intended to help students plan, monitor, and evaluate their own learning. *Cognitive strategies* such as grouping, note-taking, imagery, and inferencing encourage students to manipulate content material in different ways. *Social-affective strategies* like cooperative learning give students a chance to interact in order to ask questions and clarify the content.

A CALLA lesson is organized into five parts: preparation, presentation, practice, evaluation, and expansion. In the *preparation* phase, the teacher discovers what students already know about the content to ascertain the gaps in students' prior knowledge and to build on what students already know. In the *presentation* stage the material is presented using different techniques to make it comprehensible. The *practice* phase allows students to engage in hands-on activities in cooperative groups as they go over the content. *Evaluation* may be individual, cooperative, or teacher directed. However, the emphasis is on helping students to self-evaluate. In the final stage, *expansion*, students are encouraged to go beyond the materials to explore the content in other ways. For example, students might decide to interview family or community members about a topic discussed during a social studies lesson.

In a CALLA lesson, the goal is to provide students with different ways to practice language and learn content at the same time. Through the practice of different strategies, students are shown how to approach content in more than one way. The authors of CALLA have developed textbooks for secondary content area classrooms that follow the model. Many teachers have found both the model and the materials extremely helpful as they work to teach content to ESL students.

From a whole language perspective, CALLA builds on student strengths, involves students actively in learning, includes all four modes, and encourages social interaction. However, students have little choice about what direction the study will take or what strategies they will practice. CALLA is more content centered than student centered. Therefore, since there is a tendency to focus on details of content before students get the big picture, some of the instruction is part to whole. There is also the question of whether it is necessary to teach learning strategies directly. For example, lessons designed to teach students how to take notes appear to be useful, but students may have difficulty making the connection between practice sessions on note taking following a specified format and actual note taking to help them remember key concepts in a social studies class. In whole language classes, teachers provide demonstrations of strategies during content instruction and nudge students toward using them instead of directly teaching the strategies. Despite concerns about the direct teaching of strategies and a lack of student centeredness, we believe that CALLA lessons show faith that second language students can learn academic content. Teachers are given practical ideas for embedding content in context, and students can develop faith in themselves as learners because they are given useful ideas for approaching academic subjects.

Sheltered English (Comprehensible Content)

Sheltered English, more recently referred to as Comprehensible Content, is similar to CALLA, but, in general, sheltered instruction is not as structured as CALLA. In Sheltered English, teachers help students comprehend the English of their content area material by using a variety of techniques to make the content comprehensible.

There are two basic Sheltered English models. Students in the first model are "sheltered" in the sense that they do not compete with native English speakers. All the students in these classes are second language learners. This model follows the Canadian French immersion programs discussed in Chapter 6. In Canadian classes, students who speak English are instructed entirely in French for all content areas. There are no native French speakers in these classes, so students may be said to be sheltered from competition with native speakers.

In the Canadian sheltered programs, English speakers add French as a second language. However, in the U.S. English immersion programs, minority language speakers often lose their first languages and cultures in the process of learning English. In addition, students in English immersion programs are isloated from the rest of the student body.

For these reasons a second model of Sheltered English, a model more compatible with whole language principles, has been developed. In this model, teachers shelter the instruction for all students by using different kinds of techniques to make the content comprehensible. Second language students can learn content and learn English at the same time. Many teachers have found that these sheltered techniques make learning easier for all students, not just those who are Limited English Proficient.

The teachers in some Sheltered English classes may be assisted by paraprofessionals who are native speakers of the students' primary language. These paraprofessionals, cross-age tutors or peer tutors can provide overviews and individual instruction in the students' first language, which makes later instruction in English more comprehensible. The regular classroom teacher in a sheltered class uses specific techniques to ensure that all students understand the lessons. These techniques provide context for the academic content. Teachers have found the following suggestions for sheltering helpful:

- If possible preview the content in the student's first language. You may use a student to do this.
- Use visuals and realia.
- Move from the concrete to the abstract.
- Use gestures and body language.
- Speak clearly and pause often.
- Say the same thing in different ways.
- Make frequent comprehension checks.

- Have students explain main concepts to one another working in pairs or small groups. They can do this in their first language. Then have students report back to the class.
- Have students read and write about things that are relevant and important to them and their own lives.
- Keep oral presentations or reading assignments short.
- Use collaborative activities more often than lectures or assigned readings.
- If possible, review the lesson in the students' first language.

The goal of sheltered teaching is to teach both content and language to students who are not fully proficient in the language of instruction. While Comprehensible Content teaching programs have proven to be especially successful in developing academic competence for bilingual students, sheltering techniques have been found to be an effective way of teaching all students, both second language learners and native English speakers.

Comprehensible Units

Rhoda, a fifth grade teacher in a school with a majority of students from Hispanic and Punjabi backgrounds, was sensitive to the needs of her second language learners as she planned her curriculum. Of her twenty-six students only eight were native English speakers. Ten of her Hispanic and Punjabi students were labeled as Limited or Non-English Proficient and four others were considered to have learning disabilities. Rhoda knew she would need to involve all of her students in meaningful content activities to help them understand academic subjects and learn English at the same time. Rhoda understood the principles of whole language and was aware of the techniques that help make content comprehensible.

The social studies content for fifth grade is U.S. history. In order for the many isolated facts presented in the textbook about the history of the United States to have meaning, Rhoda reasoned that her students needed to understand the big picture first. To teach from whole to part, Rhoda organized the year around major themes. She knew that theme study would be especially helpful to her second language students because there would be a natural repetition of vocabulary as concepts developed. Rhoda proposed projects centered around different themes including the people in the United States, the geography, and historical incidents.

The class began the year by reading and discussing literature about different Native American groups across the United States and Canada, such as *Annie and the Old One* (Miles 1971), *The Sign of the Beaver* (Speare 1983), *I Heard the Owl Call My Name* (Craven 1973), *Ishi* (Kroeber 1964), and *Calico Captive* (Speare 1957). This led to comparing and contrasting the life-styles of the different Native American groups, including discovering how the geography of where they lived influenced how they lived.

Another major topic during the year was slavery. Again students read literature books including the stories of famous slaves. The class then followed the escape route of one slave from Louisiana to Canada. A final major project was an Oregon Trail simulation in which groups of students formed wagon trains, took on pioneer personalities, and solved problems as they moved across the United States. Students planned the supplies they needed, calculated costs, and wrote about and discussed their feelings and emotions as they encountered simulated obstacles similar to those that the original pioneers faced.

Thoughout the year students worked collaboratively as they read, wrote, and discussed. Groups produced reports for each major project. For the first project, students drew a web, or semantic map, which included the different ideas they had developed about Native Americans and how the environment influenced their life-styles. In the second major report of the year, Rhoda encouraged students to create a table of contents for their reports on slavery and to divide their work into chapters. The final report was a state report. The students chose a state and were encouraged to organize their report by themseleves in any way they wished. Many of the reports contained not only a table of contents and chapters but also a bibliography. Students who felt less confident about their command of English made travel brochures. Rhoda was pleased and excited about the development of content and language these reports revealed.

Rhoda's class was organized to make the content comprehensible. Students focused on one topic at a time. They read and discussed works of fiction that helped provide context for the nonfiction textbook. Their projects were done in heterogeneous, collaborative groups. Many visuals and hands-on activities were used. Because of the community spirit that Rhoda created in the classroom, students less fluent in English were supported by peers in both their first and second languages. Rhoda had high expectations for her students and showed them she had faith that they could and would learn the content. By the end of the year, all the students in Rhoda's class were proud that they had learned so much about U.S. history. They felt good about themselves as learners. Rhoda's faith in her students helped them develop their potential and develop faith in themselves.

Teachers Showing Faith in Their Learners

Rhoda is an exceptional teacher, but she is not really an exception. As we have worked with teachers, we have become increasingly aware of how many of them expand the potential of their bilingual students by showing faith in their abilities and engaging them in meaningful content.

Michael, a high school and junior college English teacher who works with many second language learners, recently shared how his growing understanding of whole language is affecting the way he views curriculum:

> As I am growing more and more into the understanding of whole language, I am better able to see methods I can easily apply to my high school English classes at all levels and with much interest and enthusiasm gained. This coming fall, with both Honors English and English Proficiency, the high and the low, I have great plans. For one thing, I plan on taking similar attitudes with both classes—that all of my students can learn equally well if given the chance (faith in the learner) and that all of my students can accomplish critical tasks which ask them to think on their own. I would especially like to begin with both an autobiographical collection of student writings and a newsletter. I have also made plans with another teacher to team teach units which incorporate local history with student writing, very much like the Foxfire series (Wigginton 1985), but with the addition of audiovisual documentaries done by the students about their families. I thought it would be a great idea to videotape interviews my students have with the elders of their rural community, many of whom are Mexican immigrants who contain within them ancient stories and folklore which would be wonderful to save both in writing and on tape.

Michael is applying all of the whole language principles as he plans for next year, but, most of all, it is clear that Michael has faith in his students. Instead of limiting what he would plan for students in the "low" group, he is offering the same rich curriculum to all his students because he has faith in their potential.

Kay, the bilingual resource teacher who organized the Teachers of Tomorrow Club discussed in chapter 4, also believes that all students, including bilingual students, have potential. Kay and the third grade Spanish/English bilingual students assigned her for special instruction got very involved in a unit on immigrants. Kay introduced the unit by reading part of the article that was discussed earlier in this chapter entitled, "America as Seen through Daddy's Eyes."

> Daddy did not believe that the "browning" of America invalidated the universality of the American Experience, or that non-Europeans were only good for cheap labor. Within living memory the same was said about Jews and Italians; in the nineteenth century they said it about the Irish, and in the eighteenth about practically everybody. . . . When we stop taking in immigrants, that's when we stop being great. (Blum 1991)

Kay talked to her students about the many immigrants who have come to America and asked her students what they thought about the statement, "When we stop taking in immigrants, that's when we stop being great." The children discussed this in both Spanish and English and decided to talk with their families about why they came to America. The next day Kay read the students a book about immigrants, *Mira, Cómo Salen las Estrellas* (Look How the Stars Come Out) (Levinson 1987). After the reading, the children brainstormed in Spanish what they remembered about this story in which two immigrant children come alone to the United States in the early 1900s on a large ship filled with other immigrants. Kay wrote their ideas on a large piece of butcher paper, and the students decided to write and illustrate their own Spanish book that summarized the story in their own words.

The following day Kay read *How Many Days to America?* (Bunting 1988) in English to her group and asked the students how the two stories about immigrants were the same and how they were different. Kay recorded their responses in both Spanish and English using a Venn diagram. One child's summary in Spanish of *How Many Days to America?* shows a thorough understanding: "La niña no quería ir a América pero cuando llegaron, estaba feliz" (The little girl didn't want to go to America but when they arrived she was happy). When Kay asked how the two books were the same, students picked out both obvious and important similiarities: "Los dos tienen una niña y un niño" (The two have a girl and a boy in them); "Ambas historias son sobre un viaje a América" (Both stories are about a trip to America); and "Los dos se tratan de tristeza" (The two are about sadness).

After Kay's students discussed the newspaper article about immigrants, wrote their own summaries and stories in Spanish, and compared the Spanish and English books, Kay asked her students if they wanted to share their summary and their conclusions with the other third graders. The response was enthusiastic. Kay and her pull-out students decided that their entire class, including nonfluent Spanish speakers, should hear in English *How Many Days to America?* (Bunting 1988), read copies of their Spanish version of *Mira, Cómo Salen las Estrellas* (Levinson 1987), and then listen to the original book in Spanish. After these activities, Kay's students felt the rest of their class would better be able to understand the presentation of their book comparisons in Spanish. Far from being insecure about being less fluent in English than their peers, these students have developed a pride in their first language and in what they have been learning in both Spanish and English.

The students in this pull-out classroom, who spend only thirty minutes a day with Kay, are often described as deprived children. They are labeled as either LEP (Limited English Proficient) or NEP (Non-English Proficient). Despite their lack of experience with the English language, they are enthusiastic participants in their classroom. Kay has faith in them as learners and helps them discover their own potential. The children are engaged as they listen, speak, read, and write, because they find the activities interesting and meaningful. They are animated in their discussion, interested in what their classmates say, and attentive to their teacher. Through their involvement with literature in their first and second languages, they are developing both language and academic ability.

Kay is not deterred by labels. She encourages second language learners to develop their full potential and build their faith in themselves. When teachers like Kay view bilingual students as valuable, important, contributing members of their classroom communities, all the students benefit. .

Kay's use of the immigrant theme "When we stop taking in immigrants, that's when we stop being great" is one other teachers working with immigrant students have come to appreciate. In a recent letter to the editor in our local Central California Valley newspaper, a middle school teacher shared how much progress the Hmong immigrants in our community have made in ten short years:

> Recently I attended a party at the home of some Hmong friends. As the evening progressed, I recalled the first Hmong party I went to ten years ago. At that time there was only one person present who could speak enough English to explain to me some of the rituals and the customs being observed. I knew that every

person in my view was on welfare and would need help for years to enter American society.

At the recent party I reflected that the host had had a job for years as repairman at a large apartment complex and now works on weekends at a second job. The hostess is a substitute custodian for the local school district. Their daughter works for the welfare department and her husband works for the school district translating materials to and from Southeast Asian languages. Her husband's family pooled their resources so that now they also own and operate a small farm. . . .

The occasion for the party was to say good-bye to the host's son. He was moving . . . to Wisconsin, where he has been accepted for doctoral studies at the University of Wisconsin . . . when the son was in high school I read his account of his family's escape from communism. What a change from fleeing for one's life to flying off to a major university for advanced study. I feel privileged to have witnessed this remarkable progress. (Jackson 1991)

Wayland Jackson knows what immigrants can do, and in his own middle school class he has helped his students reflect on their experiences. Each year students publish their writing in books that are used as a reading resource in school and in the community.

Teachers who show faith in their students produce amazing individual results. Rhoda, whose class we described earlier, was concerned about one of her students, Surjit, a Punjabi from India. He was twelve years old with no literacy in his first language. Surjit had only been in the United States for five months and had attended school in this country only the last two months of the previous school year. He was entering Rhoda's classroom having already established a reputation for disturbing classmates and having little potential. The previous teacher had recommended that Surjit be tested for a learning disability.

The first month with Surjit was discouraging. His lack of previous schooling and English kept him from participating. Because he could not understand, he often wandered around the room disturbing the other students as they worked together on projects. Rhoda, however, decided she would not give up. Each time he wandered, she looked for some kind of activity in which to get him involved. She tried to find activities that had enough nonlinguistic context so that he could participate at least minimally. She set a goal for herself and Surjit: She wanted to get him to participate with other students in their group work by the end of the year.

Because Rhoda stressed the importance of community, the students in her classroom also took responsibility for Surjit. In October two girls asked if they could be Surjit's ESL teachers during writer's workshop. This was the beginning of Surjit's real integration into the classroom. He was encouraged by his peer teachers and the entire class. By Christmas he was speaking enough English for the students to communicate with him. When he wrote his first coherent story, the whole class applauded. By the end of the year, Surjit was participating in the simulation Oregon Trail project described earlier and even made a travel brochure for a state report.

Rather than being singled out as a student who has learning disabilities, Surjit was viewed by his teacher and his classmates as having real learning potential, and he showed incredible growth. Rhoda, in fact, concluded at the end of the year that he not only has potential and can achieve and participate if encouraged, but that he succeeded beyond her wildest dreams: "I think I could have expected even *more* of him!" The most important lesson we can learn as teachers is that our students have unlimited potential and that we, their teachers, must show our faith in them to allow them to show us that potential.

Conclusion

As we have worked with teachers in our graduate classes, visited classrooms in schools, and gathered examples for this book, we have become even more convinced of the importance of the faith in the learner principle for teaching all students, especially second language learners. It has become clear to us that when educators have faith in the learners they are working with, they are more likely to apply the other whole language principles with their students. Teachers who have faith that their students can and will learn, more naturally start with the whole, rather than feed students small parts. They develop learner-centered curricula drawing on the interests and needs of the students, rather than imposing only the teacher's agendas of what they assume needs to be taught. They are concerned that what happens in the classroom is meaningful to students and serves some purpose in the students' lives rather than teaching solely to meet school, district, and state curriculum mandates. Teachers with faith in students have classrooms where there is often a productive buzz of students interacting in groups, rather than maintaining silent classrooms of students in straight rows. These teachers provide opportunities for students to express themselves through reading, writing, drama, art, music, dance, exercise, and other mediums rather than insisting that students master oral language first. They find ways to provide primary language support for their second language learners because they understand that bilingual students learn more English when they can first develop concepts in their native language, rather than accepting the commonsense assumption that "more English equals more English." They have faith in the infinite possibilities of all students, including second language learners, rather than holding a limiting view of their potential.

Having faith in learners so they can build faith in themselves is not simply a passive process of holding the right thoughts or even of doing good things within a single classroom. Cazden (1986) points out that many language minority students are at risk in our schools. The risk comes from three sources: reductionist concepts of language and learning; cultural differences between teachers and students; and inadequate communication among the different adults in students' lives.

Cazden urges teachers to be "language advocates for children" (p. 10). By this she means that teachers need to involve students in rich learning environments rather than reducing learning to bits and pieces of meaningless information. They must work to break down cultural barriers and build a true classroom community. And they should act as advocates for their students with other teachers, paraprofessionals, counselors, administrators, parents, and communities to ensure that second language students have access to the human and material resources they need to achieve school success.

Whole language teachers who have faith in their students and who want to build students' faith in themselves are willing to take the risks involved with advocacy. If they feel that systems for assessing students' language proficiency are inadequate, they join committees to review those measures and help design new ways to test students. If they feel that standardized tests for second language students only serve to reinforce an impression that these students are below the norm, they work to exempt bilingual students from having to take the tests. In schools with traditional grading systems, they join task forces to develop portfolio assessments. Whole language teachers organize collaboration at their school sites as they encourage their colleagues to plan theme cycles, read and talk about the latest research, and share personal writing with one another. If their schools do not have materials that reflect their students' first languages and cultures, they find ways to get those important resources. Whole language teachers are excellent teachers in their own classrooms, and they are willing to extend their efforts beyond the classroom to the school community to help create a positive atmosphere where there are high expectations for all students, and particularly for language minority students.

Whole language teachers of second language students must be advocates. We opened this chapter with the story of Toua. There are many such success stories in whole language classrooms. However, some stories have unhappy endings. In her case study on a bilingual student, Cathy, a student teacher, tells of seven-year-old María, whose physical appearance, personal history, and school records doom her to failure unless she finds someone who will have faith in her:

> María is quite thin and her eyes are markedly crossed . . . her manner of dress is significantly different because she lives in low income housing surrounded by upper class income family homes and her clothes come from thrift shops . . . this child has at various times attended four different schools in her short career. . . . Her teacher feels that language is not the problem and that María probably has some degree of learning disability. . . . Her interactions with adults are undemanding, quiet and respectful. In class the most likely characterization of María is that she is invisible.

Yet, Cathy has learned the important lesson of faith in the learner by working closely with María.

> My view of María is somewhat different. . . . Having talked with her, worked with her, not only for reading, but for math and science as well, I have found that when challenged and encouraged she responds well and has no more difficulty than her American-born peers. I think there are many reasons to express concern (her socioeconomic status, her unstable family situation, her physical condition, school attendance record are but a few), but her ability to learn is not among them.

Cathy sums up her conclusions for María's potential for success: "For María, contact with a teacher (or some other advocate) who will support her and her family and help her make the connections that will allow her successful academic and personal experience will be critical if she is to avoid the cracks that have swallowed up so many others."

Many stories, fortunately, have the potential of happy endings. They have the potential of happy endings because of the kinds of things teachers are doing with their second language students. We would like to end this book with a tribute to all the teachers who have shared their stories with us to make this book possible. It is because of the incredible creativity, concern, and dedication of teachers like these that we see hope for meeting the needs of our diverse student population. These teachers were working with a variety of students in a variety of settings: Sam, the bilingual first grade master teacher was working with Blanca and Carolina, bilingual student teachers who taught him as much as he taught them. Charlene and Vince were teaching upper grades in inner city schools with a majority of Southeast Asian students. René, Nancy, Teresa, and Katie were teaching similar populations of primary age children. Karen, Lorna, Nancy, JoAnne, Mary, Susan, Irene, Steve, Kelly, Linda, Rhoda, and Sonia were teaching from kindergarten to fifth grade in farming communities with very high Hispanic populations. Kay, Jill, Jane, and Rose Marie were resource specialists in those same kinds of farming communities. Michael, Arnie, Julie, Charlotte, Bunny, Wayland, Lonna, Marilyn, Linda, Cyn, and Barbara were working with second language students in junior high and high schools. Miriam, George, and Ellen were teaching ESL to adults. Denette, Julie, Diane, Alan, Steve, and Cathy were student teachers working with bilingual students.

Some of these teachers have changed schools and responsibilities, but all of them continue to be advocates for second language students. Though their grade levels and student populations differ, these teachers have much in common. They all share a vision of what teaching second language students should and can be. They all share an understanding of whole language principles, which they work to implement in their classrooms. They all share a belief in their students' potential. We are grateful to them for providing us with real examples of ways to help second language students, because through their work, they have taught all of us what whole language for second language learners really is.

References

Allen, D. (1991). Vermont's Portfolio Assessment Goes Statewide. *The Council Chronicle*. Urbana, IL: National Council of Teachers of English. P. 4.

Asher, J. 1977. *Learning another language through actions: The complete teacher's guide*. Los Gatos, CA: Sky Oaks Publications.

Au, K. (1980). Participation structures in a reading lesson with Hawaiian children: Analysis of a culturally appropriate instructional event. *Anthropology and Education Quarterly* 11, 91–115.

Baker, K. A., and A. A. de Kanter. 1981. *Effectiveness of bilingual education: A review of the literature*. Office of Planning and Budget, U.S. Department of Education.

Barrera, R. 1983. Bilingual reading in the primary grades: Some questions about questionable views and practices. In *Early childhood bilingual education: A Hispanic perspective*, edited by T. Escobedo, 165. New York: Columbia University Press.

Barrs, M. 1990. The Primary Language Record: Reflection of issues in evaluation. *Language Arts* 67(3): 244–253.

Barrs, M., S. Ellis, H. Hester, and A. Thomas. 1988. *The primary language record: Handbook for teachers*. Portsmouth, NH: Heinemann.

Bennett, W. 1985. Press release of address to Association for a Better New York.

Bird, L., and L. Alvarez. 1987. Beyond comprehension: The power of literature study for language minority students. *Elementary ESOL Education News*, 10(1): 1–3.

Blum, R. 1991. America as seen through daddy's eyes. *The Fresno Bee*. (13 January): H1, H4.

Brown, H. D. 1980. *Principles of language learning and teaching*. Englewood Cliffs, NJ: Prentice-Hall.

Brumfit, C. J. 1979. "Communicative" language teaching: An educational perspective. In *The communicative approach to language teaching*, edited by C. J. Brumfit and K. Johnson, 183–191. Oxford: Oxford University Press.

Bunting, E. 1988. *How many days to America?* Boston: Clarion Books.

Calkins, L. 1986. *The art of teaching writing*. Portsmouth, NH: Heinemann.

Cambourne, B. and J. Turbill. 1987. *Coping with chaos*. Portsmouth, NH: Heinemann.

Carasusan, G. *Los tres osos y bucles de oro*. Barcelona, Spain: Editorial Juventud.

Cazden, C. 1986. ESL teachers as language advocates for children. In *ESL children's writing: What we've learned, what we're learning*, edited by P. Rigg, and S. Enright, 9–21. Washington, DC: TESOL.

———. 1988. *Classroom discourse: The language of teaching and learning.* Portsmouth, NH: Heinemann.

Chamot, A., and M. O'Malley. 1989. The cognitive academic language learning approach. In *When they don't all speak English: Integrating the ESL student into the regular classroom,* edited by P. Rigg and V. Allen, 108–125. Urbana, IL: NCTE.

Chastain, K. 1976. *Developing second language skills: Theory to practice* (2nd ed.). Boston: Houghton Mifflin.

Claret, M. *Los tres osos y ricitos de oro.* Barcelona, Spain: Editorial Juventud.

Clark, E. 1988. The search for a new educational paradigm: Implications of new assumptions about thinking and learning. *Holistic Education Review* 1(1): 18–30.

Cochrane, O., D. Cochrane, S. Scalena, and E. Buchanan. 1984. *Reading, writing, and caring.* Winnipeg: Whole Language Consultants Ltd.

Cohen, S. A. 1988. *Tests: Marked for life?* New York: Scholastic.

Collier, V. 1989. How long? A synthesis of research on academic achievement in a second language. *TESOL Quarterly* 23:509–531.

Coulthard, M. 1985. *An introduction to discourse analysis.* New York: Longman.

Craven, M. 1973. *I heard the owl call my name.* New York: Dell.

Crawford, J. 1989. *Bilingual education: History, politics, theory and practice.* Trenton, NJ: Crane.

Cummins, J. 1981. The role of primary language development in promoting educational success for language minority students. In *Schooling and language minority students: A theoretical framework,* 3–49. Los Angeles, CA: Evaluation, Dissemination and Assessment Center California State University, Los Angeles.

———. 1984. *Bilingualism and special education: Issues in assessment and pedagogy.* Clevedon, England: Multilingual Matters.

———. 1989a. *Empowering minority students.* Sacramento: CABE.

———. 1989b. The sanitized curriculum: Educational disempowerment in a nation at risk. In *Richness in writing: Empowering ESL students,* edited by D. Johnson and D. Roen, 19–38. New York: Longman.

Danoff, M. V., G. J. Coles, D. H. McLaughlin, and D.J. Reynolds. 1977, 1978. *Evaluation of the impact of ESEA Title VII Spanish/English bilingual education program.* American Institutes for Research.

Dewey, J. 1929. *My pedagogic creed.* Washington, DC: The Progressive Education Association.

Diller, K. 1978. *The language teaching controversy* . Rowley, MA: Newbury House.

Doorn, D. 1991. The seed pod travelers: A literacy exchange program for second language learners. *TESOL Matters* 1(2): 2.

Edelsky, C. 1986. *Writing in the bilingual classroom: Había una vez.* Norwood, NJ: Ablex.

————. 1989. Bilingual children's writing: Fact and fiction. In *Richness in writing: Empowering ESL students*, edited by D. Johnson and D. Roen, 165–176. New York: Longman.

Edelsky, C., B. Altwerger, and B. Flores. 1991. *Whole language: What's the difference?* Portsmouth, NH: Heinemann.

Educators criticize national tests. (1991). *Rethinking Schools* (May/June): 5.

Egan, K. 1986. *Teaching as story telling: An alternative approach to teaching and curriculum in the elementary school.* London, Ontario. Althouse Press, University of Western Ontario.

English-language arts framework. 1987. Sacramento, CA: California State Department of Education.

Epstein, N. 1977. *Language, ethnicity, and the schools.* Washington, DC: Institute for Educational Leadership.

Estes, E. 1944. *The hundred dresses.* New York: Harcourt Brace Jovanovich.

Fast food. 1989. Rosemont, IL: National Dairy Council.

Ferreiro, E., and A. Teberosky. 1982. *Literacy before schooling.* Portsmouth, NH: Heinemann.

Flores, B. 1982. *Language interference or influence: Toward a theory of Hispanic bilingualism.* Ph.D. diss. University of Arizona, Tucson, Arizona.

Freeman, D. E. (1988). Assignment of pronoun reference: Evidence that young readers control cohesion. *Linguistics and Education. 1*(2), 153–176.

————. 1991. Teaching vocabulary: What's in a word? In *The whole language catalog*, edited by K. L. Goodman, L. Bird, and Y. Goodman, 110–111. Santa Rosa, CA: American School Publishers.

Freeman, D. and Y. S. Freeman. 1988. Whole language content lessons. *ESOL Newsletter* (Summer): 1–2.

————. 1989. A road to success for language minority high school students. In *When they don't all speak English: Integrating the ESL student into the regular classroom*, edited by P. Rigg and V. Allen, 126–139. Urbana, IL: NCTE.

————. 1990. Whole language for the bilingual student. *CABE Newsletter* 13(2): 8–9.

Freeman, D., & K. Goodman. In press. What's simple in simplified language? In *Aspects of and issues in simplification.* Edited by Makhan Tickoo. Singapore: Regional Language Centre.

Freeman, Y. S. 1987. The contemporary Spanish basal in the United States. Ph.D. diss., University of Arizona, Tucson, Arizona.

————. 1988a. The contemporary Spanish basal reader in the U.S.: How does it reflect current knowledge of the reading process? *NABE Journal* 13:59–74.

———. 1988b. Do Spanish methods and materials reflect current understanding of the reading process? *The Reading Teacher:* 654–662.

———. 1988c. Métodos de lectura en español: Reflejan nuestro conocimiento actual del proceso de lectura? *Lectura y Vida* 9:20–28.

Freeman, Y. S., and C. Cervantes. 1991. *Literature books en español for whole language bilingual classrooms.* Tucson, AZ: University of Arizona.

Freeman, Y. S., and D. E. Freeman. 1989a. Bilingual learners: How our assumptions limit their world. *Holistic Education Review* (Winter): 33–39.

———. 1989b. Changing contexts in secondary classes by altering teacher assumptions. *The CATESOL Journal* 2(1): 27–43.

———. 1989c. Evaluation of second-language junior and senior high school students. In *The whole language evaluation book*, edited by K. Goodman, Y. Goodman, and W. Hood, 141–151. Portsmouth, NH: Heinemann.

———. 1989d. Whole language approaches to writing with secondary ESL students. In *Richness in writing: Empowering ESL students*, edited by D. Johnson and D. Roen, 177–193. New York: Longman.

———. 1991a. Bilingual learners: How our assumptions limit their world. In *New directions in education: Selections from Holistic Education Review*, edited by R. Miller, 186–198. Brandon, VT: Holistic Education Press.

———. 1991b. Ten tips for monolingual teachers of bilingual students. In *The whole language catalog*, edited by K. Goodman, L. Bird, and Y. Goodman, 90. Santa Rosa, CA: American School Publishers.

———. 1991c. Doing social studies: Whole language lessons to promote social action. *Social Education* 55(1): 29–32, 66.

Freeman, Y. S. and Y. M. Goodman. In press. Revaluing the bilingual learner through a literature reading program. *Journal of Reading, Writing, and Learning Disabilities.*

Freeman, Y. S., and B. Mason. 1991. Organizing units around powerful contrasts, concepts, and content. In *The Whole Language Catalog*, edited by K. Goodman, L. Bird, and Y. Goodman, 294. Santa Rosa, CA: American School Publishers.

Freeman, Y. S. and S. Nofziger. 1991. WalkM To RnM 33: Vien vinidos al cualTo 33. In *Organizing for whole language*, edited by Y. Goodman, W. Hood, and K. Goodman, 65–83. Portsmouth, NH: Heinemann.

Freire, P. 1970. *Pedagogy of the oppressed.* New York: Continuum.

García, E. (Erminda), B. Rasmussen, C. Stobbe, and E. (Eugene) Garcia (1900) Portfolios: An assessment tool in support of instruction. In special edition "New Conceptions of Achievement and Reasoning" edited by A. Paliscnar. *International Journal of Educational Research* Vol. 14, No. 5, 431–436.

Gardner, H. 1984. *Frames of Mind.* New York: Basic Books.

Gay, K., and L. Sintetos. 1985. *I like English.* Glenview, IL: Scott, Foresman and Company.

Genesee, F. 1984. Historical and theoretical foundations of immersion education. In *Studies on immersion education,* edited by D. Dolson, Sacramento, CA.: California State Department of Education.

Gonzalez, J. (1979). Coming of age in bilingual/bicultural education: A historical perspective. In *Bilingual multicultural education and the professional: From theory to practice.* Edited by H. Trueba and C. Barnett-Mizrahi. Rowley, MA: Newbury House, p. 3.

Goodman, K. 1984. Unity in reading. In *Becoming readers in a complex society,* edited by A. Purves and O. Niles, 79–114. Chicago: University of Chicago Press.

———. 1986b. *What's whole in whole language?* Portsmouth, NH: Heinemann.

———. 1988. Language and learning: Toward a social-personal view. Paper presented at Brisbane Conference on Language and Learning.

———. (1991). Revaluing readers and reading. In S. Stires (Ed.), *With promise: Redefining reading and writing for "special" students,* 127–133. Portsmouth, NH: Heinemann.

Goodman, K., L. B. Bird, and Y. M. Goodman. 1991. *The whole language catalog.* Santa Rosa, CA: American School Publishers.

Goodman, K., Y. M. Goodman, and B. Flores. 1979. *Reading in the bilingual classroom: Literacy and biliteracy.* Rosslyn, VA: National Clearinghouse for Bilingual Education.

Goodman, K., P. Shannon, Y. Freeman, and S. Murphy. 1988. *Report card on basal readers.* New York: Richard C. Owen.

Goodman, K., E. B. Smith, R. Meredith, and Y. Goodman. 1987. *Language and thinking in school: A whole language curriculum* (3rd ed.). New York: Richard C. Owen.

Goodman, Y. 1985. Kidwatching: Observing children in the classroom. In *Observing the language learner,* edited by A. Jaggar and M. T. Smith-Burke, 9–18. Newark, DE and Urbana, IL: International Reading Association and the National Council of Teachers of English.

———. (1989). Evaluation of students: Evaluation of teachers. In *The Whole Language Evaluation Book* edited by K. Goodman, Y. Goodman, and W. Hood. Portsmouth, NH: Heinemann. pp. 3–14.

Graves, D. 1983. *Writing: Teachers and children at work.* Portsmouth, NH: Heinemann.

Hakuta, K. 1986. *Mirror of language: The debate on bilingualism.* New York: Basic Books.

Halliday, M. 1975. *Learning how to mean.* London: Edward Arnold.

———. 1984. Three aspects of children's language development: Learning language, learning through language, and learning about language. In

Oral and written language development research: Implications for instruction. Urbana, IL: NCTE.

Hamayan, E. 1989. Keynote address. Teach your children well. Twelfth annual statewide conference for teachers of limited English proficient students. Oak Brook, IL.

Harste, J. and L. Mikulecky. 1984. "The context of literacy in our society. In *Becoming readers in a complex society: NSSE Yearbook, 1984*, edited by A. Purves and O. Niles. Chicago, IL: University of Chicago Press.

Harste, J., V. Woodward, and C. Burke. 1984. *Language stories and literacy lessons.* Portsmouth, NH: Heinemann.

Heath, S. 1983. *Ways with words: Language, life, and work in communities and classrooms.* Cambridge, England: Cambridge University Press.

————. 1990. Talk given at TESOL convention, San Francisco.

Hernández-Chávez, E. 1984. The inadequacy of English immersion education as an educational approach for language minority students in the United States. In *Studies on immersion education*, edited by D. Dolson, 144–183. Sacramento, CA: California State Department of Education.

Herr, S. 1959. *Improve your reading through phonics.* Los Angeles: Instructional Materials and Equipment Distributors.

Hudelson, S. 1981–82. An examination of children's invented spelling in Spanish. *National Association for Bilingual Education Journal* 6:53–68.

————. 1984. Kan yu ret an rayt en ingles: Children become literate in English as a second language. *TESOL Quarterly* 18(2): 221–237.

————. 1987. The role of native language literacy in the education of language minority children. *Language Arts* 64(8): 827–840.

————. 1989. A tale of two children: Individual differences in ESL children's writing. In *Richness in writing: Empowering ESL students*, edited by D. Johnson and D. Roen, 84–99. New York: Longman.

Hymes, D. 1970. On communicative competence. In *Directions in sociolinguistics* edited by J. Gumperz and D. Hymes, 35–71. New York: Holt, Rinehart and Winston.

Imhoff, G. 1990. The position of U.S. English on bilingual education. In *English plus: Issues in bilingual education. Annals of the American Academy of Political Science*, edited by C. Cazden and C. Snow, 48–61. Newbury Park, CA.: Sage Publications.

Interactions/Mosaic. 1985. Hightstown, NJ: McGraw-Hill.

Jackson, W. 1991. Letter to editor. *Fresno Bee* 137 (4 February): B.5, No. 24830.

Jongsma, K. 1989. Questions and answers: Portfolio assessment. *The Reading Teacher* 43 (3): 264.

Kagan, S. 1986. Cooperative learning and sociocultural factors in schooling. In *Beyond language: Social and cultural factors in schooling language minority students*, edited by California State Dept. of Education, 231–298. Los Angeles: Evaluation, Dissemination and Assessment Center.

Kolers, P. A. 1973. Three stages of reading. In *Psycholinguistics and reading*, edited by F. Smith, New York: Holt, Rhinehart and Winston.

Kollars, D. 1988. *State school reforms leave disadvantaged behind*. Fresno, CA: *Fresno Bee*, Dec. 18.

Krashen, S. 1982. *Principles and practice in second language acquisition*. New York: Pergamon Press.

———. 1985. *Inquiries and insights*. Haywood, CA: Alemany Press.

———. 1990. The case against bilingual education. Speech presented at 1990 NABE Conference, Tucson, Az.

Krashen, S. and D. Biber. 1988. *On course*. Sacramento, CA: CABE.

Krashen, S. and T. Terrell. 1983. *The natural approach: Language acquisition in the classroom*. Hayward, CA: Alemany Press.

Kroeber, T. 1964. *Ishi: Last of his tribe*. New York: Bantam.

Labbo, L. and W. Teale, 1990. Cross-age reading: A strategy for helping poor readers. *The Reading Teacher* 43(6): 362–369.

Larsen-Freeman, D. 1986. *Techniques and principles in language teaching*. Oxford: Oxford University Press.

Lebsock, R. 1988. A classroom of authors. Video, Fresno, CA.

Levinson, R. 1987. *Mira, cómo salen las estrellas*. Madrid, Spain: Ediciones Altea.

Lozanov, F. 1982. Suggestology and suggestopedy. In *Innovative approaches to language teaching*, edited by R. Blair, Rowley, MA: Newbury House.

Lucas, I. 1981. Bilingual education and the melting pot: Getting burned. *The Illinois Issues Humanities Essays: 5*. Champaign, IL: Illinois Humanities Council.

Lucas, T., R. Henze, and R. Donato. 1990. Promoting the success of Latino language-minority students: An exploratory study of six high schools. *Harvard Educational Review* 60(3): 315–340.

Matthews, J. 1990. From computer management to portfolio assessment. *The Reading Teacher* 43(6): 420–421.

Miles, M. 1971. *Annie and the old one*. Boston: Joy Street Books.

Miller, R. 1990. *What are schools for: Holistic education in American culture*. Brandon, VT: Holistic Education Press.

———. 1991. Pioneers. In *The whole language catalog*, edited by K. Goodman, L. Bird, and Y. Goodman, 29, 54, 109, 139, 169, 204, 219, 243, 367, 393. Santa Rosa, CA: American School Publishers.

Morrice, C., and M. Simmons. 1991. Beyond reading buddies: A whole language cross-age program. *The Reading Teacher* 44(8): 572–577.

Morrissey, M. 1989. When "Shut Up" is a Sign of Growth. In *The whole language evaluation book*, edited by K. Goodman, Y. Goodman, and W. Hood, 85–97. Portsmouth, NH: Heinemann.

National Commission on Excellence in Education. 1983. *A nation at risk: The imperative for educational reform.* Washington, DC: U.S. Government Printing Office.

National Geographic World. Washington, DC: National Geographic Society.

Newman, J., and S. Church. 1990. Commentary: Myths of whole language. *The Reading Teacher* 44(1): 20–26.

Olsen, L. 1988. *Crossing the schoolhouse border: Immigrant students and the California public schools.* San Francisco: California Tomorrow.

———. 1989. *Bridges: Promising programs for the education of immigrant children.* San Francisco: California Tomorrow.

Olsen, L., and N. Mullen. 1990. *Embracing diversity: Teacher's voices from California classrooms.* San Francisco: California Tomorrow.

Olsen, R. 1991. Results of a K-12 and adult ESL survey—1991. *TESOL Matters* 1(5): 4.

Ovando, C., and V. Collier. 1985. *Bilingual and ESL classrooms: Teaching in multicultural contexts.* New York: McGraw-Hill.

Paley, V. 1981. *Wally's stories.* Cambridge, MA: Harvard University Press.

Phillips, S. 1972. Participant structures and communicative competence: Warm Spring children in community and classroom. In *Functions of language in the classroom,* edited by C. Cazden, V. John, and D. Hymes, 370–394. New York: Teachers College Press.

Piaget, J. 1955. *The language and thought of the child.* New York: Meridian Books.

Porter, R. 1990. *Forked tongue: The politics of bilingual education.* New York: Basic Books.

Ramírez, J. D. (1991). *Final Report: Longitudinal study of structured English immersion strategy, early-exit and late-exit bilingual education programs* (300-87-0156). U.S. Department of Education.

Rigg, P. 1986. Reading in ESL: Learning from kids. In *Children and ESL: Integrating perspectives,* edited by P. Rigg and S. Enright, 55–92. Washington, DC: TESOL.

Rigg, P., and V. Allen. 1989. Introduction. In *When they don't all speak English,* edited by P. Rigg and V. Allen, vii–xx. Urbana, IL: National Council of Teachers of English.

Rigg, P. and S. Hudelson, 1986. One child doesn't speak English. *Australian Journal of Reading,* 1, 3, 116–125.

Romijn, E., and C. Seely. 1979. *Live action English.* San Francisco, CA: Alemany Press.

Rose, M. 1989. *Lives on the boundary.* New York: Penguin.

Rosenblatt, L. 1978. *The reader, the text, the poem: The transactional theory of the literary work.* Carbondale, IL: Southern Illinois University Press.

Rothman, R. 1990a. Ford study urges new test system to "open gates of opportunity" *Education Week* IX (36): 1,12.

———. 1990b. New York chief outlines plan for "results" system. *Education Week* IX (36): 1, 16.

Scarcella, R. 1990. *Teaching language minority students in the multicultural classroom.* Englewood Cliffs, NJ: Prentice-Hall Regents.

Segal, B. 1983. *Teaching English through action.* Brea, CA: Berty Segal, Inc.

Shannon, P. 1989. *Broken promises: Reading instruction in twentieth-century America.* Granby, MA: Bergin and Garvey.

———. 1990. *The struggle to continue: Progressive reading instruction in the United States.* Portsmouth, New Hampshire: Heinemann.

Sinclair, J., and R. M. Coulthard. 1975. *Towards an analysis of discourse: The English used by teachers and pupils.* Oxford: Oxford University Press.

Sizer, T. 1990. Student as worker, teacher as coach. Viewer's guide to teleconference. New York: Simon and Schuster.

Skinner, B. F. 1957. *Verbal behavior.* New York: Appleton-Century-Crofts.

Skutnabb-Kangas, T. 1983. *Bilingualism or not: The education of minorities.* Clevedon, England: Multilingual Matters.

Smith, F. 1982. *Writing and the writer.* New York: Holt, Rinehart and Winston.

———. 1983. *Essays into literacy: Selected papers and some afterthoughts.* Portsmouth, NH: Heinemann.

———. 1985. *Reading without nonsense* (2nd ed.). New York: Teachers College Press.

———. 1986. *Insult to intelligence: The bureaucratic invasion of our classrooms.* Portsmouth, NH: Heinemann.

———. 1990. *To think.* New York: Teachers College Press.

Speare, E. G. 1957. *Calico captive.* New York: Dell.

———. 1983. *The sign of the beaver.* New York: Dell.

Spier, P. 1980. *People.* Garden City, NY: Doubleday.

Stevick, E. 1976. *Memory, meaning and method.* Rowley, MA: Newbury House.

Swain, M., S. Lapkin, S. Rowen, and D. Hart. 1990. The role of mother tongue literacy in third language learning. *Language, Culture, and Curriculum* 3:65–81.

Taylor, D. 1990. Teaching without testing: Assessing the complexity of children's literacy learning. *English Education* 22(1): 4–74.

Taylor, T. (1969). *The cay.* New York: Avon.

———. 1991. *Learning denied.* Portsmouth, NH: Heinemann.

Urzúa, C. 1989. I grow for a living. In *When they don't all speak English: Integrating the ESL student into the regular classroom,* edited by P. Rigg and V. Allen, 15–38. Urbana, IL: NCTE.

————. 1990, March. "Read to me!" tutoring at its best. Paper presented at annual conference of Teachers of English to Speakers of Other Languages, San Francisco, CA.

Valette, R. M. 1977. *Modern language testing*. New York: Harcourt Brace Jovanovich.

Wald, B. (1984). A sociolinguistic perspective on Cummins' current framework for relating language proficiency to academic achievement. In C. Rivera (Ed.), *Language proficiency and academic achievement* (pp. 55–70). Clevedon, England: Multilingual Matters Ltd.

Vygotsky, L. 1962. *Thought and language*. Cambridge, MA: MIT Press.

————. 1978. *Mind in society: The development of higher psychological processes*. Cambridge, MA: Harvard University Press.

Wallerstein, N. 1987. Problem-posing education: Freire's method for transformation. In *Freire for the classroom: A sourcebook for liberatory teaching*, edited by I. Shor, 33–44. Portsmouth, NH: Heinemann.

Watson, D., C. Burke, and J. Harste. 1989. *Whole language: Inquiring voices*. New York: Scholastic.

Weaver, C. 1988. *Reading process and practice: From socio-psycholinguistics to whole language*. Portsmouth, NH: Heinemann.

————. 1990. *Understanding whole language: From principles to practice*. Portsmouth, NH: Heinemann.

Widdowson, H. 1978. *Teaching language as communication*. Oxford: Oxford University Press.

Wigginton, E. 1985. *Sometimes a shining moment: The foxfire experience*. New York: Doubleday.

Wilde, S. 1989. Looking at invented spelling: A kidwatcher's guide to spelling, parts 1 and 2. In *The whole language evaluation book*, edited by K. Goodman, Y. Goodman, and W. Hood, 213–236. Portsmouth, NH: Heinemann.

Wilkins, D. A. 1976. *Notional syllabuses*. Oxford: Oxford University Press.

Willig, A. 1985. A meta-analysis of selected studies on the effectiveness of bilingual education. *Review of Educational Research* 55: 269–317.

Willis, J. D. 1983. The implications of discourse analysis for teaching oral communication. Unpublished M.A. thesis, University of Birmingham.

You. 1986. Rosemont, IL: National Dairy Council.

Index